Ego-Oriented Casework: Problems and Perspectives

Ego-Oriented Casework: Problems and Perspectives

Papers from the Smith College
School for Social Work

Editors
Howard J. Parad
Roger R. Miller

FAMILY SERVICE ASSOCIATION OF AMERICA
44 East 23 Street   New York, N.Y. 10010

Seventh Printing, 1976

ISBN: 0–87304–011–2

Library of Congress Catalog Number: 63–14026

Printed in the U.S.A.

To the Members of the
Smith College School for Social Work
Alumnae Association

Contributors

Lucille N. Austin, Professor of Social Work, New York School of Social Work, Columbia University

Charlotte G. Babcock, Professor of Psychiatry and Associate Director, Pittsburgh Psychoanalytic Institute, School of Medicine, University of Pittsburgh

Bernard Bandler, Professor and Chairman, Division of Psychiatry, Boston University School of Medicine, and Psychiatrist-in-Chief, Massachusetts Memorial Hospitals, Boston University Medical Center

Louise Bandler, Lecturer on Social Casework, Simmons College School of Social Work, and Casework Consultant and Supervisor, South End Family Program, Boston

Virginia S. Bellsmith, Professor of Social Work, New York School of Social Work, Columbia University

Yonata Feldman, Case Consultant, Madeleine Borg Child Guidance Institute, Jewish Board of Guardians, and faculty member, Smith College School for Social Work

Selma Fraiberg, Supervising Child Analyst, Baltimore Psychoanalytic Institute, Lecturer, New Orleans Psychoanalytic Institute, and Case Consultant, Family Service Society and Children's Bureau of New Orleans

Florence Hollis, Professor of Social Work, New York School of Social Work, Columbia University

Irving Kaufman, Director, Clinical Services to Children, Massachusetts Division of Legal Medicine, and Lecturer, Smith College School for Social Work

John A. MacLeod, Associate Professor of Psychiatry, College of Medicine, University of Cincinnati

CONTRIBUTORS

Roger R. Miller, Director of Research, Smith College School for Social Work, and Editor, _Smith College Studies in Social Work_

Howard J. Parad, Director, Smith College School for Social Work

Helen Pinkus, Associate Professor of Social Work, Smith College School for Social Work

Frances H. Scherz, Director of Casework, Jewish Family and Community Service, Chicago, and member of the graduate seminar faculty, Smith College School for Social Work

Herman D. Stein, Professor of Social Work, New York School of Social Work, Columbia University, and Visiting Lecturer, Smith College School for Social Work

S. Michael Turner, Director, Family Life Education and Group Treatment, Family Service of the Cincinnati Area

Contents

CONTENTS

Introduction

INTENDED AS A companion volume to our earlier collection of Smith papers, *Ego Psychology and Dynamic Casework,* this book offers a number of contributions to the ongoing reformulation of the relationship between ego psychology and casework practice. The *problems* considered are those encountered in the search for an increasingly exact correspondence between theory and practice. The *perspectives* presented are those of the individual authors, whose interests have engaged them in the study of a variety of specific practice issues concerned with learning, teaching, studying, and doing casework.

The network of ideas comprising ego psychology is undergoing extensive elaboration. Even if previous conceptions of ego properties and functions had been fully exploited—which is by no means the case—the advent of new formulations would require sustained and careful study. The dynamic character and complexities of ego psychology have resulted, at times, in the oversimplification of the conceptual system to a conscious problem-solving mechanism, the introduction of artificial stability by reification of the ego, and even the outright rejection of the ego concept as viable and open to inquiry! Therefore, the observations and experiences of serious students of the practice implications of ego psychology are all the more timely.

The developmental process that intervenes between the exposition of an idea system and its eventual incorporation in the professional

1

equipment of the practitioner is a lengthy one and derives many benefits from widespread professional participation. The work presented here illustrates the potential yield of practice wisdom and offers a number of models for the further pursuit of an exciting and challenging enterprise.

We have divided the seventeen papers of this collection into four sections: (1) An Overview; (2) Theoretical Considerations; (3) Practice Applications; and (4) Learning and Teaching in Casework. The allocation of material to Parts II and III was based on the relative emphasis of papers on either conceptual elaboration or practice implementation. Since most of the papers in these two sections are both practice-oriented and theory-related, a different distribution would obviously have been possible.

Part I surveys a number of vital issues confronting casework education and practice. Locating the study of ego psychology in a larger context of professional concerns, this introductory paper identifies a variety of specific problems, many of which are addressed in subsequent chapters.

Part II is concerned with the investigation of selected aspects of the knowledge base of social work, an obvious prerequisite if we are to gain new vantage points for the study of practice. The advantages of conceptual clarification are well illustrated in a discussion of ego support. The analysis and definition of this elusive but central concept constitute an important addition to practice theory; a broad metapsychological framework provides the rationale for techniques of support useful in mobilizing ego forces. The response to stress, viewed as an ego phenomenon, provides a convenient focal point for examination of interacting psychological, physiological, and social forces. Guidelines are offered for the integration of dynamic perspectives with other conceptual schemes. A review of a range of social science concepts enhances the practitioner's diagnostic perspectives and points up an unresolved problem that is symptomatic of the state of current knowledge: the need to develop and substantiate the theoretical linkage between social science perspectives and psychological conceptions. The section includes a paper in which the stages and mechanisms of sublimation, a subject rarely treated in a systematic way in casework literature, are defined and elaborated. The illustrative case material is a highly useful increment in delineation of an increasingly precise theory of differential treatment. The final paper in this section describes a project which has undertaken to study some dimensions of ego functioning and which offers possibilities for a systematic investigation of the relationship between dynamic theory and practice problems with a view toward facilitating further work in this direction.

Part III is primarily concerned with the use of theoretical formulations, that is, the application of the insights of ego psychology to practice. Here is reflected the excitement of discovery as social work practice ventures into challenging areas, some untried and some tried with a still incomplete knowledge base: family-centered casework, drawing on social science concepts to advance the study of family communication and interaction patterns; brief casework, using the concept of stress for the development of strategy and tactics for crisis intervention; the creative modification of treatment arrangements to meet the needs of clients with limited ego capacity; the management of group treatment processes for clients with character disorders; a differential approach to protective casework, with the caseworker assuming auxiliary ego functions to help the inadequate parent; and, finally, a test of the exportability of dynamic casework which provides a check on the practical application of the American model to the needs found in a different culture.

Part IV begins with a discussion of the process by which the educator may facilitate the students' integration of ego-dystonic content when they confront the disquieting propositions of psychoanalysis. Another important contribution toward a dynamic theory of learning is offered in an appraisal of the relevance of analytic theory to casework education and practice. A somewhat different approach to education for casework, presented in the next paper, describes a casework sequence augmented by the introduction of extensive theory from the social sciences. The last two chapters tackle issues in supervision, still a subject for lively debate. An examination of supervision within the context of organizational theory proposes the division of customary supervisory responsibilities into discrete teaching and administrative functions, and foresees the development of new arrangements to keep pace with the changing role of the supervisor. And the final paper, viewing supervision in terms of the learner's ego involvement, builds a strong case for the retention and strengthening of an extended supervisory program.

Acknowledgments

As with our earlier collection of Smith papers, *Ego Psychology and Dynamic Casework*, the stimulus for the present volume derives largely from the many requests we have received for papers presented at benefit lectures sponsored by chapters of the Smith College School for Social Work Alumnae Association. We are deeply grateful to our contributors who have given so generously of their time and wisdom in furthering professional knowledge.

We acknowledge our appreciation to many others who contributed to this collective effort: Libbie G. Parad for her editorial assistance and for doing the index; Cora Kasius and Shirley M. Martin of the Family Service Association of America for their encouragement and practical help; and Betty H. Vogel and Jacqueline Van Voris for patiently and cheerfully typing the manuscripts.

HOWARD J. PARAD
ROGER R. MILLER

Northampton, Massachusetts
March, 1963

Part 1

An Overview

1. Contemporary Issues for Caseworkers*

Florence Hollis

A MOST IMPORTANT DEVELOPMENT in casework during the past forty years has been its gradual assimilation of the theories of dynamic psychiatry. One of the cornerstones of the fruitful collaboration between the two professions was laid by the psychiatrists and caseworkers who formed the early teaching staff of the Smith College School for Social Work.

Dynamic Psychiatry in Perspective

The period of the twenties must have been one of great ferment. It is easy to imagine not only the excitement over those new ideas, but also the anxiety of student supervisors and faculty as new and strange ideas flooded in. It is common knowledge that many of the leading social workers of the day were extremely distrustful of these new ideas, especially the "weird" Freudian notions—so shocking in themselves, so disputed, and so lacking in what the scientist calls established validity. It is small wonder that Mary Richmond, who had spent her life persuading caseworkers to gather facts, verify them, distinguish them from inferences, and to draw conclusions carefully, regarded with dismay the inroads of a theory said to rest on dreams and slips of the tongue.

* Reprinted from *Smith College Studies in Social Work*, Vol. XXX, No. 2 (1960).

Why did psychoanalytic theory rather than some other survive in casework? In the twenties it was not a theory of great prestige. Psychologists, then teaching in departments of philosophy, ridiculed it; all but a handful of psychiatrists fought it tooth and nail. It certainly had not been subjected to rigorous scientific testing and validation. We still cannot say that we base our casework methods on Freudian psychology because it has been proved beyond the shadow of a doubt that all Freud's hypotheses are true. The truth of the matter is that *no* theory of behavior, no theory of society, has been proved to be true. Data are being gathered systematically; they are being classified; theories are being evolved; fragments of theory have been tested; techniques for more extensive testing are being slowly and painfully worked out. Sociologists, psychologists, psychiatrists, caseworkers—all are groping toward ways of testing and validating our theories. Meanwhile, psychiatrists and caseworkers must treat patients and clients. We do not have the scientific aloofness of the laboratory and the library, the objective scrutiny of non-participants, the safety of paper and pencil tests on willing college students. We must be *doing* something, trying to bring about change, engaging actively in the lives of fellow human beings who are shaping the lives of their children, marrying and unmarrying, submitting or refusing to submit to frightening and painful medical treatment, who are in fact anxious, belligerent, weeping, loving, striving. And, for better or worse, we must do something about their problems. If we do nothing, we are still doing *something;* and doing nothing may be just the wrong thing. In the field of human relations we cannot wait for absolute certainty before we act; we are fortunate when we feel reasonably sure of the wisdom of a course of action, and not infrequently we are only slightly certain that one procedure is better than another.

Why, of all the unproved theories available, did casework choose psychoanalysis? A complete answer to that question would take us into a fascinating study of personalites and organizations, and of the social and philosophical trends of the times. For our purposes a few of the many threads in the strand will suffice. Despite its great interest in environmental causation in the early part of this century, casework had never really lost its interest in the part played by individual personality differences in social adjustment. Terminology was certainly different from that of today. What we now refer to as ego and superego is rather close to what our predecessors embraced in the term "character." Just as we today are concerned about the client's ego strengths and his better use of them in the solution of his problems, so social workers then were concerned with strengthening character. Then, as later, some workers tried to modify character by doing things *to* people while others drew people out into fuller and more constructive use of their own powers.

A great temptation, yielded to more often than resisted, leads each generation to enhance its own self-esteem by emphasizing the shortcomings of its predecessors. Hence it has become popular to think of the early caseworker as an interfering busy-body, an authoritative do-gooder imposing his own rigid, moralistic, upper-middle-class ways of life on the helpless poverty-ridden widow. Every distortion has its elements of truth. No doubt early in the century the average social worker had much greater confidence in the magic of advice-giving than we have today. It is also true, however, that many workers were painfully aware of their failures and that this feeling was one ingredient in the readiness for a new theory offering alternative courses of action.

Fortunately, advice-giving and kindred forms of manipulation were even then only part of the social worker's treatment kit. A careful reading of the early writings of people like Octavia Hill, Zilpha Smith, Francis H. McLean, and Mary Richmond demonstrates keen awareness of the importance of the client-worker relationship, and of respect for the individual, his own aims and hopes, of unlocking his strengths, and of gaining his trust. They speak of listening to him, of understanding and sympathizing with his concerns and his aspirations. The term "acceptance" may not have been coined, but the good will now designated by that symbol is clearly to be seen in many of the early writings. Underlying both emphases was true concern for others, a clear desire to help, and a constant groping for better ways of doing this.

While psychoanalysis brought to light facts that previously had escaped attention, pointed out connections never before seen, and provided explanations previously unimagined, its basic point of view toward people was in harmony with the best social work tradition. In early associations with Freudian-trained analysts the caseworker recognized a deep desire to help, appreciation for the stress and suffering of other human beings, understanding rather than condemnation of weakness, willingness to invest long hours in understanding and treatment, rather than a search for quick tricks of cure. Here were kindred spirits. These early analysts were generous in sharing their knowledge and skill with caseworkers; some today would say too generous. I do not share that view. It was for casework itself to find its own place in the Freudian framework. Perhaps the analyst, too, surrounded as he was by so much harsh rejection in his own profession, felt kinship in the caseworker.

Another less worthy basis for our affinity to psychoanalysts must be acknowledged. Dependence! Norman Polansky has recently pointed out that many caseworkers tend to be orally dependent characters—we smoke too much, we drink quite enough, we talk incessantly, we like to give and also to be given to.[1] Perhaps we also tend to devour new theory—to swallow more than we have chewed. Perhaps we also overidentify, lose our ego boundaries, and incorporate rather than assimilate. Whatever tendencies we have toward dependence are certainly mobilized by the size of the task by which the social worker is daily confronted. Constantly we are faced with problems we do not yet know how to solve. Constantly we act upon probabilites rather than certainties. Small wonder that we are ready to lean on other broad shoulders, glad to be told that others hold solutions for our problems, willing to ascribe magical powers never claimed by the recipients of our dependence.

It would be a travesty of the truth if the case were allowed to rest here. Whatever affinities and subjective needs may have brought about our addiction to psychoanalysis it is the empirically tested usefulness of the theory itself that has been the main determinant of the wide and long-lasting influence analysis has had on casework. First of all, it taught us to listen. Whatever the shortcomings of that much maligned passivity it was a splendid antidote for advice-giving. As we listened and clients felt permitted to express themselves freely we were astonished at the extent to which

[1] Norman A. Polansky, "The Professional Identity in Social Work," *Issues in American Social Work*, Alfred J. Kahn (ed.), Columbia University Press, New York, 1959, p. 302.

10

their verbalizations were consonant with Freudian ideas. Suppressed ideation of both the client and the worker began to come to the fore, and the various components of relationship, including transference and countertransference, began to be understood. With this came a renewal of the emphasis upon acceptance. What had previously been an intuitive and philosophical attribute of the best caseworkers now was articulated and could be taught on empirical grounds. As hostility began to emerge freely, the need-frustration-aggression cycle, with its boomerang of loss of love and need for more love, was demonstrated over and over again; the value of catharsis with acceptance was repeatedly demonstrated. Later, when the ego was more fully understood and diagnosis in the "clinical" sense emerged, we again had the experience of cumulative data that matched Freudian descriptions and took on significance for treatment steps when understood in Freudian terms.

We would do our predecessors and ourselves a grave injustice if we assumed that casework was a mere passive consumer of Freudian dogma. It was only because these observations were verified in our own experience and usefully explained by analytic theory that so many caseworkers accepted this rather than some other theory of personality. Let no one suppose that workers were ignorant of rival theories. Adler's ideas were well known and fairly widely used, as were those of Adolph Meyer. There was a reading acquaintance with Jung. Sullivan was followed with interest. Rank impressed a segment of the field as having ideas of greater usefulness than those of Freud.

However, this empirical type of evaluation, as we know, does not constitute rigorous scientific validation. When our research techniques reach the point of being equal to the task, such testing must be done. But meanwhile let us not discount the honest observant human mind as an evaluator of theory. It has its pitfalls and sources of error—but so do these other tools. Ultimately it is always the human mind that not only devises the tools but judges the worth of the tool itself, draws conclusions from its findings and decides whether the evidence is sufficiently strong to be convincing. Who decides whether to act upon a finding when its probability is at the .01 level of significance, the .05 level, or some other level? The *consumer* of research—either on his own independent judgment or on that of some other expert whose judgment he considers better than his own. Doubting Thomas had to feel with his own fingers. Others are willing to believe their eyes and ears.

The Impact of New Knowledge

My reason for introducing all this background in a paper dealing with contemporary issues is that this, too, is a period of ferment in social work. Old knowledge and old ways are being challenged. New knowledge is flooding in, new ways are being tried. Understanding our past may help us act wisely in the present. One great challenge comes from the field of social science; another with many facets comes from within our own ranks and constitutes a demand for various types of short cut. Together they comprise a broad-fronted demand for re-evaluation and revision of certain aspects of social work theory and practice.

We must try to meet the challenge honestly, thoughtfully, with good will and without neurotic defensiveness. The ultimate responsiblity of social work is to the client or patient. Every item in theory or practice must be measured ultimately against a single criterion—will it enable us to help clients more effectively? This means that we must substitute new ways for old only when there is reason to believe that clients will be benefited by this change. An equal responsibility rests upon us to study new proposals and willingly grasp for our use those that show promise of being beneficial.

We all acknowledge that self-awareness is a necessary prerequisite for objectivity. This is true not only in work with clients but also in the study of general issues. What are the pitfalls into which we are likely to fall? First, we may become frightened. The combination discussed earlier of heavy responsibility with far less than absolute certainty about much of our methodology makes us particularly vulnerable to anxiety. What inappropriate defenses are we likely to use? First, defensive hostility. We are frightened, so we attack. We belittle the new idea: "pretentious gobbledygook, evolved by arm-chair theorists who have never had to deal with a real problem." Second, projection: "They are attacking us, trying to belittle our theories, wanting to displace us." Third, identification with the aggressor: "They are so much more scientific than we.

12

Quick, we must learn all about it; let's get on the bandwagon."
(Charlotte Towle and Norman Polansky in recent papers have both
warned against this fallacy.[2] Polansky notes our tendency to fads
and relates this to dependency traits.) Fourth, denial: "There's
nothing new in this idea. We've been doing it all along." Fifth,
turning against the self: "Yes, of course; casework is unscientific.
We have no proof for what we do. It's just rule of thumb, tradition, and ideas we've borrowed from other people. What has casework ever developed that's really new?"

What can the healthy part of our embattled egos do about it?
First look the facts in the face and stop being so uneasy. Casework
is not hopelessly behind the social sciences in the stage of validation
it has achieved. Casework is strong in rule-of-thumb research—
the collection of meaningful observations, testing and refining of
treatment methods in practice, the assembling of findings concerning
small groups of cases, seen always against the background of what
other practitioners have observed and published, and against the
background of relevant theories. Much knowledge is passed on by
word of mouth in supervisory conferences and classroom teaching.
Systematic pondering over these findings has produced a wealth of
significant hypotheses awaiting more rigorous study. As a profession we have rightly made use of the findings of the behavioral sciences, particularly in the area of personality theory.

Casework is a scientific art. Certainly since the days of Mary
Richmond we have been committed to objective examination of the
facts of each case. We draw inferences from those facts, we diagnose,
we view the individual case against a frame of reference which is
itself the product of informal research. We constantly alert ourselves to sources of error such as insufficient evidence or distortion
on the part of the client; bias or countertransference reactions on
the part of the worker. We have kept records for many decades—
more detailed and more universally than any other profession dealing with human adjustment. We have used supervision for the
purpose of increasing objectivity and devising suitable treatment
plans more extensively than any other profession. Indeed, our concept of supervision can be considered one of our major contribu-

[2] Charlotte Towle, "Implications of Contemporary Human and Social Values
for Selection of Social Work Students," *Social Service Review*, Vol. XXXIII, No.
3 (1959), p. 264. Norman A. Polansky, *op. cit.*

tions to the professions. With the exception of psychoanalysis, the therapeutic professions only recently have begun to approximate our standards in field work training and subsequent controlled practice. Methods of field teaching have nowhere been studied and articulated so extensively as in casework.

We have developed child placement from a mere dumping of needy children on receptive foster parents to a controlled process with criteria for both the need for placement and the suitability of a home. We have developed standards and procedures for the giving of financial assistance which have brought public assistance from a political handout and pork-barrel standard to an honest, need-centered operation. We have explored the social component in illness and to a significant degree have contributed to its inclusion in diagnosis and treatment in the modern hospital. In collaboration with psychiatry we have illuminated the role of parents in the problems of children and developed techniques for work with parents. We have been in the vanguard in studying effective ways of lessening marital disharmony. The importance of the caseworker's relating to the family as a whole and understanding the interaction between different family members has been part of casework theory for many years; the concept of family equilibrium appeared in our literature at least ten years ago. The concept of internal and external stresses—the person-in-his-situation—has been basic to casework for so long that most of us feel it came with our mother's milk.

We have been developing, and are now becoming more articulate about, a middle-range treatment method which does not require the uncovering of deeply unconscious material but depends very heavily upon rational, rather than directive and manipulatory, techniques.

Perhaps it sounds as if the writer's defense is flight into grandeur. Let us admit that rule-of-thumb research is the beginning, not the end, of knowledge. Hypotheses arise primarily from such small-scale, informal research. The first testing of ideas in isolated cases occurs at this point. It is here that imagination, originality, and integrative capacities of mind are most needed. Here ideas are developed to the point of discovering whether they are worthy of proof (as Alfred North Whitehead once put it). But eventually

14

formal, rigorous research must follow. We are now ready for that in casework. The social scientist has gone much farther than we have in developing tools for such study. We cannot take these tools over in unmodified form. Collaboration between social work and social science is needed for adapting research methods to the problems we need studied. At present this is often awkwardly done, owing largely to the fact that social workers do not have sufficient sophistication to help in the retooling process. Hence our great need at this point for doctoral training. We especially need this training for mature students well grounded in social work practice, with sufficient confidence in their own profession to continue to represent it and to insist on modifying the tools to study social work, not social work to fit the tools. Innumerable hypotheses and propositions in casework are ready for testing. Social scientist and social work scientist collaborating as different but equal partners have a fertile and exciting field before them. Let me stress again that the social work researcher must be a true expert in social work. This means that his level of competence in social work itself must be substantially beyond that achieved by master's work. Advanced social work content as well as more knowledge of the social sciences must therefore be part of his doctoral work.

Some of our pet hypotheses may prove invalid; many will need modification and further development. I believe most of them, if properly tested, will hold up very well. If they do not, the sooner we are rid of them the better. Surely we are not afraid to put them to the test.

The Contribution of the Social Sciences *

What about social science theory *per se?* Especially what about those parts of social science that deal with man's relationship to his environment and the effect of the environment upon him? There need be no essential incompatibility between these branches of social science and social work. Our conception of the person-in-the-situation has always emphasized the importance of the environment, the necessity of estimating internal disturbance only in the light of the situational pressures to which the individual is being sub-

* *Editor's Note:* For an elaboration of this subject, see Herman D. Stein, Chapter 4 of this volume.

jected. We have stressed the importance of life experiences in shaping personality. This is true of the Freudian framework, too, though it is often not recognized. The world was so shocked and hypnotized by Freud's illumination of instinctual life that it sometimes forgets that interpersonal, especially intrafamilial, experiences are at the core of his theory of causation. Nor was he ignorant of the effect of later life experiences outside the immediate family.

It is only recently that sociological theory has begun to catch up with personality theory in developing material of use to the caseworker. As some of the methods of the cultural anthropologists permeated sociology the latter field began to evolve some theories that had much pertinence to social work. It is no accident that this sociocultural material attracted our attention. We very much need this material to understand norms of behavior as they are affected by ethnic and class factors. Variations between classes, for instance in the norms for the expression of both aggressive and instinctual behavior, have direct implications in both personality development and the significance of deviant behavior. They certainly have implications, by no means fully understood as yet, for treatment. Defenses undoubtedly differ greatly between classes; what is normal and healthy behavior for one may be pathological for another. The more accurate material the sociologists can give us on these matters the better.

Superego formation is undoubtedly subject to cultural influences both through the culturally influenced standards of the parents and through peer and other extra-family identifications.

Even perception is culturally influenced. We see only partly what is there; objective reality is distorted by what we expect to see. There are undoubtedly cultural determinants in these expectations. What the client sees in the caseworker is partly class-conditioned. The norms against which he measures the caseworker are affected by what is understood as kindness and competence by people of his class. On all these matters sociological inquiry can throw light.

Other areas of interest to casework include: the sociology of the professions, which can help us to understand ourselves and help us enormously in our collaboration with other professions; reference group theory, which enlarges our understanding of group elements in various aspects of identification; and role theory, which can throw

16

new light on social components in perception of self and others and expectation of self and others. Theories and observations about bureaucracies can help us understand the agencies in which we work; studies of the internal social structure of institutions such as mental hospitals, prisons, training schools for children, can throw much light on a side of treatment that has scarcely been touched by social work theory.

The Assimilation of New Knowledge

The mere listing of these areas brings to mind one of our sources of resistance to this new material. How on earth are we ever going to learn it all? Not all of us are going to learn it all. Social workers particularly interested in this material and social scientists interested in and sympathetic with social work will have to study the available data—some, one part of it and others, another—winnowing out those parts that are of real significance for social work.

Are there any principles that can guide us in this assimilation? First of all, the final decisions as to what is useful and what is not must be made by social work itself. We must be responsible for our own practice, for judging whether or not this new material will enable us to help our clients more effectively. Second, we must take responsibility for learning about these new data and theories and evaluating them carefully and honestly. Third, we must ask ourselves: How well established is this material? Does it have a large body of evidence behind it or is it extremely hypothetical or controversial within its own field? How much is fact and how much theory? Fourth, how much is really new in these ideas? There is no sense in substituting elaborately worded propositions for ideas that, in simpler language, are already a part of casework understanding. Profundity is not a function of polysyllabism.

Fifth, do new theories offer a more convincing, a clearer or simpler, explanation of events than we already have? Do they offer plausible explanations of things we previously could not understand or deal with? Do they bring within our view potentially significant aspects of the problem previously unperceived or ignored? Pollak has pointed out that observations tend not to be used or even comprehended until we have a frame of reference into which to fit

17

them.[3] This is an extremely pertinent observation. Although case-work has theoretically stressed the importance of the total family and emphasized that its problems may be partially caused by external pressures, we have lacked a framework for adequately structuring this knowledge and therefore in actual practice have not made full use of it.

Sixth, is the new theory expressed economically and concisely? Does it lead us to conclusions and action by a shorter route? I recently read an article that took the reader all around Robin Hood's barn in the form of pages of role theory to understand what was evident in the first few paragraphs of the case presentation—that the wife in the family probably had castration tendencies of unknown strength and was displacing rivalrous feelings originally felt toward her brother onto her husband and son. On the whole, the role theory presented was accurate and pertinent but it added little of treatment value to the understanding of the case and tended instead to waste energy and divert attention from the essence of social study and treatment. That men and women expect and are expected to function differently in many respects and that they hurt each other and suffer themselves when they do not do so is hardly a new idea for casework.

Seventh, we must keep a sharp eye open for contradictions and inconsistencies. For the most part, sociological material offers enrichment to present-day social work knowledge. Certain theories, however, run diametrically opposite to our own. For instance, as long as environmental influences are seen operating along with constitutional, instinctual, and other intrapsychic elements in causation —as they *are* seen by many sociologists—they enrich our understanding and are easily absorbed in our present framework. But social theorists who hold the view that personality is entirely the result of environmental conditioning demand the scrapping of our basic premises. Short of this extreme are rival propositions demanding different degrees of emphasis on internal and external causation. The possibility of flight from the instincts into the environment offers a recurring temptation. "It is not in any way my fault, it is just what people have done to me." We who have spent our lives

[3] Otto Pollak, *Integrating Sociological and Psychoanalytic Concepts*, Russell Sage Foundation, New York, 1956, p. 196.

18

working with people have seen too much evidence on the other side, too many people who have survived pressures to which others succumb, to accept the extreme environmentalist position until it is supported by far more cogent evidence than has so far been uncovered. At times, however, it is quite possible that we have not sufficiently understood environmental influences and therefore not given them sufficient weight in either diagnosis or treatment. Concerning this we must be open minded.

Fortunately there are now a number of social scientists who see the possibility of fruitful collaboration with casework, who want an opportunity to convey their ideas to us and who also recognize and respect our contribution and the bodies of knowledge on which we have heretofore based our practice. Together we may contribute to the assimilation of useful social science theory by social work, to the organization, definition, testing, and validation of our own data and theories, and to the joint development of new theory.

Short Cuts

In the limited space available I shall deal very briefly with the second type of challenge by which casework is currently confronted —the challenge of the short cut. Three proposals have been presented to us as short cuts to expanded services but all have dangerous potentials for undermining the effectiveness of our work with clients. The first concerns recording, the second supervision, and the third modification of the master's program.

1. *Recording*

Recording is undoubtedly time-consuming and hence expensive. The increased use of periodic summaries has a number of advantages, especially when summaries are written from informal notes jotted down immediately after the interview and written in such a way that they serve the purpose of organizing the diagnostic data and clearly outlining trends in treatment. Recently, however, there has been word of agencies where dictation is done only at six-month intervals or even delayed until the closing of the case. The danger here is very great that the record will become a statement merely of what the worker hopes he has done rather than of what actually occurred.

19

Our real need is for differential dictation. The more skilled the worker, the more summarized recording can be relied upon. Frequency of summarization should vary directly with the complexity of the case. Furthermore, enough primary data should be included even in summaries to give the reader direct evidence of some of the treatment process. In addition, every worker should regularly dictate at least a few records in process form. The less experienced and skilled the worker, the more essential is this practice. It is easy to dictate, "I reassured" or "I helped him to understand" or even "I handled his resistance." The important question is, "How?" To answer this there is no substitute for process recording. Countertransference reactions, too, tend to be completely obscured by greatly abbreviated summarization. Skill does not lie only in diagnostic thinking and broad treatment planning. To an equal if not greater extent it is found in the *art* of the treatment process. This skill can be improved only by studying the fine details of our work and for this most of us need detailed recording. This useful tool for improving therapeutic techniques was first developed in casework. We can modify it and improve it, but we must not so debase it that in effect we abandon it. To do so brings us perilously close to irresponsible practice.

2. *Supervision*

Supervision has been under criticism in recent years partly because it is expensive and takes time away from direct work with clients and partly because it is said to encourage dependence, which is not only distasteful to experienced workers but prevents them from making independent contributions to professional practice.*

Because there is some truth to these contentions we are moving toward the conception of a senior caseworker who is ready to carry full responsibility for his own casework procedures and to seek consultation on cases as he needs it rather than continuing under close supervision. In agency practice there is no way of sidestepping the ultimate responsibility of the agency for the quality and scope of its work. Certain administrative checks and procedures are necessary, but it is entirely possible for an agency to designate a point of competence at which the worker in day-to-day practice carries

* *Editor's Note:* See Lucille N. Austin, Chapter 16 of this volume.

full responsibility for his own direct work with clients, seeking consultation only as he himself feels the need for it. Two safeguards, however, must be taken when this is done. First, sufficient provision must be made for regular consultation. Experienced workers carry extremely difficult and challenging cases; they, too, need checks to correct subjectivity and are not invulnerable to countertransference. Agencies will need to budget approximately two hours per worker every two weeks for consultation. The consultant will need additional time for reading the material to be discussed.

Second, care must be taken not to shift workers to this senior status until they are ready for it. An agency that uses this plan for young workers fresh from master's training is guilty of malpractice. It probably takes four years at the minimum and often five or six for the average worker to qualify for a complete shift to consultation rather than supervision. Some workers never do acquire this degree of skill. We very much need criteria for this level of performance by means of which we can determine when workers are ready to substitute consultation for supervision.

3. *Professional Training*

From time to time plans are proposed for modifying the basic training for social work. Insofar as these have to do with enriching the curriculum and raising the standard of performance they are worthy of consideration and experimentation. It is my impression that schools of social work on the whole do not demand as high a level of intellectual performance as the average student in the school is capable of. This is true in part because students come from very different backgrounds, and courses must often be geared to fill in the gaps for students who do not have appropriate undergraduate training. Some solution for this problem must be found. We shall either have to provide special supplementary instruction for the poorly prepared student or have to stratify the classes to provide more advanced studies for the well prepared student. Absolute prerequisites in the behavioral sciences might seem to be the solution, but unfortunately the quality of undergraduate teaching varies to such a degree that the number of courses taken by a student is no measure of the content he has covered.

I am convinced that many students need and would welcome a greater intellectual challenge, and that considerably more content could be injected into the curriculum without increasing the number of class hours. The additional content need not alter the basic structure of social work education. In some schools this additional content might focus on social science; in others it might be used to strengthen the psychiatric sequence, depending upon the needs of the individual school.

From time to time inroads are proposed on the amount of time devoted to field work. Field work too can be strengthened. In most schools of social work students could carry heavier caseloads, especially in the first year, thus giving them wider experience and preparing them better for the job pressures they will later face. Close co-ordination between field and classroom instructors could eliminate the apprenticeship quality of field work and strengthen its intellectual content. Material from courses other than casework could be integrated into field teaching if the agency and community aspects of field work were more fully developed. The total time given to field work should not be decreased. Indeed in many schools it should be increased for it is only as classroom knowledge is converted into practical skill that it has achieved its purpose. Both breadth and length of field experience under educational supervision are necessary.

The great demand for trained social workers sometimes tempts schools to introduce short cuts that inevitably lead to inferior training. If the field must use workers without adequate preparation— as, for the present, it obviously must—it is far better that such people be honestly recognized as technicians who do not have full training than that we give the name of graduate social worker to undertrained personnel. Shorter school programs will not in the long run attract the type of college graduate we need for social work.

Rather we need to win more respect among good undergraduates and college faculty members who play such a large part in the career choices of good students. There is reason to believe that the development of doctoral programs is increasing interest in social work. Undergraduate instructors in the social sciences should be advising their best students to enter social work, not those whom they believe not good enough for college teaching and doctoral work. We desperately need more men in the field, but easy training plans are not the way to attract men of the caliber needed.

On the monetary side, we must put more money into fellowships, and secure more fellowships without agency strings attached to them. And we must continue the current upward thrust in salaries. A cheapened degree would be likely to have a negative rather than a positive effect on salaries.

Above all, we need more well-trained graduates and more scholarly and experienced social workers ready to take advanced training which will equip them for the caliber of leadership in practice, research, and teaching which will bring well-earned repute to our field.

Conclusion

This paper has ranged over many topics: casework and psychoanalysis, social science, and short cuts—some already undertaken in practice and others proposed. I trust that a certain underlying point of view has become apparent. Casework has developed a body of knowledge and skill in which it can justly place confidence; it must continue to develop by keeping a non-defensive, intellectually receptive attitude toward potentially useful new ideas. Casework must be willing to modify its own methods and procedures. Each such change must be measured realistically against the single criterion of its effect upon our ability to help the client. Casework itself must make such decisions. We must neither resist new ideas nor succumb to them too readily. Above all, we must not lose respect for well-demonstrated principles of casework, and must be sturdy and hard-headed in standing for these principles and practices when this stand is warranted, as well as ready to modify them when there is sufficient evidence that our clients would benefit thereby.

Part II

Theoretical Considerations

2. The Concept of Ego-Supportive Psychotherapy*

Bernard Bandler

ANY SCIENTIFIC THEORY of therapy must have as its base a scientific theory of health and of disease, precise normative knowledge of the variations within the range of health throughout the life span, and a metapsychological classification of disease. Therapy is specific when directed at the basic factors in the underlying disorder and at mobilizing the forces of health. But we are confronted initially with the problem that we have no adequate nosology, no adequate classification of psychological disease, although we possess both the psychoanalytic theory of psychology and the theory of psychopathology. In the absence of any scientific etiologic classification of health and disease, and in the absence of much basic normative data, we lack a firm foundation on which to construct our principles of psychotherapy.

How, then, shall we define the term "ego-supportive psychotherapy"? From one point of view, all psychological forms of therapy are "ego-supportive." None of them aims to weaken or to overthrow the ego. This fact may seem too obvious to mention, except that one of the great contributions of ego psychology is the recognition that our therapeutic efforts are focused upon the ego. The most frequent error in the beginning therapist is unwittingly to

* Presented at a meeting sponsored by the New England Chapter of the Smith College School for Social Work Alumnae Association, Boston, May 19, 1961.

side with the id, superego, or reality against the ego. The "wild" psychoanalysis described by Freud still has its contemporary counterpart in wild psychotherapies.[1] Who has not seen the psychotherapy that identifies too early with the reality of other people in the client's life, or with sexual strivings or aggressive trends, or adopts attitudes that reinforce the client's sense of guilt? Psychoanalysis is also ego-supportive. In the first phase, one establishes a therapeutic alliance with the ego which is profoundly ego-supportive. Throughout analysis one endeavors always to maintain the threshold of anxiety at a level that will not overwhelm the ego. Psychoanalysis obviously is more than just ego-supportive, but psychoanalysis is to be distinguished from all forms of psychotherapy and not merely differentiated from ego-supportive activities.

A Clinical Analysis of Supportive Therapy

We thus turn necessarily to our clinical experience to see to what extent we can generalize from our practice in our efforts to define ego-supportive psychotheraphy. The situations in which we are most obviously supportive are those moments of crisis in which the ego is overwhelmed or is about to be. Here all our efforts initially are expended on helping the ego maintain itself; we employ every device at our command to forestall its disruption. We do not, in these patients, explore the id, but rather come to the ego's rescue in its defensive operations against the id. We are all on the ego's side against the superego. We do everything possible to mitigate the demands of reality and to assist the ego in remaining in some contact with it. Ego-supportive therapy, in these instances, would fall easily on the repressive side of the dichotomy between repressive and expressive psychotherapy. Or one might say that ego-supportive means ego-restitutive or ego-conservative.

There are other situations, however, if not of crisis at least of considerable momentary stress, in which the client comes to us when the ego is not in such danger; when, in fact, it is relatively intact. I am thinking of our experiences with college students who increasingly turn to psychiatric and casework counseling services for

[1] Sigmund Freud, "Observations on 'Wild' Psycho-Analysis," *International Psycho-Analytical Library*, No. 8, Ernest Jones (ed.), Hogarth Press, London, 1949, pp. 297–304.

28

assistance and are often helped in the course of a few interviews. Our observation indicates that many of their episodes of anxiety and psychosomatic symptoms are transient and within the range of normal behavior, like the universal nightmares and transient phobias of childhood. Probably no one would dignify the brief psychotherapy consisting of five sessions with a more elevated title than ego-supportive. But if we analyze what is achieved in these sessions, the definition of support becomes far from simple. In a way, this type of support now seems the antithesis of support as represented in our previous example, when the ego was threatened with dissolution.

With what problems do these students confront us? Typically they are in a temporarily acute phase of trying to cope with such problems as separation from home, re-examination of values, realization of sexual drives, the struggle between strivings for dependence and independence, problems of identity, choice of career, and decisions about marriage. And what do we talk about with these students? Usually about these very things. We help the ego to recognize these issues, to identify them, to see them in perspective, and to cope with them. We deal with id and superego. Our therapy is not ego-restitutive, but ego-progressive; it is not repressive but, within the limits of time, expressive.[2] It is true, of course, that we deal only with certain facets of experience and that we do not go very far—if by far we are thinking of psychoanalysis as our model. But we clarify, possibly even interpret, and at times work with the preconscious; our activity may facilitate ego growth and ego synthesis of id and superego.

Our goals in these two situations seem very different. In the first it was ego-maintaining or restitutive, or ego-conservative in the broadest sense. In the second, it was a change or growth in the ego, an enlargement of its synthetic capacities, an ego-progressive psychotherapy. Should we then consider ego-supportive psychotherapy that form of psychotherapy whose goal is ego-conservative and contrast it with ego-progressive psychotherapy whose goals are a change or growth in the ego, a development of new capacities, functioning, and sublimations? This differentiation

[2] See Heinz Hartmann, *Ego Psychology and the Problem of Adaptation,* International Universities Press, New York, 1958, p. 36.

could then be elaborated further by referring to the techniques that are most appropriate and common to the two forms. The over-all *repressive* methods, including the techniques of suggestion, mobilization, and manipulation would be the techniques of choice for ego-supportive, ego-conservative psychotherapy. The *uncovering* techniques of clarification, and particularly of interpretation, would be those appropriate for ego-progressive psychotherapy.

Although this distinction, in terms of goals, has much to commend it, it strikes us as oversimplified. The example of student counseling was given as a clinical illustration of supportive psychotherapy. In spite of its obvious differences from the kind of support offered in a crisis situation, both types seem to belong together when contrasted with those intensive forms of psychotherapy whose goals are a more radical alteration of the structural relationships in the psychic apparatus with respect to ego, id, and superego and whose techniques consist more extensively of clarification and interpretation, and aim at greater self-knowledge. But we should caution ourselves not to be betrayed by words. "Radical alteration" sounds profound; if, however, we compare the results of our work with some of our patients in ego-supportive psychotherapy with that of our most successful patients in prolonged intensive psychotherapy, can we so easily determine whose egos have grown more and have undergone more change?

If goals do not enable us to define ego-supportive psychotherapy, possibly we can arrive at an understanding of the term by referring to techniques. Among the various techniques such as mobilization, manipulation, suggestion, clarification, and interpretation which aim at insight, there may be one, or a preferential grouping of a number, that constitutes the essence of supportive psychotherapy. Yet, if we look at practice, all these techniques are employed, although to varying degrees with different clients. There is such a continuum in what we actually do with clients that, although at one time our emphasis may be on one or another technique, there is often an overlap and interplay over a span of time. And, if we consider a theoretical approach, we find that a definition whose essence lies in a particular technique would inevitably be partial and arbitrary. It would, for example, be like defining psychoanalysis in

30

terms of the technique of interpretation aiming at insight. It is true that interpretation is the basic technique of psychoanalysis; it is not true that psychoanalysis can be defined essentially in terms of interpretation whose aim is insight.

In moments of semantic stress, one turns to the dictionary. When we consult the Oxford Dictionary we note that support means to maintain, to endure, to strengthen, to furnish food or sustenance.[3] We might comment that support is here given significant maternal functions. The dictionary further attributes to support the function of propping up, of keeping from falling, of bearing the weight of, and of sustaining. Support is here given significant paternal functions. In addition, support prevents giving way, and keeps from being exhausted and perishing. Finally, the dictionary defines support as "spiritual help and mental comfort" Any form of therapy that furnishes sustenance, strengthens, keeps from perishing, maintains, furnishes spiritual help and mental comfort, is obviously a basic form of therapy. "Maternal functions" and "paternal functions" were used in comment on some of the definitions; as we list all the functions of support—parental, progressive, developmental, and educational—the term "life functions" comes more appropriately to mind.

The Life Model

When we review these functions we seem suddenly removed from the terminology we have hitherto been utilizing—for example, ego, insight, and clarification—to another frame of reference, the frame of reference of life. We realize suddenly that we are confronted with the question of models, a question that is in the forefront of current scientific concern. Are there any models of ego-supportive psychotherapy? And have we implicitly been following them? The answer to both questions, I believe, is "Yes." But the two questions can be answered in another way. The implicit model, at least for many psychiatrists, if not for social workers, is psychoanalysis. The ideal model, I believe, is life itself, the natural processes of growth and development and the rich trajectory of the life span.

[3] *The Oxford English Dictionary*, Vol. X, Clarendon Press, Oxford, 1933, pp. 207–209.

Children do grow and solve problems and resolve conflicts with the aid of parents and teachers, without the benefit of psychotherapy. Parents do help their children to mature without technical guides and professional counseling. The ideal of psychic normality is never fully realized any more than is the ideal of absolute health either in life or in therapy. But life itself, its processes and almost infinite successful experiments, can be our model, and the goals of psychotherapy are to approximate arduously what is accomplished ideally in living.

If we take seriously the proposition that life, its processes and successful methods of solving problems and resolving conflicts, is our model for psychotherapy, we are confronted by a significant phenomenon. Some of the most important experiences of conflict, resolution, and growth take place entirely in the unconscious. In their deepest roots they are alien to awareness and to self-knowledge. They leave, as a result, no traces that are accessible to memory. Although unconscious, these conflicts are far from silent. They are lived through their derivatives. It is with the derivatives that children struggle and it is the derivatives that parents influence. The oedipus complex is a classical example. How do successful parents in different cultures help children to solve the oedipal problem? We know a certain amount about how children accomplish this feat through the reconstruction of childhood in adult analyses, as well as by the direct observation and analysis of children. We still have much to learn. But to what extent and in what detail have we studied the contributions of parents, not to psychopathology but to the fruition of normal functioning and of growth? I believe there is a considerable lack in our knowledge in this area compared to our knowledge of psychopathology. It is superfluous to add that the methods employed by parents are not simply manipulative and that talking things over is the human method of problem-solving *par excellence*.

The extensive research on child development conducted in centers throughout the country during the past ten years is yielding invaluable data on the earliest phases of life, the unfolding processes of growth and maturation, and the matrix of relationships that nourish, sustain, facilitate, impede, and distort develop-

32

ment.[4] Much of the data still awaits precise analysis, interpretation, and evaluation; it will be years before all the definitive conclusions can be drawn. Only with the completion of the life span of those children now being studied can we firmly evaluate the relative interplay of constitution and environment and the extent to which one phase of development is incidental and peripheral to the personality or predisposing and determining for the future. I believe that these studies will eventually make the most significant contributions to psychotherapy, and the more we learn about the optimal conditions for human growth—the psychophysiology of health, the normal methods of satisfying needs, ways of learning to achieve sublimations, and problem- and conflict-solving—the more shall we be able to utilize this knowledge as the model for our psychotherapy.

There are two assumptions underlining my argument which should be made explicit. The first is that there are two major tendencies in all people from birth to death which are ceaselessly in opposition. These might well be termed the progressive and regressive trends in human nature. Our lives are circumscribed by these polarities. The second assumption is that, other things being equal, progressive forces are the stronger. Growing up, all education, and that special form of education known as psychotherapy, are based upon such forces. Viewed in this framework, mental illness would then be an expression of blocks, obstructions, interferences, arrests and fixations of the progressive forces, which leads to and results in a strengthening and reinforcement of the regressive trends. Our therapeutic task, then, is twofold. First, we must identify and help remove the blocks and obstacles; with our typical orientation to pathology this is often the major focus of many psychotherapists. Second, we must identify the progressive forces with which we can ally ourselves and which, at the appropriate time, we can help mobilize. This aspect of our therapeutic task tends to be relatively neglected. Yet it may be the most effective instrument for the removal of obstacles. Of all these forces love is the most effective antidote to anxiety.

[4] See, for example, John D. Benjamin, "Prediction and Psychopathological Theory" in *Dynamic Psychopathology in Childhood*, Lucie Jessner and Eleanor Pavenstedt, (eds.), Grune and Stratton, New York, 1959, pp. 6–77.

33

The Psychoanalytic Model

By and large, life has not been taken as the model for ego-supportive psychotherapy. The implicit model, as suggested earlier, has been psychoanalysis. I realize that social workers, although deeply versed in psychoanalytic theory, have taken an independent and original course in their development of casework treatment. Most psychiatrists, however, have followed a different direction. It is to psychiatry, therefore, that I am primarily referring when I suggest that psychoanalysis has been the main implicit model which all other forms of psychotherapy approximate and by which they are judged. Furthermore, I believe it is much truer of the psychiatrist than of the social worker to say that the psychoanalyst and the fantasy of a psychoanalyst form the model on which he bases his therapeutic efforts.

In this connection we can no longer defer dealing with the distinction between psychoanalysis and psychotherapy. Rangell's definition of psychoanalysis is as follows:

Psychoanalysis is a method of therapy *whereby* conditions are brought about favorable for the development of a transference neurosis, in which the past is restored in the present, *in order that,* through a systematic interpretive attack on the resistances which oppose it, there occurs a resolution of that neurosis (transference *and* infantile) *to the end* of bringing about structural changes in the mental apparatus of the patient to make the latter capable of optimum adaptation to life.[5]

I would add to this definition only "through free association." Psychoanalysis thus involves a progressive rollback of the personality to the infantile, most deeply unconscious sources of conflict, including unconscious fantasy, and to the geneses (so far as they are reachable by psychological techniques), of the methods of adaptation, the forms of relating, as well as to the origins of the defenses and character formation. Psychoanalysis in theory thus seeks to effect a basic modification in character, to undo fixations and to interrupt the repetition compulsion, making optional and elective what was hitherto obligatory. Its primary technique is insight through interpretation.

[5] Leo Rangell, "Similarities and Differences Between Psychoanalysis and Dynamic Psychotherapy," *Journal of the American Psychoanalytic Association,* Vol. II, No. 4 (1954), pp. 734–744.

From this point of view, it would seem that even the most profound psychotherapies are superficial and palliative. Because of the differences in method, they would be unable to penetrate deeply into the unconscious (except as wild psychotherapy), to trace back conflicts to their earliest origins, and to understand the infantile roots of character and of the defenses. How, then, could they undo fixations, abolish the repetition compulsion, and modify the methods of adaptation and of the defenses? Yet we know from experience what profound changes occur in the personality and what progressive development takes place in the course of or in consequence of psychotherapy. The theoretical problem remains: How is it possible and how is it accomplished? The approach to the answer lies, I believe, in turning again to the model of life rather than to the model of psychoanalysis. In this paper, however, we can only acknowledge the profound theoretical problems involved; we cannot undertake their solution.

A Metapsychological Approach

We mentioned at the beginning of this paper that one of the bases for a scientific theory of therapy is a metapsychological classification of disease. We do not have such a classification at the present time. It might be instructive, however, to examine the psychotherapies from a metapsychological point of view; that is, from the structural, genetic, topographical, dynamic, and economic points of view. Most writing on the psychotherapies focuses on the structural point of view. This is quite natural since we tend to think most often in structural terms of the ego, id, and superego in relationship to each other and to reality. The psychotherapies, however, have many facets, many partial goals, and a variety of methods. They are so various, in fact, that we can think of the definition and classification of the psychotherapies in terms of the problem on which our attention is primarily focused: the general and specific *goals* and the general and specific *techniques*. If the primary threat to the ego, for example, is in its relationship to reality, our general goal is ego-conservative or restitutive. This danger often involves the actual or imminent threat of disruption of the ego and the loss of its control in its own psychic house in relationship

35

to the other intra-psychic structures—a situation prevailing in psychosis or in threatened psychosis.

In addition to the over-all ego-restorative goal, there may be subsidiary goals, such as the enhancement or restoration of specific ego functions concerning reality-perception, reality-testing, and the development of trust in interpersonal relationships. The techniques used to achieve such a goal involve mobilization directed toward the actual environment and those forces within the personality (for example, repression) that facilitate the restoration of balance. An over-all classification of this type of psychotherapy might be as follows: Major goal—ego-restitutive; subsidiary goals—restitution and enhancement of the ego functions of perception and trust. The techniques by which these goals can be realized would include manipulation, mobilization through strengthening of repressive forces, and an increase of self-esteem and of self-identity.

There are many other familiar clinical situations exclusive of psychosis, in which the client is so threatened by reality or so mired in its importunate demands that apparently little can be done except to listen, or to attempt to lighten burdens. This is particularly true when there are few or no satisfactory relationships, the ego is rigid and lacking plasticity, the tolerance for anxiety is low, the threat from aggressive drives is great, and denial and projection play massive defensive roles. In these cases of threats from reality, our goals again appear to be ego-conservative or restitutive and our techniques those of relationship, nurture, mobilization, and limited clarification. Yet, even here it is easy to oversimplify. Both the processes of life and the processes of the therapeutic interaction are often more complex, fluid, and mobile than our most refined terminology. Even in these most difficult cases, our goals are not infrequently to assist the client in some facets of his relationships, to moderate to some extent his most unfavorable adaptive patterns, and help to achieve some satisfactions. Obviously, not everything is worked on simultaneously and some areas of functioning that show improvement may not even have been touched on at all. One of the most remarkable facts of psychotherapy is that an advance in one area of functioning—the achievement of a satisfactory relationship, the accomplishment of a sublimation—can release the progressive forces and effect a redistribution of energies which is reflected in an improvement of functioning in many areas with which we have not been directly concerned. Nor do I believe that a close study of the exchanges between worker and client over a long-term period will show that the only techniques employed in the ambiance of the relationship are those of mobilization and suggestion. Some understanding, along with the feeling of "being understood," is also communicated although clarification and explicit interpretation may have been minimal.

Still within the framework of the structural point of view, we now turn our attention from the relationship of the ego to reality to its relationship with the id and the superego. There is no need to underline the significance of guilt in the lives of our clients. Its manifestations are ubiquitous. (Yet I often wonder if the pendulum of interest has swung too far in the direction of guilt and the aggressive drives, with resultant neglect and underplaying of the significance of the libidinal forces.) What are some of the more simple ways with which we deal with guilt in psychotherapy? First, of course, is the attitude we display in the therapeutic alliance of worker and client, of worker and self, in the relationship and in the ensuing transference. Tone and attitude can at times do much to mitigate superego excesses. The restoration of self-esteem through tactful appreciation of accomplishments, both past and present, may also gradually ameliorate the sense of guilt. And if, as frequently happens, guilt is mediated by an identification with a lost object, then helping the client to become aware of the very fact of identification may moderate the sense of guilt. Nothing has been said so far of the client's masochism, ambivalence, and often deep-seated aggression. The client's aggression is often so strong and so rigidly repudiated that it may never be touched. In such clients, the goals may be an improvement of some relationships and the attainment of sublimations. In others, however, at the appropriate time, it may be possible to permit some derivative expressions of aggression, perhaps directed at some secondary figure rather than the primary initial object of hostility.

How can we generalize these random examples of some of our methods of dealing with the relationship between ego and superego into some valid statements about psychotherapy? Our over-all goal is largely one of conservation. It is to restore the previous balance between ego and superego. Our more immediate goals may be to moderate the superego through the client's identification with our attitudes in the transference, enhance the client's self-esteem, or loosen a pathological identification. And what about our techniques? At this point, we may begin to feel (to paraphrase Churchill) that "never before did so few accomplish so much." Have we perhaps been too schematic and over-reduced our technical armamentarium to manipulation, mobilization, suggestion, clarification, and interpretation? Certainly all techniques, except interpretation, are very much involved in the above example of dealing with guilt. And to what technique shall we ascribe making the patient aware of an identification of which he was oblivious? The exposure of concealed pathological identification is often the critical phase in our work with many patients. How does this jibe with the dichotomy that equates supportive therapy with repressive techniques as opposed to expressive or uncovering techniques? Certainly making the patient conscious of such an identification utilizes expressive and uncovering techniques, although the expression need not extend to the aggressive drives themselves. But in using the word "conscious" with its implied relationship to the preconscious and unconscious, I have unwittingly shifted my metapsychological stance. I have moved from a structural point of view to a topographical one.

However, before discussing ego-supportive psychotherapy from the topographical point of view, I should like to comment again on the relationship between the ego and the superego. The cases we have been discussing have all been characterized by an excess of superego. There is also the problem of superego defect, of a deficit in the superego. In our work with delinquents, for example, we encounter this phenomenon daily. Our goal is not restitutive or conservative, but progressive. Our task is to create something new. Through the transference we serve as auxiliary ego ideals which mark the halfway point in the development of a new superego, a new self-image. And what techniques do we use? Here less than anywhere do we use interpretations and development of insight to make the unconscious conscious, although we so often associate interpretation and insight with our goals of profound and creative personality changes.

Our brief discussion of psychotherapy from the topographical point of view—that is, the relationships, forms of communication, and barriers between conscious, preconscious, and unconscious—is based on the realization that a complete analysis of the psychotherapies would have to include a systematic analysis of their principles in their relationship to psychic topography.

When Freud introduced the structural point of view with his series of books on the ego, beginning with *Group Psychology and the Analysis of the Ego*,[6] and came to the realization that much of the ego and of the superego (as well as the id) are unconscious, he changed his formula for the goals of analysis from making the unconscious conscious to "Where id was, there shall ego be."[7] Topography, however, has retained its basic importance. How far into the unconscious can psychotherapy penetrate? Or, put in another way, how much of the deep unconscious can psychotherapy make conscious? I believe the differences between psychotherapy and psychoanalysis introduce a significant limiting factor. Only psychoanalysis, I believe, will give systematic access to the deepest stratum of the unconscious. Psychotherapy, even with interpretation, has access largely to the preconscious and limited sectors of the unconscious. Wild psychotherapy is a different matter. A more interesting question is whether the topographical point of view permits a classification of the psychotherapies. Would they then fall into two major categories: the *conservative* or restitutive (characterized by repressive goals, the primary grouping of the techniques of mobilization, manipulation, and suggestion, and work with the conscious and preconscious) and the *progressive* (characterized by expressive goals, the primary grouping of the techniques of clarification and interpretation, and more extensive work with the preconscious and the unconscious)? Much of our experience, viewed roughly, might fit into such schemata. My doubts about these subdivisions of psychotherapy are that many cases, when viewed closely, contain elements that require both types of treatment, although to different degrees. A pluralistic formulation of

[6] Sigmund Freud, *International Psycho-Analytical Library, No. 6*, Ernest Jones (ed.), Hogarth Press, London, 1948.
[7] Sigmund Freud, *New Introductory Lectures on Psycho-Analysis*, W. W. Norton and Company, New York, 1933, p. 112.

39

the psychotherapies, I believe, will come closer to the truth and may be of greater help in our application to clinical practice.

By the genetic point of view, I refer, not to the current dynamics of the client's dysfunction, but to the temporal origins of the psychic structure, their vicissitudes and development. Here again the theoretical difference between psychoanalysis and ego-supportive psychotherapy is clear. Psychoanalysis enables one—in optimal cases—to roll back each facet and modality of the personality to the nuclear conflicts of infancy.[8] Psychotherapy obviously reaches into the past, but more commonly only to adolescence and latency; the barriers of infantile amnesia are largely impenetrable by it. As a result, the basic fixations are inaccessible to us. The full scope of the infantile neurosis will not be re-experienced in the transference. Even if some facets of the infantile neurosis find expression in the transference and in acting out, they will, in the main, not be intelligible to us.

What theoretical implications concerning the principles and classification of the psychotherapies follow from these facts? One that suggests itself immediately is that they may be differentiated according to the extent and degree to which they deal with the potentially accessible genetic factors. The crucial phrase here is "deal with." We obviously have to know about the relevant past and some of the genetic factors in order to understand the client. Hence, all forms of psychotherapy deal with the genetic factors in this sense. The basic issue is: What use do we make of the understanding? Do we utilize our understanding without referring to it in our interviews? Do we establish linkages for the client between present and past? Or do we try to resolve some of the conflicts of the patient, not *via* current figures alone, but through direct work with the conflictual relationships to the primary persons (in the historical and genetic sense) of the patient's life? It can be argued that the ego-conservative, supportive form of psychotherapy confines itself more to the current scene, and the ego-progressive form with its expressive techniques gives greater scope to genetic factors. My own preference is again toward the pluralistic rather than the dualistic view of psychotherapies. There are many in-

---

[8] For a discussion of the conflict-free area of the ego see Heinz Hartmann, *op. cit.*, pp. 3–21.

stances of work with clients where our goals are restitutive, our technique largely manipulative and mobilizational, and where there is some outstanding event from the past which dominates the current scene and with which we must deal. In attempting to attain theoretical simplicity and tidiness we risk distorting and doing violence to the richness and variety of our clinical experience. My thesis is that we should include the genetic point of view explicitly both in our principles of psychotherapy and in their application to the over-all casework planning for each individual client.

Everything genetic in the client's personality, however, is not operative in his current dysfunction. The past is not only silent, much of it may also be quiescent. What is genetically determined in the formation of the personality is not necessarily dynamically relevant. Thus, consideration of the genetic point of view brings us inevitably to the dynamic point of view—to the needs, problems, and conflicts of the client, and to those clashing forces within the ego, id, and superego with which we deal daily in our psychotherapies. The significance of the psychodynamic point of view requires no elaboration here. Psychoanalysis can again be differentiated theoretically from psychotherapy; in the course of psychoanalysis a more comprehensive part of the genetically-determined past becomes dynamically re-activated, especially in the transference neurosis. But not necessarily all, as Freud pointed out in "Analysis Terminable and Interminable." [9] The dynamic point of view, however, can make its contribution to the classification of the psychotherapies.

The economic point of view will be mentioned, not only to complete the categories, but because it is, I believe, the one least taken into account in our theoretical considerations. The economic concept deals with psychic energies in their quantitative aspects, their distribution and availability. Ultimately, in our diagnosis, in our planning, and in our therapy we are confronted by the question of quantity. Our basic everyday vocabulary is saturated with quantitative terms. We speak of the strength of the drives, the strength or weakness of the ego, the strength of the superego, and the strength of the transference. Ultimately, as Freud said, quoting Napoleon,

[9] Sigmund Freud, *International Psycho-Analytical Library, No. 37*, Ernest Jones (ed.), Hogarth Press, London, 1950, pp. 316–357.

41

"Victory lies with the largest battalions." Space, unfortunately, does not permit an elaboration of the economic point of view. We are reminded, however, with respect to its significance, that the full title of Freud's classic paper on masochism is "The Economic Problem in Masochism." [10]

Summary

The first problem confronting any theory of psychotherapy is the absence of any adequate theoretical classification of disease. A rational rather than an empirical discussion of the principles of ego-supportive psychotherapy would necessarily have such a classification of disease as its base. In the absence of a metapsychological theory of the classification of disease, the principles of psychotherapy have no firm theoretical foundation. We can and do turn to our rich clinical experience and attempt to generalize from our practices. These generalizations, while useful in clarifying our understanding of what we do in teaching and in supervision, run the risk of arbitrariness and oversimplification. This risk entails the danger of distorting our understanding and our analyses of clinical experience. There is the further danger of oversimplified concepts of practice, which, while relatively easy to master intellectually, may be applied too literally and hence lead to an impoverishment of casework rather than its enrichment.

The second problem confronting a discussion of the principles of ego-supportive psychotherapy is the absence of any conceptual analysis of the meaning of "supportive." How can one discuss principles if there is not some consensus as to the meaning of the term and hence to the area of clinical experience relevant to our discourse? Considerable time was spent, consequently, on a critical analysis of the meaning of support. The concept of support was extended to embrace parental, progressive, educational, and life functions. Viewed in this larger sense, then, all psychotherapy is ego-supportive.

It was suggested that the model to which we turn should be, not the implicit model of the psychoanalyst, but life itself, its processes of growth, development, and decline, its methods of problem-solving and need-satisfaction as understood in the trajectory of the

[10] *International Psycho-Analytical Library, No. 8,* Ernest Jones (ed.), Hogarth Press, London, 1933, pp. 255–268.

life span. That model, I believe, will help us to understand the release of progressive forces and the growth of personality that ensues—often to our surprise—after we have undertaken a limited piece of work in ego-restitutive psychotherapy. I should like to make one point very clear. When I speak of discarding the psychoanalyst as our model and using as our model life itself, I am not speaking of discarding psychoanalytic understanding and psychoanalytic theory, which we all use in our attempt to understand our clients, our casework practices, and the processes of the life span.

The psychotherapies were then contrasted with psychoanalysis. No experienced psychiatrist or caseworker, of course, confuses the two in practice, but it is essential to distinguish between the two in theory if we are to have a firm grasp of the principles with which we work.

It was then suggested that our guideline to the understanding and classification of the psychotherapies be a metapsychological one, and that a comprehensive picture of each include the structural, topographical, genetic, dynamic, and economic points of view. These profiles of the forms of psychotherapy would include statements about (1) general goals, (2) subsidiary and specific goals, (3) general techniques, and (4) specific techniques.

Where, in these forms of psychotherapy, does ego-supportive psychotherapy fit and what is our concept of it? My argument has been in favor of the pluralistic view of the psychotherapies rather than a dualistic one. I would even suggest that we discard the term ego support if I did not know that many others find it useful and clarifying. The concept of ego-supportive psychotherapy suggested here is that it is the form of psychotherapy that deals with the goals of ego-conservation or ego-restitution; aims at restoring the defenses; emphasizes the techniques of mobilization, manipulation, and suggestion; topographically deals with the conscious rather than the preconscious or unconscious; and dynamically deals with the present rather than the past, with conflicts in relationship to current derivative figures rather than to those of a primary genetic nature.

But something vital, essential, omnipresent has been left out, as if we were to discuss the principles of parenthood without talking about the parent-child relationship. We all know and acknowledge

43

the basic importance of the worker-client relationship. It is the medium in which everything happens; without it nothing happens. We all know about transference cures; we usually speak of them disparagingly as something incomplete and transient. Yet I wonder whether sometimes in our analyses of our case material, in our focus on principles, goals, and techniques, we neglect the significance of relationship in the therapeutic process and in the therapeutic results. The reciprocal relationship is not merely the medium in which restitution and growth take place; we, as the objects to whom the patient relates (like parents and educators, *via* identification), take our place in his personality and contribute to its consolidation and modification. Therefore a complete statement of the principles of psychotherapies must accord primacy, among techniques, to the therapist's conscious use of his personality in the relationship.

3. Inner Stress in Illness and Disability*

Charlotte G. Babcock

AMONG THE MANY conceptions of stress that appear in professional literature, those related to ego operations seem most relevant to clinical problems. Under most circumstances stress remains manageable as long as the integrative capacity of the ego is greater than the integrative task presented to it. The concept that growth occurs in response to a degree of stress commensurate with the individual potential to bear it is equally well known. The ego can assist itself from past and present experience and may call into action inactive or undeveloped internal resources to increase its span. Or it can be helped to increase its reserve and thus its span through resources external to it, as exemplified by the interaction that ensues when a client makes known a problem and receives psychological and material help from the social worker.

Relation of Stress to the Ego Functions

The usefulness of this orientation to the interplay between stress and ego functions lies chiefly in the questions it raises. What are the forces that affect the integrative task imposed by stress and the integrative capacity of the individual? How do these forces interact to yield the resolutions we observe in our work and how may

* This material is based on a paper presented at the Annette Garrett Memorial Institute sponsored by the Michigan Chapter of the Smith College School for Social Work Alumnae Association, Detroit, November 8, 1960.

45

this complex process be influenced? Let us try to examine these questions through study of the stress created by an illness or disability.

For our purpose, stress is any stimulus, or series of stimuli, initiated from within or external to the individual, which is experienced as a potential or actual threat toward his basic urges and needs, rather than toward those perceived as less vital to his existence.[1] Such stressors threaten the span of those capacities or mechanisms that ordinarily can regulate pressure (load) or traffic (ordering of stimuli). Stress is experienced in terms of time (duration) and intensity; thus we speak of illness as acute or chronic, and as mild, moderate, or severe. In addition to the duration and the intensity of the illness or disability, we must take into consideration the characteristics of the individual as reflected in his age, biological endowment, the events of his past history that give clues to his reserve factors in meeting the current stresses, and his personal experience—as well as that of significant other persons—with health and disability.

Theories and established data defining the phenomena of growth and development of the ego are frequent in the professional literature, as are those pertaining to growth and development of the derivatives of the biological drives and of the superego.[2] By use of its two perceptive "surfaces," one directed toward instinctive impulses and needs and the other toward external reality through the

[1] For further discussion of definitions and their advantages and disadvantages for operational use, see Daniel H. Funkenstein, and others, *Mastery of Stress*, Harvard University Press, Cambridge, 1957; Fred E. Horvath, "Psychological Stress: A Review of Definitions and Experimental Research," in *Yearbook of the Society for General Systems Research*, Ludvig von Bertalanffy and Anatol Rapaport (eds.), Ann Arbor, Michigan, Vol. 4 (1959), pp. 203–230; Richard S. Lazarus, and others, "The Effects of Psychological Stress upon Performance," *Psychological Bulletin*, Vol. 49 (1952), pp. 292–317; Donald Oken and others, "Stress Response in a group of Chronic Psychiatric Patients," *Archives of General Psychiatry*, Vol. 3, No. 5 (1960), pp. 451–461, and Hans Selye, *The Stress of Life*, McGraw-Hill, New York, 1956; William A. Caudill, *Effects of Social and Cultural Systems in Reaction to Stress*, Pamphlet, No. 14, Social Science Research Council, New York, 1958.

[2] See, for example, Erik H. Erikson, *Identity and the Life Cycle*, International Universities Press, New York, 1959, and David Rapaport, "Historical Survey of Psychoanalytic Ego Psychology" in the same volume; Heinz Hartmann, *Ego Psychology and the Problem of Adaptation*, International Universities Press, New York, 1958; John D. Benjamin, "The Innate and the Experiential in Child Development," in *Lectures on Experimental Psychiatry*, Henry W. Brosin, (ed.), University of Pittsburgh Press, 1961, pp. 19–42.

sensory perceptive apparatus, the ego functions to perceive, distinguish, experience, and interpret the stimuli received by the organism. It then is in a position to carry out its tasks of mediation, integration, mastery and control of voluntary psychological, intellectual, emotional, and motor behavior which constitute the stimulus response. By these means the ego keeps the individual in a state of functioning equilibrium with optimal tension to operate smoothly but free of anxiety. This process permits anxiety to be available as a signal of change from either internal or external sources. Thus the ego, deriving its energy from the biological matrix and influenced by its developed superego and ego-ideal activity, and the environment, relates the organism to the reality principle. It should be clear that a large part of these processes and interlinkings occur at less than conscious levels. Although conscious phenomena are of the greatest importance, the moment, degree, and extent of consciousness vary in the handling of each stressor and stressor response.

Stress is handled by the ego. Determinants of stress as well as of ego strength are found in the biological matrix of any given person; in the sociological structure of the relevant environment; and in the scope and ramifications of the disease process within which the disability of the individual falls.

Illness and Disability as Sources of Stress

Illness and disability create psychological strain on the adaptive capacity of the ego; first, through the threats that the stress offers to the security and integrity of the person; second, through the impact upon the body image; and third, through pain. Since each individual begins to develop in early infancy a self-concept derived from the fact that the birth-growth-death sequence orders the phenomena of life, he has a sense of life span; stimuli that interfere at any given point in the normalcy of the total life span constitute such a threat. Threats to security are posed by such factors as actual deprivation or loss of biological or social resources for fulfilling normal need; inner inhibition or inner loss to the self as experienced through disturbances to the self-image, narcissistic injury, loss of a loved person or body part; loss of a source of dependent gratification; loss of an object for the expression of love

47

or for the expression of aggression; and loss of opportunity for gratifying sensoric or motoric need, or for productive work. Maladaptation of affect also constitutes a threat as exemplified by the neurotic employment of guilt or shame in the wish to use, or the actual use of, an illness as a solution to stress, or as a punishment for past omissions or commissions of behavior. Finally, the temptation to exploit an illness for secondary gain—once the primary conflict is assuaged by the illness—may be a source of conflict. These reactions to stress set in motion the threat of decompensation of ego function which in turn stimulates attempts at defensive repair.

Threats to security are manifested by well-known symptoms. Anxiety, which is felt in the ego—although not always consciously —is a frequent and prompt internal response to the threat. Delayed anxiety, a common manifestation of both physical and psychological shock, may not be felt until after the period of shock has passed, regardless of whether the stress stimulus is internal or external. Anxiety may appear directly in both its physiological and psychological components or indirectly in many concealed ways, such as pre-anxious states, conversion symptoms, or absorption by the multiple ego defenses.[3]

Pain, provided as a sensory mechanism of protection, often far exceeds this function. Like anxiety, pain is subjectively experienced. It is difficult both for the ego of the sufferer and for the external witness of the pain to measure and modulate it. Analogously, as the ego reacts to anxiety, so it reacts to pain as something startling, frightening, hurting, difficult to endure, and anxiety-producing. As does psychic pain and anxiety, physical pain acts as a message from the body to the ego, pleading for help. The adaptive mechanisms are stimulated by the pain and anxiety. Unless the ego is totally overwhelmed by the shock of these feelings, efforts at communication with the self-resources or with the outside world are immediately mobilized.[4] In order to understand

[3] Phyllis Greenacre, "The Predisposition to Anxiety" (Part I), *Psychoanalytic Quarterly*, Vol. 10, No. 1 (1941) pp. 66–94.

[4] Henry W. Brosin, "The Reciprocal Relations between Incentives, Motivation and Strain in Acute and Chronic Stressful Situations," pp. 209–218, and John P. Spiegel, "Psychological Transactions in Situations of Acute Stress," pp. 103–112, in *Symposium on Stress*, Division of Medical Science, National Research Council and Army Medical Service Graduate School, Walter Reed Medical Center, Washington, D.C., 1953.

patients who complain of pain, no matter how trivial or seemingly unrelated to what the observer can perceive in his examination of the situation, the observer must always keep in mind that the complaint is a message. It is a signal that something is out of balance in one of the patient's functioning systems.

Response of the Ego

Often, the steps taken in adaptation to the stress stimulus can be delineated. Take the instance of a major illness such as an acute attack of gall-bladder disease which might result in surgical intervention, or an automobile accident in which the person is threatened with the loss of an extremity. Pain brings not only its own suffering, but the prompt concern with actual or possible change to the body and the body image. Fear is present, usually fear of the pain, and of the uncertainty that it produces regarding possible change in the self and the self's relation to its environment; there is fear of the possible or actual loss, or of the fantasies that these possibilities stimulate. Anxiety accompanies both the pain and the fear. Hostile feelings appear simultaneously, or very soon and, with them, the anger, guilt, and perhaps shame for having been neglectful of oneself or others. Self-punitive fantasies may quickly express the feeling that one deserves what has happened.

In the moments or hours or days of the first shock of illness or accident, the ego musters its defenses. In the instance of the loss of a body part, one routinely and normally finds a series of defenses in operation, each of an intensity compatible not only with the character of the patient and the degree of injury, but also with the reacting environment which may be helpfully informative or confusingly silent or even distortive in its approach to the patient. Denial is almost immediate ("It isn't so; it didn't happen"); repression of details as to how "it" did happen and of experiences preceding and following the event occurs. In their place comes acute anxiety, or devotion to trivial details that stand out with plaguing clarity. Projection (the feeling that "This did not happen to me—it must have happened to someone else") is frequent; correspondingly, where the loss is recognized and accepted, the projection then may extend to the lost part. One sees the frequent distress of amputees anxious to know whether or not the lost part has been properly buried and treated with the respect that belongs, not to the part, but to the person involved. Regression to omnipotent and superstitious fantasies, and to infantile and dependent behavior, with some feeling that a loss of a part causes the person to become a child again, is not unusual. Often there is overcompensation in the form of obsessive attention to the injured part or to some other part of the body. Many times there is mourning for the injured part as well as for the actual injury, with frank depression and weeping.

But the defenses of the ego are useful, and in a reasonably healthy person and healthy environment the ego strengths begin to assert themselves. The individual discovers other assets and begins to delimit the injury to the part of himself that has been injured rather than to his total self, rebuild a body image compatible with his present state, and make an adaptive adjustment to an altered reality. His natural recuperative powers, strengthened by past experience and fortified by help from the environment, help him to return to a different but valid equilibrium. The professional person or team must be alert to recognize the signs of movement from stage to stage of recovery. The healers must not only allow such movement but must also provide the individual with adequate care. The team must have an awareness of normal dependent and regressive need in illness, and provide opportunity for their fulfilment. It is essential that change in degree or quality of the need be recognized; if it becomes more pathological, the causes should be sought and treatment instituted. But sensitivity to signs of recuperative movement is equally important. Recognition of these states is paramount both to recovery and to the prevention of future psychological as well as physiological complications.

Response of the Environment

With the onset of a member's illness, the defenses of the family are mobilized. Always, there is anxiety. There may be shame and guilt as the threat to a previously existing state of stabilization occurs. Members of the family often feel guilt for their own misdeeds, or shame for their relief that the misfortune happened to another person; many times an injury to one person constitutes a narcissistic injury to other members of the family. Family members may actively or without conscious intent conceal knowledge of the injury from themselves or from sources of help, thus reinforcing the patient's helplessness and intensifying his use of denial and regression. Sometimes they overcompensate in sacrifice and rely heavily upon religious and other acceptable cultural defenses. Often the family, in shock itself, is as unaware of the shock to the patient as is the patient. And sometimes illness of one member of a family activates illness in other family members.

The demands for a shift of energies within the personality of the individual who becomes ill or injured are prominent in the stress picture. In both patient and family the margin between illness and health is often narrow. For example, menstruation, pregnancy, and delivery are normal, as are voice changing, bearding, and balding. But in a moment of acute or chronic internal or external stress, any of these may pass the border to become pathological, and the feelings and reactions about them may correspondingly fluctuate between the normal and the pathological.

The Pre-Illness Personality

Before we discuss specific reaction patterns to stress, the pre-illness personality and its methods of conflict solution must be considered. The conflict of competition with the father provides an example. The normal individual eventually reaches a state of emancipation in which he no longer needs either to feel intimidated within himself or depreciative of the father. Usually he finds ways not only to be productive but to cease provocative fighting with the father sufficiently so that they can live in peace with each other. The individual in neurotic conflict may find himself with an obsession that drives him to a meticulous accuracy beyond job demands, or a phobia of knives, or a hysterical avoidance of the problem projected onto a part of himself so that he may have a paralyzed arm, or be chronically fatigued. The psychotic may solve the conflict with a frank delusion that the father is dead, or with hallucinations of a deity's voice. The individual with a character disorder may be the most repressive top sergeant in an army group, or may, in chronic defiance of authority, repeatedly lose jobs because he reacts to the boss as though he were the father.

Now let us add a disabling illness to each of these personality

51

problems. The anxiety and pain are typically handled by the defense system already characteristic of this sick person. Thus, the phobic person may well project so that more areas or persons are involved in the phobic avoidance; not only can he not bear to look at the injured part but he becomes afraid of a specific symbol—the hypodermic needle, the night nurse, or the doctor. The paranoid person may discover by magical omnipotence that the doctor himself is really the reincarnation of the hated father and thus subtly attack the doctor by signing his hospital release, or openly threaten the doctor. Similarly, some of the recovery defenses are predictably related to both the pathological and the healthy portions of the ego of each of these persons.

Knowledge about a specific culture enables us to perceive further clues that signal the ego's reaction to inner stress.[5] Patient A, for example, is a neurotic individual of Old American background who reacts to antagonism with the father by meticulous conformity to detail, and by behavior designed to please his superior. If beset with a crippling injury he is likely to be detached, take it like a good soldier, be uncomplaining, and insist that he will do whatever the "good doctor" says. He may regard emotionality as wasteful and shameful and, in conformity with his culture, may act like an upright citizen and father even in the presence of pain. Or he may react in exactly the opposite way, as though the illness gave him permission to regress and be helplessly dependent and infantile. Patient B, with a different cultural orientation, is a neurotically dependent individual whose anxiety is equally severe as that of the Old American; he may have a present-oriented apprehension and immediacy of pain experience, with acute disturbance in response to the actual pain sensation, which he vocalizes articulately in whining or raging words, or inarticulately in anguished or outraged cries. Such a patient may accept drugs very readily, and be as tunefully happy when he is relieved as he is ready to cry when in pain. He has confidence in the doctor and accepts dependency upon him without importunate gestures. He does not worry about whether or not he receives approval for being a "good patient" as the Old American does.

A member of still another group, patient C, has a neurotic attach-

[5] Mark Zborowski, "Cultural Components in Responses to Pain," *Journal of Social Issues*, Vol. 8, No. 4 (1952), pp. 16–30.

ment to his body functioning which may be focused on the symptomatic meaning of the pain. Quite apart from the reality and degree of the injury, he may feel it as a catastrophe. He wails loudly, is reluctant to accept drugs (or if he does accept them, is sure they will not relieve the pain) or he may insist that it is his lot to suffer pain. He is openly skeptical of the doctor, although he has insisted upon having the "top man" and may talk pridefully to his friends or family about having such a physician. This patient is less concerned with the acute pain sensations and more with future-oriented anxiety.

Patient A is openly concerned with efforts to conceal that he feels the pain. Neither Patient B nor Patient C is ashamed of open expression of pain but B needs to try to relieve pain in the present and is free of anxiety as long as he does not have pain. C, on the other hand, is much more anxious because of both the positive and the negative meanings for him of anticipated recurrent or continued pain and hence is less responsive to measures that relieve the pain of the moment. In a phobic state, patient A concentrates on his phobia and drains off his anxiety by use of it and by conformity to his ideal. If B has a phobia, he does not connect the pain and the phobia, but deals with them separately and is likely not to mention his phobia to the doctor but to avoid the pain of his phobia by attention to his actual physical pain. C becomes more diffusely apprehensive. All three patients are influenced, in addition to these cultural factors, by such other determinants as age, the degree of occupational and economic threat, and past experiences with physical pain.

The Specific Reaction Patterns

Within the specific reaction patterns of any character structure, whether the reaction is healthy or pathological, one may see shifts in the inner alignments as the ego attempts to cope with the stress of illness. These patterns must always be seen as dynamic interacting clusters of behavior, now partially to fully conscious, now partially or totally unconscious, and always significant only in the context of the specifics of the individual's endowment and experience in interchange with his own culture. Study of these patterns provides the therapist with the possibility of predicting behavior and thus manipulating in varying degree those internal and external factors that will restore equilibrium and promote health.

The Self-Concept Pattern

Since pain and anxiety are felt as signals in the ego, reaction patterns centering on the self-concept appear almost simultaneously with the impact of injury or illness. Proper understanding of this pattern can be fostered if the reader will recall his last minor mishap with a knife, a hot oven, or a burning matchbook. Pain, anxiety, concern about the extent of the damage, examination of the injured area, momentary loss of contact with the total context of the situation, self-reproach, and anger are entailed in the self-preoccupation that is instantaneous and automatic. Given a greater stimulus, the ego, overwhelmed with more signals than it can readily process at any given moment, may respond to the pain not only with appropriate but also with neurotic anxiety. Furthermore, the ego may be limited by absence of, or by inaccurate, information. Out of these complications, disturbances of the self-concept extend beyond those appropriate to the situation. Thus, because of fear, distortion of the source and extent of injury, of the duration of the pain, and of danger is frequent. Secondary defense efforts may include withdrawal and inhibition, acting out, or fantasy and thought disturbances. There is a tendency to minimize the potential or actual danger as the threat draws closer, or to avoid it altogether by dissolution into panic. In many patients, disturbances in the self-concept take the form of partializations. They worry lest parts of the body will not "behave" in socially acceptable ways, or in ways that the doctor expects. For example, loss of sphincter control is always disturbing to the concept of an integrated self. Considerable patience is needed to help the colostomy patient or the diabetic patient feel that those things that were under voluntary control will again come under management, if not control. Loss of voluntary control also activates fears of dependency needs.

Since hope, goal, and zest are such vital components of human well-being, and since the need to be intact and "complete" is so compelling, the patient tends to looks for ways to compensate for his injury. The injury activates childhood memories of threatening situations and his fantasy about these may provide either a resource

54

or a deterrent to his recovery. Thus, the food in any institution is always unsatisfactory and that longed for or brought from home is much better, because the patient is nostalgic for home and mother.

A further disturbance to the self-image may result when the patient who is approaching physical normalcy finds himself beset by the anxiety and fear that would have been appropriate at the time of the injury. The delayed reaction increases the normal anxiety about ambulation and return to work. Partial inadequacies of the past are now seen as imminently total; the self-concept again tends to become partialized or to be conceived of as damaged, whether or not there is permanent disability of a body area; and the individual retreats before the onslaught of his fears. Many times the delayed reaction causes disturbances in the self-concept because the illness brings forth feelings that are totally unacceptable to the patient ("I didn't think I could be like this"). This feeling may be accompanied by self-castigation, or when the injury is partially repaired there is a release of sufficient energy for the patient to give attention to his latent feelings of anger and resentment. Thus, patients who seem calm and able to cope with the immediate disaster may later have disturbing and painful irritability and depression.

The Narcissistic Object-Relation Pattern

Concern with the value of the self in relation to others is a frequent reaction. Illness may bring either a return to earlier narcissistic patterns or a defensive denial of narcissistic needs. On the whole, the patient who can be actively concerned with the injury to his body and can attend to his self-image, as it were, is sooner able to invest in his recovery. If he can establish a pattern of relating the now-dependent self in a manner analogous to a prior helpful experience, he is able to meet his narcissistic need with a greater feeling of security that he will not at the same time lose his relationship to his internalized object choice, nor to those objects he has in the current reality.

Some patients find themselves in greater need for nursing care of a physical nature and can accept it from any well-disciplined and gentle person, while others experience more specific psychological need such as reassurance and support from a father figure, be that person the doctor or the boss. The shifting nature of these needs and the frequency with which both the internalized and reality objects change must be understood by members of the medical team. It is essential that the caretakers realize that the patient's changing preferences for members of the team or family may represent shifts of a transference-like nature resulting from the patient's changing internalized object and need. Otherwise, competition for the right to care for the patient may arise among members of the team, or between the team and the family.

Furthermore, when the patient is more narcissistically oriented, he is less able to relate to several people at once. He tends to turn his interest first to himself. In the initial stages of injury or illness, after the passing of the acute pre-operative anxiety or the panic of accident, the patient's self-interest is often so internalized that he is listless, fatigued, apparently helpless, and totally disinterested in his world. This phase passes shortly and he becomes object-related to himself, a phase characterized by preoccupation with the physical pain and the sensations accompanying body change.

In a few days another shift occurs, and the individual begins to relate in a fashion more compatible with his level of maturity and is able to consider a one-to-one relationship. Even though he may be in actual contact with several people and handling himself with the usual social conventions, these early relationships are often partialized. He tends to limit them in terms of the function of each person. Often we see three excellent nurses working around-the-clock shifts, but only one to whom the patient is attached. His relationship to the doctor also is very specific. In this phase, he may resent social remarks made to him by the doctor until he can give attention to more than the combination of the doctor-and-his-wounded-self. As recovery occurs, the individual is better able to tolerate and relate to people in groups.

Awareness of these essential narcissistic shifts and of the slow rate at which they may occur in the chronically ill patient is extremely important to the success of vocational and social rehabilitation programs. Adults recovering from a severe illness often react —although with age-appropriate behavior—like the shy child who, in the mother's arms, turns its head away at the first introduction to a new person or situation but, held in security by the mother, gradually lifts the head to look, explore, and eventually participate.

56

The affect resulting from narcissistic injury may be focused on inanimate objects. Thus, the individual becomes preoccupied with a clock, a vase, or a religious object, and reacts with feelings of loss or disorientation if its position is altered or it is removed. He may become similarly attached to new ideas or philosophical systems, regardless of the level of his intellectual sophistication. Fantasy is as important as it is highly personal; if the individual has suffered delirium he is often frightened yet profoundly interested in the strange things that he thought, "experienced," and reported to hearers who may or may not have been present when he was in the delirious state. Again, affect may be displaced, particularly from things and persons invested with any kind of deep feeling, to less self-related things. The patient is able to cry over a tragedy about which he reads in the paper, or "nag" the nurse about a sick child whose cry penetrates his room. But he is unable to cry with pain or in disappointment in the presence of his wife, his best friend, or his therapist. Frequently there is a reactivation of childhood fears of parental abandonment. The patient who is unwilling for his wife or other members of his family to leave the hospital is usually suffering, without awareness, from the fears of abandonment that he experienced in the past. He has a great need for reassurance by people who "belong" to him and also by persons unrelated to him but upon whom he is economically, physically, and emotionally dependent.

The Dependency-Independency Pattern

Shock may be reacted to by a period of overactivity or of overt helplessness, depending upon the general defense pattern of the ego. On the whole the healthier ego tends in the direction of appropriate activity in the presence of stress. A healthy adult may act very adequately, though defensively, against shock or pain until the emergency is past, at which time he becomes able to respond to his own dependency needs. He may attempt to conceal his marked anxiety out of fears of becoming dependent. For example, a skier who had often worked as part of a ski rescue-team walked down a mountain assuring himself that his severed Achilles tendon was a "sprained ankle." His greatest concern was that he might be in the humiliating position of having to be picked up by the ski-patrol

57

which would inconvenience the patrol in the regular performance of its duties.

Guilt and uneasiness regarding the dependent state and the expression of fears and fantasies about it are frequent. The fear of loss of love through being dependent is high, and the fear that the ill person will anger those dependent upon him is even higher. The dependency-independency struggle in the ill person is accented through his searching of the environment for the "right" attitude. The patient's anxiety becomes focused on the question of how an ill person "is supposed to behave." Without adequate cues from the environment, he is apt to act out his prior experience as an ill person, usually in the direction of dependency. Although his past experience with illness may be of help, the repetitive nature of such acting out and its concomitant lack of flexibility may result in inappropriate behavior in the current situation. Projection of responsibility upon another person (the object of the dependent needs) rather than recognition of the actual causative factor is frequent. Thus, illness may be denied until a signal that was important to the mother or the childhood doctor appears ("If you have a fever, you can stay in bed."). At such a point, the patient seems to have received permission to recognize and accept care for his illness. The patient may use many persons and objects constructively or regressively as replacements for needed love-objects on which to depend. Familiar personal objects in the hospital room decrease the number of new and stress-producing stimuli as well as provide constant stimuli for orientation.

The Passivity-Aggressiveness Pattern

Either axis of the passivity-aggressiveness pattern may be accentuated depending upon which axis has been more consciously used or more unconsciously repressed prior to the illness. To many people, illness represents an attack of an intensely personal nature. Often it is intimidating beyond its reality threat. As a result, withdrawal, inhibition, and dependency become greatly increased, not always usefully. There is a tendency to a more total reaction, in the form of massive passivity or outburst of uncontrolled emotion. Fearfulness may activate psychosomatic discharge or the passivity-aggressiveness conflict may assert itself through bitterness or paranoid trends. Startle reactions (as contrasted to frank anxiety phenomena) reappear, asserting both the primitiveness of the response to the illness and the registering of "surprise" and instability.

Often one sees a disengagement from the self; the individual states he will never be sexual or angry or able to work again. Sometimes he regards his symptomatic solution as a source of strength and develops a character response in which he takes pride, after the manner of a New Year's resolution. He may find a kind of strength and courage in renouncing a previously enjoyed activity or in mastery of an ambivalently acquired skill. Aggressive impulses are frequently modulated from direct expression to indirect expression. In an individual not too greatly intimidated by the illness, such character responses may lead to a resurgence or a development of new patterns of search for use of the resources of the self. New eagerness for friendships, jobs, or leisure-time pursuits may appear as the aggressive impulses experienced in the illness become a part of reaction formation or of sublimatory growth.

Affect Pattern

Alternation of the affect phenomena of human behavior has been repeatedly mentioned in our previous discussion. Pathways that provide for expression of or inhibition of tender feelings, irritated, resentful, or openly angry feelings, shame or guilt, grief or joy, are uniquely culture-linked. The impact of feelings ranging from pity to revulsion sometimes is first felt in response to an illness or injury stimulus. Many patients and their family members dread illness not only because it will stir up unwanted and painful feelings, but because they fear that their response to these feelings will not conform to public expectation. The appearance of affect may be as frightening and disturbing to equilibrium as the affect itself. This is particularly true of those individuals who have poor integration of affects and whose tendency to magical and infantile intellectual response to affect is still present; or in those whose adequate control is maintained by defensive measures, without sufficient insight to use intellect

59

and emotion in harmony for the management of difficult and painful situations. The more experience with sickness he had as a child or observed in a sibling, the greater the patient's tendency to rely on early learned expressions of defense.

Feelings of being an "outcast" are common since illness tends to break the continuity of the patient's unique feelings of belonging. If the injury or illness is mutilating, feelings of self-aversion and anticipated aversion by others are particularly intense. Conscious feelings of shame about a disability often arouse deep unconscious shame, guilt, and anger. As a result, severe depression or acting out of the immediate conflict may occur. Caretakers are especially apt to be seen as rejecting or punishing parents and are scrutinized constantly for clues as to how they feel toward the patient. The anxious patient may interpret the slightest gesture of the helping person as derogatory or rejecting. The greater the repressed fear activated by the injury the more the efforts at reality reassurance will be misinterpreted. Shock and grief may be masked by the more frequently and perhaps more recently felt feelings of guilt, shame, or anger. In both acute and chronic disorders, information about the patient's recent past, gleaned fortuitously or by interview with family or friends, gives clues to the emotional framework in which the misfortune occurred. Phrases such as "He just got over" or "He was just starting" or "This isn't his year" are most revealing leads about the kind of affect that may cover the shock and fear, or may be accentuated by them.

Finally, the fact that other specific reaction patterns to illness may be delineated in a given individual should be noted. One should not be bound by the common clusters discussed here in thinking about an ill individual, since the variability and range of human behavior under stress are enormous. Growth and ego-integration phenomena, including the enrichment of preconscious and unconscious sublimative trends that the illness may stimulate in the individual, have not been discussed.

Evaluation of Inner Stress

Diagnosis and evaluation of inner stress require the same broad foundation as does precise evaluation in any other instance.[6]

60

Through observation and examination, facts must be collected, correlations and interpretation integrated, decisions made, a plan of action instituted. Two factors are of immense importance: (1) in an acute illness the patient or client may be in a highly fluctuant state—what was pertinent an hour ago or yesterday may change in significance; (2) if the situation is chronic, the current data may contain only clues to, or condensations of, the facts and feelings of trauma, the details having been lost from memory or contaminated. The overwhelming feelings from the multitude of stimuli, in the first instance, or the blocking of painful memory, in the second, cause distortion and blurring. Moreover, operation of defenses such as denial, projection, repression, and symptom formation makes it necessary for the data-gatherer to evaluate the presently observed phenomena in the context of the passage of time. Needless to say, in either acute or chronic illness, the caseworker must be attuned to the pertinent and usually shifting reality. The essential differential diagnosis may lie between an inner stress reaction to a current traumatic experience and a prior or an on-going state that simulates a response to a trauma.

Using diagnostic skill, acumen, and experience as the essential background, the caseworker may find some of the following signs helpful in evaluating the level of inner stress. Mild or severe signs of anxiety or lability of affect, as well as any inappropriate affect or behavioral response that does not seem consonant with the realities of the trauma or reactive shock should be noted. The length of time necessary to develop the initial shock reaction and the intensity or range of the initial response are variables to be considered. Since persons in his environment often sense the inner stress before the patient does and are made anxious by it, one should look for clues from the environment, particularly concealment, exaggeration, or overprotectiveness about the sick individual. Loss of, or failure to establish, communication is always an important indicator. The shifts between effort and inactivity, buoyancy and hopelessness, on the part of both the

[6] For another useful frame of reference for evaluation of stress see Howard J. Parad and Gerald Caplan, "A Framework for Studying Families in Crisis," *Social Work*, Vol. 5, No. 3 (1960), pp. 3–15.

patient and those around him provide another index. Finally, when there is no adequate response to therapeutic efforts, and the organic condition is not worsening, it is probable that the inner stress is increasing.

Conclusions

Caseworkers, like other therapists, need to remind themselves of the seriousness of the wound to the spirit as well as the body when illness or injury occurs. Inner stress is inevitable; no one knows how much pain another has. Our concern is to decrease pain and suffering and to prevent the development of further pathology. Always the initial shock of trauma produces a loss of confidence in one's ability to be effective and to maintain one's independence. This ability, hard won in the struggle against one's infantile omnipotence and the tremendous blows to one's self-esteem incurred in becoming socialized, is relatively fragile under the impact of injury. Hence, prompt attention to the psychological and physiological ramifications of shock as well as injury is very important. Prompt treatment of a third degree burn may well mean recovery; delay of even an hour or two may mean serious complications or death. Timing and use of adequate measures are of equal importance in psychological injury. Anxiety handled today, stimuli decreased, or sleep promoted may help prevent intensification of the trauma through the development of fantasy tomorrow or next week.

Freedom from concern about the fulfilment of the patient's dependent needs on the part of caretaking personnel must be encouraged, since some regression from his usual social behavior and ways of thinking and feeling is essential to the patient's recovery. The clinical team must study not only the patterns of breakdown but also the patterns of reconstruction for, just as the processes of breakdown are initiated by trauma, so are the forces of reconstruction. Close attention should be paid to any clues that indicate shifts toward health and independent action. Like the leaf buds on a growing plant these are small; they need protection and encouragement before they can become sturdy. As soon as it can be seen as other than a defensive conforming measure, independent action in areas other than that traumatized should be encouraged.

The person's expectation of his course of behavior should be studied by paying attention to time span. When an individual can handle five minutes well, some progress has been made. When he can anticipate and plan for a longer span of time, growth is being achieved. When the cardiac patient can think of going home planfully rather than anxiously, when he can see it as logical rather than as "a test," recovery is well established. When a patient who has had a psychotic episode can think of going home for a week and plan for it, and when his family can think of bearing him for that much time without being driven to overanxiety, a great deal has been accomplished. Attention must be given to whether the patient's expectation of his course of behavior is compatible with his capacity. It may be beyond his capacity, but far more frequently it is below his capacity. Often this tendency is reinforced by the anxious family or community which, having risen to the emergency, may now be some weeks behind the patient in its own recovery, and thus be blinded to the patient's progress.

The caseworker needs to be clear not only as to what the pre-illness adjustment was, but what it might have been, whether the present illness incapacitates the patient below that level, or whether he can reach the same level or a higher one when he is recovered. The worker and eventually the patient must evaluate whether he is productive, trainable, and able to work. Long-term goals must be taken into account and opportunity for exploration of them provided. Attention to the adaptation, not only to the handicap or illness, but also to the adjustment to other problems, is vital. This means that the worker may well initiate with the patient study of areas of the patient's life where, prior to the trauma, there was pathological difficulty, such as poor family adjustment or personal or social inhibition. And, obviously, the worker as well as the patient and the patient's environment must distinguish the handicap from the person. The worker must be aware that the handicap need not be all-pervasive in the individual's remaining life span. The future must be made pertinent, especially in the light of the past and

63

present. The tasks of repair, retraining, and relearning require of the caseworker great patience, astute observation, and skill. One has to individualize each case and find for each one its sense of time and pace. Caseworker help, focused on sound interpretation of the relationship between inner and outer stresses and the proper use of resources, is a priceless ingredient in the patient's return to health.

4. The Concept of the Social Environment in Social Work Practice*

Herman D. Stein

THERE IS HARDLY ONE national or state conference that does not today have an appreciable segment of its program devoted to consideration of the relationship of social science theory and research to social work practice. Institutes and workshops with social science themes and social science participants are proliferating, schools of social work are increasingly more cognizant of this content in master's as well as doctoral programs, and our journals reflect similar growing awareness. It is pertinent to note also that trends within the field of psychiatry have had some effect on social work in this regard, as in so many others. It might be fair to say that an even more intensive interaction with the social sciences has developed within psychiatry than within social work. There is no escaping the conclusion that the social sciences are with us, and we cannot look to psychiatry as a haven against these new winds that are blowing our way. They are blowing just as strongly within psychiatry. One may note, as illustrations, several recent works that reflect the growing collaboration between psychiatrists and social scientists.[1]

* Reprinted from *Smith College Studies in Social Work*, Vol. XXX, No. 3 (1960).

Social Science and Social Work

The relevance of social science to social work may no longer be questioned. What is important is how we prepare ourselves to be selective and judicious about what we choose to accept, how we choose to integrate and apply what we accept, and what we ourselves decide to test.

Before proceeding to comment on some of the implications of this growing involvement with the social sciences for our theory and practice, I should like to state certain propositions, simply to make my premises clear.[2]

First, I do not consider social work an applied social science. I consider the social and behavioral sciences indispensable to our basic knowledge, but social work derives as well from other scientific disciplines, and in some respects social work is not wholly based on scientific knowledge or approaches. Such respects include our system of values and ethics, and the initiative and artistic elements in any professional practice that do not lend themselves to being pinned down by logic or experiment. I do believe that increasing our scientific base will be a never-ending need, and that part of this need—but only part—will be met through greater comprehension of what the social sciences now have to offer, and what we may develop in the

[1] Alexander H. Leighton, John A. Clausen, and Robert N. Wilson, *Explorations in Social Psychiatry*, Basic Books, New York, 1957; Alfred H. Stanton and Morris S. Schwartz, *The Mental Hospital—A Study of Institutional Participation in Psychiatric Illness and Treatment*, Basic Books, New York, 1954; August B. Hollingshead and Fredrick C. Redlich, *Social Class and Mental Illness: A Community Study*, John Wiley and Sons, New York, 1958; William A. Caudill, *The Psychiatric Hospital as a Small Society*, Harvard University Press, Cambridge, Mass., 1958; Otto Pollak, *Integrating Sociological and Psychoanalytical Concepts*, Russell Sage Foundation, New York, 1956; Nathan W. Ackerman, *The Psychodynamics of Family Life*, Basic Books, New York, 1958.

The recent contributions listed follow a long development of thought and research in the attempt to bring together psychological and social scientific perspectives for a more integrated view of human behavior. In the history of this development since the 1920's, particularly in the relationship of psychoanalytic to anthropological approaches, should be included the works of Ruth Benedict, John Dollard, Erik Erikson, Lawrence Frank, Abram Kardiner, Ralph Linton, Margaret Mead, James Plant, and others.

[2] The discussion of these points draws in part from the author's paper, "Social Science in Social Work Practice and Education," in *Ego Psychology and Dynamic Casework*, Howard J. Parad (ed.), Family Service Association of America, New York, 1958. For an extended appraisal of social science in social work education, see Grace Longwell Coyle, *Social Science in the Professional Education of Social Workers*, Council on Social Work Education, New York, 1958.

66

future through our own efforts and through our utilization of other appropriate disciplines.

Second, a social worker in his capacity as a social worker is not a social scientist. His role as a practitioner is not primarily composed of observing, understanding, doing research, and developing theory. As a practitioner he must act, and act with whatever tools and knowledge he has at his command. Certainly, a given social worker may be able to function in an alternate role as a social scientist, and vice versa, but in his relationship with a client, a group, an organization, or a community it would be difficult to maintain at one and the same time both an academic and a professional role.

Third, the primary value of social science content for social work, as would be true for any other scientific content, is its relevance to practice. The ultimate test of such relevance is what difference the content can make in social work's capacity to help people.

Fourth, this test of relevance should be applied within the function and competence of the social work practitioner. The cultural anthropologist, the sociologist, or the social psychologist cannot be held responsible for guiding social work in how to select or to use the ideas and the research from their respective disciplines. It is the practitioner who will have the responsibility for integration —for determining what concepts and knowledge to use and how to use them.

Fifth, generalizations about group behavior stemming from social science theory and research remain generalizations. They should not be used to ascribe to every individual who fits into a group designation certain inevitable modes of behavior or attitudes. The social sciences ask what the consequences are of being located in different positions in the social structure; they do not suggest that any given individual necessarily reflects group norms.

Social Work and the Social Environment

I should like to turn now to what I believe is the over-riding contribution of the social sciences to our field, and that is the enrichment and clarification of our conception of the social environment. Certain inappropriate ways of thinking about the social environment have crept not only into our literature but into much of our approach to practice. These underlying conceptions require sharp re-examination, and are due for drastic revision as we become increasingly exposed to the new theoretical currents. Such outdated concepts include:

1. The social environment seen as restricted to what is accessible to immediate perception, and open to direct modification. Thus, the social environment has often been viewed in our literature as those elements that are relatively concrete, visible, and almost palpable—such as housing, jobs, neighborhood, health services [3] —and relationships that are immediate and face to face, such as those in the family. The very phrase "environmental manipulation" is suggestive of this sense of concreteness and specificity in the environment. It connotes the way in which a social worker can affect jobs, housing, child placement, and so on.

2. The social environment seen as external to the individual, epitomized in the phrase "helping the individual adjust to his environment." The suggestion is that the individual stands alone, an isolated complex of intra-psychic processes with a psychosexual history; that he must, from time to time, wade into his environment and cope with it as best he can, leaving this environment behind when he enters, for example, the sanctum of the caseworker's office. This view does not take into account how much of the social environment has been transmitted to the individual, internalized and transmuted by him; how the environment affects his values, his self-image, his opportunities for meeting his needs, and his choice of symptoms.

3. The social environment perceived as static. The environment exists, and individuals and groups have to do the best they can with it or get themselves changed so they can adjust better. With this orientation we fail to give recognition not only to the changing

[3] This listing is not to suggest that housing, jobs, health services, and so on, are in any way less *significant* than the less concrete manifestations of the social environment with which this paper is concerned. On the contrary, social work should give such problems as housing and employment continued and vigorous attention as objectives for the improvement of social welfare. It is the fallacy of assuming that the social environment is limited to what is visible and palpable to which this paragraph is directed.

quality of environmental factors, but also to the possibility of inducing change in the environment.

These assumptions have, at least in part, been either expicitly stated or are implicit in social work writing.[4] I do not wish to set up a "straw man" to attack, or to belabor the presence of such inadequate conceptions, because they have clearly been giving way, but I should like to indicate briefly their significance historically in the development of social work.

A recent article on the influence of Freud [5] on social work is quite suggestive in this regard. The author states: "With the turn into the twentieth century, social work moved into what has been termed the sociological stage." He defines this stage as being concerned with the social order and the growing conviction that man's life experience is environmentally determined. Thus, he notes, there was emphasis on modification of the environment in terms of child placement, changing jobs, moving the family, separating individuals in the home, and so forth. This, he terms a movement away from "individualization," and suggests that this sociological and environmental approach was reflected "at its best" in Mary Richmond's *Social Diagnosis*. In the twenties, he goes on, "Social workers, already suspicious that environmental manipulation was not enough, grasped the opportunity of learning more about the emotional factors in human behavior." The thirties, he indicates, saw "the psychiatric deluge," but the depression reminded social workers again of "the environment."

What is significant about this article for our present purpose is that it highlights the two distinct traditional strains in social work development, that of social reform and social action, on the one hand, and that of concentration on the psychological and emotional factors in the individual on the other; and that in relation to both,

---

[4] Erikson refers to a similar neglect of the social environment until recent years in the mainstream of psychoanalytic thought. "The phenomenon and the concept of *social organization*, and its bearing on the individual ego was . . . for the longest time shunted off by patronizing tributes to the existence of 'social factors.'" Erik H. Erikson, "Identity and the Life Cycle," *Psychological Issues*, Vol. 1, No. 1, International Universities Press, New York, 1959, p. 19.

[5] Gordon J. Aldridge, "The Influence of Freud on Social Work," *Mental Hygiene*, Vol. 42, No. 2 (1958), pp. 284–288.

despite the merits of the historical overview, a highly restricted view of the social environment is communicated which is reflected in many other social work writings. The environment is seen again as relatively concrete, and so, with a so-called "environmental approach," one helps people by doing something specific about their environment, helping them to move from one place to another, from one job to another, from one home to another. The psychological-individualistic approach, on the other hand, in this author's view, aims at change within the individual, with "environmental manipulation" seen as supplementary where it is appropriate at all.

I suggest that greater understanding of social science theory and research is rapidly changing not only this mechanistic view of the social environment, but may have the effect of providing more of a bridge than now exists between these two traditions of environmental change and psychological treatment.

One may conceive of the social environment as a series of concentric circles of systems of influence, all interacting. At the outer extreme is society as a whole—in our case the United States—particularly its effects on patterns of human behavior. We then look at regional variations and those of urban, small town, and rural life. As we move closer toward the center of the individual's life experience we reach the neighborhood, or community, level with its specific conditioning patterns. The influences of peer groups, of recreational and institutional settings in which the individual may be located, are closely involved, and at the very center of the social environment of the individual we find his family, the one in which he grew up, and the one in which he became a parent.

The influences of these aspects of the social environment are variously incorporated or otherwise reacted to by each individual in different ways because of his unique hereditary endowment and life experiences. In a sense, therefore, each individual has his own social environment, which changes as he moves through life. This environment provides the central values to which he reacts and his patterns of behavior for meeting basic needs; induces clear, confused, or conflicting modes of conduct; affects his aspirations and ambitions and the character of his relationships with others. An understanding of the social environment of a given individual does

70

not tell us all we need to know about him, nor can it explain him fully, but it can indicate some of the sources of his strengths and weaknesses, his clarity, and his confusions.

I should like to comment briefly on some of the environmental elements noted in this network of circles of influence.

As we look at the larger dimensions of the American society we are to an extent involved in an examination of national character, a field of study that only gradually and recently has been approached systematically. Here we are concerned with those central currents in national life which brush every man, woman, and child, and leave an indelible impression, despite the fact that reactions to such influences will vary greatly among different segments of the population. We refer, for example, to such pivotal values in American life as the accent on achievement and success, an orientation to the future, individualism, the kinds of values communicated by our mass media and our educational system. These values are, in turn, transmitted by our parents and serve to differentiate the individuals growing up in one country from those growing up in another. Here we rely heavily on cultural anthropology, on the studies, for example, by Margaret Mead,[6] those of Research in Contemporary Cultures, which she directs, and which were initiated by the late Ruth Benedict, in cross-national comparisons, and on the work of such sociologists as Robin Williams [7] in his analysis of value orientations in American life. We rely on such studies to provide insights that illuminate polar tendencies shaping our value system and consequently the efforts of people to assimilate, reject, or become confused by contradictory pulls. We are also aided greatly in understanding the kinds of dilemmas in acculturation faced by migrant and immigrant groups who come with orientations to life, to success goals and ethical standards, for example, that may differ sharply from those built into American life.

[6] Margaret Mead, *And Keep Your Powder Dry,* William Morrow, New York, 1942. Margaret Mead and Martha Wolfenstein (eds.), *Childhood in Contemporary Cultures,* University of Chicago Press, Chicago, 1955.

[7] Robin M. Williams, Jr., *American Society, A Sociological Interpretation,* Alfred A. Knopf, New York, 1951. See also Florence Rockwood Kluckhohn, "Variations in the Basic Values of Family Systems," *Social Casework,* Vol. XXXIX, Nos. 2–3 (1958), pp. 63–72.

Social Class Influences

Within the famework of the larger American society the social class system operates to register distinctive influences on people as they are located at different levels in the social structure, and as they attempt to move into different class positions. This area of social stratification is complex and there are many different points of view about it. Theoretical orientations are diverse and sometimes conflicting, and there are consequently wide variations as well in the methods used for locating people in class positions and in defining class levels. Nevertheless, there are also wide areas of agreement; in the fact, for example, that there *is* such a thing as social stratification, and that there are significant differences in the attitudes and behavior of people which are related to their social class position. There is, moreover, an abundance of research in this branch of sociology in such areas, for example, as differences in parental relationships, participation in voluntary associations, child-rearing practices, rates and types of mental illness, peer-group relationships, and the like. Not all the findings are consistent. Differences in research design, as well as differences in the definition of social class, account for some of these inconsistencies. But there is much that is consistent and of direct relevance to social work interests.

It is noteworthy that until relatively recently there was virtually no reference in social work literature to such studies, a reflection perhaps of an underlying suspicion that social stratification is an "undemocratic" concept, which is hardly the case, since a ranking system of some kind exists in every complex society. At any rate, the implications involved in social class differences have begun to filter into social work, and this development has no doubt been accelerated by the fact that some segments of psychiatry have given it quite serious recognition as a vital aspect of social environment of both patients and therapists. I note here again the pioneer work of Hollingshead and Redlich in their study of *Social Class and Mental Illness*. A list of other material on social class which is of direct interest to social workers would be too lengthy to be included in this article.

We are now mindful of the probability that social class differences supersede ethnic differences in child rearing. We are becoming

72

increasingly cognizant of the ways in which values associated with class position become transmitted within the family and variously incorporated into the self-image of individuals; of the diverse manner in which many who are located in lower social class positions react to what they perceive as a limited or closed opportunity structure; of the personality strains inherent in the process of upward social mobility; of the value conflicts that may be present when husband and wife identify themselves with different social class levels; with the intensity with which individuals in depressed minority groups who move into middle-class positions attempt to live up to the norms of middle-class society. There is little question that in social class we have a striking source of influence in the social environment of individuals and groups, a source of influence which is not readily accessible to the naked eye.

As we move toward increased recognition of these social class factors we shall be faced with value dilemmas of no mean order. Should we stimulate individuals to higher achievement when they have the potential for such achievement, even when they are reconciled to lower aspirations and when higher aspirations mean more strain and anxiety? In a recreational center in a lower-class area do we conform within the institution to patterns of behavior that are accepted in the community, or do we insist on norms more consistent with the values of the professionals and the members of the board? Do we deal with existing patterns of participation in voluntary groups by drawing on the greater readiness of middle-class people to join, of upwardly mobile people to assume more responsibility, and of lower-class people to be relatively less eager for participation and for assumption of leadership responsibility; or do we attempt to change such patterns of involvement even though short-range community organization efforts may suffer?

In addition to providing us with a whole set of valuable clues to understanding sources of strain as well as satisfaction in individual and group life and, in turn, intensifying questions of policy, our exposure to the area of social stratification makes us increasingly conscious of our own biases related to social class backgrounds which may affect our professional orientation. The Introduction to *Explorations in Social Psychiatry* [8] notes, for example, "If the

[8] Leighton and others, *op. cit.*, p. 10.

therapist's implicit model of healthy, desirable behavior is postulated on the preferred life patterns of the educated professional subculture, he may inadvertently guide his patients toward goals that are inappropriate in the patient's subculture."

It would be foolish to suggest that we know all that we should about the way in which social class influences operate or, indeed, about the nature of the differences. It is clear, however, that knowledge already developing in this field is of utmost significance to our understanding both of client groups and of ourselves and our professional ideology.

Ethnicity

The existence of ethnic influences in personality and behavior comes as no news to the field of social work. Our field has long been aware of diverse patterns of behavior in, for example, various immigrant and migrant groups. What social science theory and research present to us, however, is a more careful and intensive analysis of the complexity and ramifications of ethnic subcultural influences and of the diversity of cultural patterns *within* ethnic groups, based on social class, regional, and religious differences. We have more precise and penetrating studies of such groups as Puerto Ricans and other Spanish-speaking Americans, Negroes, Jews of Eastern European origin, Americans of Southern Italian background, and others. We have a clearer picture of value orientations based on ethnic backgrounds, of differing predispositions to the use of professional help, of ethnic differences in reactions to illness and in response to medical care, of differences in parental rela tionships and parent-child relationships in child rearing, and in the structure of the family. We are beginning to have explanations for differing rates and kinds of mental illness, of alcoholism, drug addiction, delinquency, illegitimacy, and other forms of deviant behavior, partly in terms of the variations in the cultural systems involved.

Ethnic influences run deep. We see them most clearly in first generation families of migrant and immigrant groups, less clearly in second and third generations; and much more research is needed to understand the extent to which ethnic influences persist through the generations. Issues of self-identification and self-acceptance in ethnic cultural terms become increasingly important to our understanding of the individual personality and of the relationship between minority groups, and their relationship, in turn, to the larger cultural system. The day is long past when agencies that deal with substantial segments of one or more ethnic groups can afford to be without the best knowledge available of the cultural patterns and their variations within such a group, whether it is second-generation Eastern European Jewish, lower-class Negro, first generation Puerto Rican, or migrants to northern cities from the Kentucky hills. We need far more understanding than we now have, too, as to the factors involved when both worker and client or worker and group have the same ethnic identifications. Our literature has only scratched the surface of understanding in these areas.

It becomes important, as well, as we gain understanding into ethnic group differences, to be more wary than ever of stereotyping and to recognize the infinite variety in human beings in their responses and modes of incorporation of all environmental influences. We realize, too, that ethnic cultural influence may be used pathologically, and that cultural conformity is not the same as health, any more than deviance is the same as pathology, as is amply illustrated in a recent volume edited by Georgene Seward.[9] But we must recognize as well that these pervasive ethnic influences and patterns do exist, that they affect personality development, that they help shape basic attitudes toward life. An understanding of the ethnic patterns to which an individual does or does not conform, and why, can enable us to get a much better perspective on the individual and on the nature of the problems he presents.

Agency Setting

The influence of the agency setting in which the helping function is provided for the clients or patients receiving service is an aspect of the social environment of the client or patient which has only recently been brought into focus. Here we are dealing with the consequences of administrative arrangements, of role definitions on the part of professional personnel, of patterns of interaction

[9] *Clinical Studies in Culture Conflict,* Georgene Seward (ed.), Ronald Press Company, New York, 1958.

between clients and patients themselves as well as interaction with staff, and of the relationship of the agency to its community. Perhaps the most noteworthy of studies in this connection has been that of *The Mental Hospital*,[10] in which it was demonstrated, for example, that the very symptoms of patients could be aggravated by the presence of disagreements among the professional personnel. As an institution the mental hospital has, indeed, been the subject of considerable scrutiny in the study of open versus closed wards and in reports such as *The Psychiatric Hospital as a Small Society*.[11] We have begun to get systematic observation of the behavior of patients in the general hospital related to attitudes of the medical staff. Studies in the effects of bureaucratic structure have indicated the extent to which the kinds of service that clients receive in public assistance, for example, are strongly influenced by administrative policy and arrangements.

We have had, however, very few systematic examinations of social work settings, despite our growing alertness to the fact that there is more to the helping function than the relationship between client and worker, or group worker and group. What has been lost and what has been gained, for example, in the professionalization of the group work setting? [12] We tend to have now in group work a defined professional hierarchy with rather clear and separate functions, as against the "old-fashioned" settlement house pattern where staff members were not as conscious of specific roles and carried on a variety of tasks in much more informal fashion. What have been the effects on service? How does the recipient of service in the bureaucratized group work institution perceive what he is getting, from whom? Have we so structured the roles of the consumers of our social work help that we are meeting needs more as *we* see them than as clients feel them? How is our intake process in casework agencies affecting the *mind-set* by which clients perceive their own roles in the agency? What is the effect of having more or less opportunity for staff participation in administrative

[10] Stanton and Schwartz, *op. cit.*
[11] William A. Caudill, *op. cit.*
[12] Richard A. Cloward, "Agency Structure as a Variable in Service to Groups," in *Group Work and Community Organization Papers*, Columbia University Press, New York, 1956.

policy? These kinds of questions require illumination so that we can better assess how the setting either facilitates or impedes the effectiveness of the services we are attempting to render.

The Family in the Social Environment

No social institution has had more concerted attention from the profession of social work over the past decades than has the family, and no social worker need be reminded of the importance of the family to the understanding of human behavior and the development of personality. It will be noted, however, that in the observations made thus far the family has been referred to not only as a matrix of highly significant and complex relationships between parents and among parents and children, but in other contexts as well. And it is in these other contexts that social science contributions make themselves felt.

First, the family is seen as the bearer and transmitter of the surrounding culture in the development of the young. It is the family more than any other institution that promotes values and attitudes peculiar to the surrounding society, so that children in our culture grow up to be Americans in their general perspectives toward life, rather than French, Mexican, or Burmese. It is the family that transmits the values and patterns of behavior associated with different class levels, and it is the family that passes on ethnic traditions and the variations in structured roles within the family which are based on ethnic determinants. The sociocultural perspective makes it possible for a caseworker to locate the family more accurately within the framework of the larger society within which it functions in order to understand more precisely the way in which each individual and the family as a group are affected.

Again, this is hardly to suggest that there is an automatic absorption by each family of surrounding influences which are then again automatically molded on to the personality of the child. Family members respond in different ways, internalize these influences variously and transmit them variously; children receive them, and absorb or reject them in highly individual terms. Although generalizations do not tell us what is happening in any one family in any one such group, and certainly do not tell us in advance how

77

any individual will react, we must be aware of the pervasive influences of the social environment in shaping parent-child relationships and the values incorporated in family life.

Thus, the GAP Report of "Integration and Conflict in Family Behavior" [13] lists five points of reference for the family: "The Individual," "The Family as a Group," "The Surrounding Social System," "The System of Values Characteristic of the Social System," and "The Geographical Setting." This analysis, stressing the concept of the family as an interacting and transacting organization suggests the diversity of values incorporated in family life due to the nature of the social environment, particularly in ethnic and social class terms with respect to the character of innate human nature, the relationship of man to nature, time orientation, activity orientation, and man's relationship to other men. The report goes on to illustrate diverse value systems by contrasting the orientations to these themes in the Spanish-American familistic societies and the American middle-class family system.

Similarly, Ackerman, in his work on family diagnosis [14] stresses the necessity of an understanding of the values in the family's surrounding social system and the way in which families incorporate and transmit them:

. . . It behooves all mental health workers, therefore, to re-examine the entire area of values—in their own lives and their own work, in their patients, in the culture and the society from which they and their patients come. No matter how technologically sound our principles, no matter how well-implemented our techniques, we cannot expect to progress toward a mentally healthy community until values are clarified and value systems defined.

We have been reminded again in different ways by Spiegel, Kluckhohn, Hill, Ackerman, Pollak, and others of the importance of seeing the family in terms of its totality, including all significant members in the household, and not necessarily parents and children alone; of kinship relationships outside the household; of a better understanding of the roles of family members, especially that of the father; of variations in family structure and their consequences, particularly contrasting extended kinship family types and the

[13] *Integration and Conflict in Family Behavior,* Report No. 27, Group for the Advancement of Psychiatry, Topeka, Kansas, 1954.
[14] Ackerman, *op. cit.,* p. 335.

78

American middle-class, nuclear family; of intergenerational influences in family life, going back three or more generations when necessary; and of the types of families most immune and most vulnerable to various kinds of stress.[15]

Implications—Some Illustrations

It may appear that the effort to span such a large canvas of variables as we have been referring to—everything from the psychological conflict of an individual to the American social system—may be paralytic in its effect for the social worker in the practice situation. Indeed, we do have a problem here, but a no greater problem than we had when our field was confronting the depth and complexity of psychological theory in order to improve our capacity to help. There is a good deal to learn and a good deal more to take into account than we have usually had to do in the past, but any profession that develops, even in part, on the basis of scientific advances in related fields, is perpetually faced with new problems of selection, adaptation, and testing. These are the kinds of problems we should have, and they are far from insuperable. To incorporate a more expanded view of the social environment does not mean forgetting what we have learned, but building further on the base that we already have. It is adding an enriched social perspective to the biological and psychological perspectives which have thus far been incorporated into our understanding of human behavior. If this perspective helps us to make clearer diagnoses, to set more realistic treatment plans, to reconsider agency policy or to plan community services more thoughtfully, we need it. Practitioners need not know all theories that may conceivably be relevant to social work needs from the social as well as the psychological sciences, but should know those concepts that flow from social science theory which have bearing on practice needs. No one theoretical system is sufficient for practice needs; to meet such needs we need grounding in the most appropriate theories but also a broad view of the central ideas stemming from other theoretical and research sources.

15 See Reuben Hill, "Social Stresses on the Family: 1. Generic Features of Families Under Stress," *Social Casework*, Vol. XXXIX, Nos. 2–3 (1958), pp. 139–50

The fact is that, in the absence of a more sophisticated and explicit approach to the utilization of sociocultural concepts, we are at the mercy not only of our special areas of ignorance but of the illusion that our assumptions are necessarily based on knowledge. Our own predispositions toward people from different class levels and ethnic origins, our own values stemming from our particular life experience as well as our "blind spots," are more apt to remain unexamined, less touched by the rigors of professional self-discipline that we attempt to apply in keeping our individual psychological needs from interfering with the process of helping others. Sociocultural considerations may, in other words, very well affect one's perceptions in casework, group work, and community organization without one's being aware of it; but if not made explicit and subject to scrutiny, such considerations run the risk of being biases subject to distortion and gross inaccuracy.

The first requisite is to know the kinds of questions to raise about the social environment of our clientele, to recognize those characteristics that appear prominently in a given agency or locale, and to know where to look for more information and more guidance. Students in our schools require this orientation so they can pursue and evaluate knowledge in this area relevant to their practice. In general, an increasingly systematic comprehension of appropriate social theory is already becoming the order of the day in our graduate schools and in professional social work circles. We are taking steps, in other words, very similar to those we have taken as we have become more sophisticated about the insights of psychiatry and their application to social work. We are not overcome either with apathy or with apprehension as we learn of advances in psychological theory and research, and we have no reason to react in this way to advances in the social sciences that create new opportunities for us to be more effective.

I should like to offer a few illustrations of some implications of the concepts we have been discussing.

The experience gained at the Northside Center for Child Development, a Child Guidance Center that serves children in the Harlem community of New York City, illustrates some of these points regarding class and ethnic factors. At the Northside Center it has become the custom "never to make a diagnosis unless some member of the staff is present who is familiar with the particular cultural background. If this cannot be achieved, the Center has sought other people in the field who are familiar with the particular cultural background, and asked their participation." [16] Such evaluation, particularly in terms of social class and ethnic background, has become an intrinsic part of diagnostic process, partly because of clinical experiences which demonstrated the possibilities of diagnostic distortion when a sociocultural perspective was not included. The therapists at this Center conclude that:

> The concept that personality emerges only in terms of its social setting means that an evaluation of the healthy or morbid psychological aspects of an individual can be made only in terms of what is appropriate and effective functioning within the specific cultural milieu. If this principle is not kept in mind, then the frequent difference between patient and psychiatrist in social, economic, or cultural status will lead the psychiatrist to make the error of using his own status as the norm. . . .[17]

We have learned a good deal from the American experience prior to World War I with such groups as the Southern Italians and Eastern European Jews. Among the lessons we have learned is that a steamroller approach to so-called Americanization with the intent of rapidly wiping out Old World cultural traits can have very damaging effects both on the newcomer and on his children. Degrading the values of the immigrant generation can lead to the rejection by their children of parental standards, the aggravation of parent-child conflict, and the destruction of one set of values before alternative values have been truly incorporated. Self-rejection and deviance from community norms have often come in the wake of a misguided effort to transform the behavior of people rapidly into our conceptions of what is proper and acceptable. In the present Puerto Rican migration many social agencies and other formal institutions are increasingly alert to the cultural patterns with which many of the migrants come, without falling into the trap of stereotyping or failing to make adequate differentiation along social class and religious lines. Thus we note in many Puerto Rican families the existence of an essentially patriarchal

---

[16] Stella Chess, Kenneth B. Clark, and Alexander Thomas, "The Importance of Cultural Evaluation in Psychiatric Diagnosis and Treatment," *Psychiatric Quarterly*, Vol. 27, No. 1 (1953), p. 109.

[17] *Ibid.*, p. 112.

structure with the wife subordinate, and the fact that this pattern is often challenged by the greater readiness with which the wife can find outside employment. The threat to parental roles is such that children can be disoriented, with the consequent waning of parental discipline and the strengthening of peer-group standards which may be in conflict with those of the family.

It is not only immigrants and migrants from other societies who confront us with the necessity for a sympathetic understanding of other background cultures. In some parts of our country we are witnessing a migration to urban centers of newcomers from the Southern Mountains region, quite indigenously American, but with family structure and social patterns quite dissimilar to those of middle-class American society. The challenge to social work in its efforts to meet the needs of these newcomers is considerable. Community organization, group work, and casework agencies are all involved. I am indebted to Professor Roscoe Giffin of Berea College, in Kentucky, for an account of the sociocultural patterns in this group, and some of the consequences of their migration to cities. In general these migrants tend to have very strong kinship relationships, and have characteristically depended on such ties when in trouble. They have not been accustomed to urban patterns of voluntary co-operation, or to dealing with a series of impersonal official figures in offices, hospitals, recreation centers, and the like, as all city dwellers do. Their previous relationships have been personal and face-to-face. In general they have not been trained in urban skills. Home is associated not only with the present family; it is the place where they grew up and where their parents and grandparents had likewise grown up. Their education tends to be less than that of urban dwellers of the same age. Problems of illness and poverty abound. In their exposure to the urban environment a number of disorganizing influences soon became felt—overcrowding in substandard housing; the necessity to relate to hundreds of strangers with the consequent feeling that the impersonality of the relationship means unfriendliness; the wife's often having to go to work, threatening the father's position in the family; the attitude of older residents who resent the fact that the newcomers do not seem to be appropriately ambitious for self-improvement; the labeling by school officers of these children as being less educable than others, and so forth—problems, it will be seen, similar to those confronting segments of the Puerto Rican population in New York City.

What are the steps that we already know may be of value in making the acculturation process, difficult at best, less disorganizing for this group and less likely to bring a high incidence of pathological and antisocial behavior in its wake? First steps are the provision of more personalized services and personalized relationships in local neighborhood organizations, individual introductions to schools and churches, simple instruction in the management of money to counteract the temptation to buy on credit all the new and glittering gadgets. Further aids would include recognizing the strengths in this family pattern and helping the father, who is the center of authority, and the mother, typically the center of warmth and affection, to understand the types of problems they and their children are likely to encounter; the provision of more adequate housing and supervised play areas; caution in the use of authority among city officials in relation to this group; and making use of the rich heritage of mountain folk games in recreation. Above all, one must respect the cultural values of these families and seek to understand the origins of behavior that might seem inappropriate in the population at large. In recognizing the strains in the current social environment of these newcomers and of other groups who face a cultural re-adjustment, social workers can perform vital functions both as helpers and as interpreters to the larger community, in how one provides health, recreational, psychological, and counseling services, and how one makes it more possible for employers, unions, hospitals, banks, and schools to receive and work with the newcomers with an appreciation of the changes in outlook to which they have gradually to become accustomed.

Another illustration, this one coming from the field of group work, concerns a non-sectarian day center for elderly people in a large metropolis. The center was designed to be self-governed by the membership, insofar as possible, with a constitution, a democratically elected president, slate of officers, chairmen for small groups, and so forth. The center has several hundred members, and the average age of the members is over 75. Although a number of other ethnic groups are represented, most of those participating

83

in the center are from East European Jewish and Italian back-grounds. The group in the center is largely from a working-class background.

The program has reflected the concern of the professional staff for general American cultural values, such as respect for individuals, belief in the democratic process, faith in the possibility of individual growth, and a concern for the well-being of others. There is also a strong accent on the importance of keeping busy, with the implication that not to be busy is to be unhappy. The professional staff anticipated acceptance of the values inherent in the program and of the forms that go with it. They were not prepared for the fact that elected leaders tended to be authoritarian; that divisions of opinion were not only common but were often accompanied by verbal aggression and name-calling. House rules of the center were often forgotten. The president of the group, a motherly women, side-stepped both staff decisions and those made by the group, in the interest of running things in the way that she felt was best for everybody. This attitude has been largely accepted by the members to the consternation of the professional staff. A group worker, who began to examine what was actually happening from the standpoint of those involved rather than from her own biases, discovered that there was much less confusion than seemed apparent. One of the processes that was apparently going on was a transfer of family roles to the center, and the din was not dissimilar to family discussion and family quarrels. To the staff members, interruptions, shouting, arguing, appeared to be hostility and disorganization; to those in the group this kind of behavior was a carry-over both of family roles and patterns of prior union activities. A more objective view also led to the recognition that the accent on constant work, on keeping busy, was not necessarily a value accepted by the participants in the center, to the same degree as it was by the achievement-oriented middle-class professionals. Those who came to the center and sat about chatting, observing their fellow members, occasionally playing cards, were not necessarily lonelier or more isolated than those who were involved in arts and crafts.

The intrusion in this case of the values of the staff in the character of self-government and the program objectives simply did not work. Gradually there was recognition that it might be best to see the program from the cultural standpoint of those for whom the program was designed. A much richer program with less wear and tear, particularly on the part of the staff, developed as there was greater recognition of the meaning of the social environment of the center's clientele.

The Social Science Emphasis and Social Reform

Now to return briefly to the issue of social science and the two social work traditions of individual psychology and social reform. There has been, from time to time, within our own profession criticism of our relative inattention to social action and social policy reform, with the onus for such neglect placed on our psychological emphasis, particularly in casework. There is some merit in this view, in the sense that concentration on intrapsychic processes places the individual as the object of change rather than the social order; and even when environmental stresses are acknowledged they tend to be perceived as inaccessible by the clinician. Thus, an exclusive concentration on psychodynamics is consistent with a conservative approach toward social change. This is not necessarily so, nor has it been consistently so in our history. Individuals dedicated to casework have acted time and again to improve social security, public assistance, settlement laws, reforms in mental institutions, and the like. What is more to the point is that in an era of relatively sparse concern with social change and social reform a purely psychological approach can provide a convenient escape for those who want an escape. It does not, however, *cause* retreat or disinterest.

Part of the merit of a sociocultural approach, integrated with the biological and psychological, is that it compels a constant and increasingly systematic concentration on the social environment of the individual or group being helped by social workers, and therefore directs our attention to deficiencies, strains, and inequities that may be contributing to the pressures our clients face. Again, this does not mean that social workers with a conservative or apathetic attitude will become involved in social action, but it means that one ideological escape hatch has been closed. I am convinced that our professional pursuits will increasingly relate us to the environment

85

in a much more penetrating way than they have in the past, and that the very process of social work will be affected by more direct intervention in the environment of our clients, as we see the environment more fully.

It will be increasingly difficult to maintain that the primary factors leading to antisocial behavior in the child are "purely psychological," and that environmental factors are important only insofar as they affect the parents' psychological rearing of the child, as one authority has it. [18] Sociological concepts, such as culture conflict, social isolation, and cultural norms, are essential to providing a more complete framework for analyzing behavior. Albert K. Cohen has suggested that psychologists and sociologists ask different questions about the same things—the one, why X is as he is, the other, what are the social conditions and the social locations within which this behavior tends to occur.[19] The social worker must ask both these questions, utilizing insights from both fields.

Implications for Practice Areas

In child welfare a better approach to the social environment will lead us to add considerations in this area to those of the physiological and psychological needs of the child. In foster care, for example, more attention will be given to class and ethnic factors in foster families in relation to the foster child's background, and changes in family balance will have to be reckoned with. In hospital social work greater attention will be given to such matters as the role relationships of hospital personnel, the nature of the patient's environment in the ward, and ethnic components in reactions to pain and illness. In family agencies we shall have more concern for all the significant figures in the client's family, and give more attention to pressures and satisfactions in occupational settings, and to social class and ethnic factors in behavior. In group

[18] See Michael Hakeem, "A Critique of the Psychiatric Approach to the Prevention of Juvenile Delinquency," *Social Problems*, Vol. 5, No. 3 (Winter, 1957–58), pp. 194–206. This article is a sharp attack on the psychiatric approach and represents what many, including a good number of sociologists, consider an extreme position. Dr. Kate Friedlander is quoted in this article as making the point noted in *The Psycho-analytical Approach to Juvenile Delinquency Theory*, International University Press, New York, 1947, pp. 274–75.
[19] Albert K. Cohen, "Sociological Research in Juvenile Delinquency," *American Journal of Orthopsychiatry*, Vol. XXVII, No. 4 (1957), pp. 781–788.

work the leader's concepts in regard to class, age, sex, ethnic, and occupational terms, program objectives and perceptions of the agency's function will become of increasing relevance. In community organization, power structure in community life, differential patterns of community participation, and class as well as ethnic factors in inter-group relations, will become increasingly important. In psychiatric clinics the significance of ethnic influences on symptom choice, of class and ethnic variables in communication, and of diagnostic perception in the relationship between therapist and patient will become increasingly prominent considerations. These considerations concern both public welfare and voluntary welfare, and in both the direction of future attention should increasingly be on the patterns and needs of lower-class groups in our society.

Some Final Observations

I have emphasized throughout the contribution from the social sciences to social work understanding of the social environment. The character of the present relationshp is, in fact, largely one through which social work selects, redefines, and attempts to apply social science concepts. We anticipate that social work increasingly will be testing social science concepts as applied to our field, rejecting as well as accepting, and we shall ourselves be conducting more empirical research based on social science theory (and thus very likely contribute to theory); and that social work data will become increasingly available and usable for social scientists, and we shall be raising the questions for which we want answers from social science. We should be reminded that the present state of knowledge within the social sciences (for example, in our understanding of lower-class subcultures) has not reached a point where we can get all the answers we need, and that there remain conflicting points of view within the various areas of social science, requiring a capacity on our part to select and appraise judiciously the various scholarly wares available to us.

Let us keep in mind, moreover, that we know relatively little of the interactions of social and personality systems; or of the personality correlates of different levels in the social structure. And, finally, while we have some understanding of how social and environmental factors can aid us diagnostically, we have far too little recorded experience with the ways in which such expanded understanding actually affects social work process and objectives in specific practical terms. It is well, however, that we move slowly and thoughtfully in this regard, and that first, as a field, we become proficient and knowledgeable in the underlying concepts and related research. May I be bold enough to predict that the resurgence of interest in basic social science concepts, particularly as they provide a deepened comprehension of the social environment, will lead very soon to expanded demonstration and experimentation in revising current patterns of social work practice, to the benefit of those we serve.

5. Some Casework Aspects of Ego Growth Through Sublimation*

Louise Bandler

THE EARLIEST ORIGINS OF ego development are still wrapped in comparative obscurity. Precisely how the primitive ego emerges from the id in the symbiosis of the mother-child relationship still awaits elucidation. Each ego seems to have its own potential and its specific range of capabilities. Further understanding of how these capacities unfold, alter, and mature, how defenses are elaborated and adaptive patterns are established, is one of the study objectives of developmental psychology. There is no question, however, that one of the most significant mechanisms for ego growth is that of sublimation.

Much has been written in psychoanalytic literature, particularly in the field of ego psychology, about the mechanisms of defense; relatively little has been written about sublimation. Casework literature, as far as I know, has not dealt systematically with this subject. Although Freud planned a special paper on sublimation, as one of his contributions to metapsychology, he never wrote it. His contributions must be gleaned from many papers.

* Presented at the Annual Supervisors' Conference, Smith College School for Social Work, Northampton, July 14, 1961.

Freud's Concept of Sublimation

In Freud's early writings, sublimation referred to certain vicissitudes of the libido, particularly those energies attached to erogenous zones and early pregenital polymorphous sexual trends. These libidinal energies are transformed and redirected from their sexual aims, goals, and objects to non-sexual aims and goals. In Freud's view, sublimation denotes the process of purification, desexualization, or distillation of these libidinal trends.[1] In the Schreber case he described how sublimation can be reversed and the energies restored to their early sexual aims and objects. When Schreber was no longer able to sublimate his unconscious homosexuality, the magnificent structure of his sublimations collapsed and his ego had to develop a psychosis to defend itself.[2] With Freud's introduction of the concept of the death instinct and the aggressive drives, the concept of sublimation was extended to include aggressive as well as libidinal energies.

The First Phase

There are three outcomes possible for instinctual drives: direct satisfaction, repression, or sublimation. The need for sublimation arises when the initial, infantile, primitive aims of the drives are no longer acceptable to the developing ego. If these drives are to escape repression, or if the ego is not to be overwhelmed by them, they must be redirected to substitute goals.

Hartmann introduced the concept of the neutralization of energy to cover the first phase of the sublimatory process whereby libidinal and aggressive drives are neutralized.[3] The specific qualities of the libido and aggression, particularly in their primitive aspects, are detached from their original aims and goals so that the energies of these drives may become available to the ego in a more neutral and utilizable form.

[1] Sigmund Freud, *The Ego and the Id*, Hogarth Press, London, 1927.
[2] Sigmund Freud, "Psychoanalytic Notes on an Autobiographical Account of a Case of Paranoia," *Collected Papers*, Hogarth Press, London, 1953, Vol. III, p. 387.
[3] Heinz Hartmann, "Notes on the Theory of Sublimation," *The Psychoanalytic Study of the Child*, Vol. X (1955), pp. 9–30.

In their papers on sublimation, Hartmann and Kris referred to identification as the primary mechanism by which neutralization takes place.[4] In this first phase of sublimation, the basic mechanism of primitive ego development—identification—utilizes a social relationship—the mother-child interaction.

The Second Phase

The description advanced thus far of the process of sublimation is incomplete. The ego has to direct the neutralized energies to aims, goals, object, and activities. The second phase of the process of transformation of energy involves the displacement of that energy to ego-syntonic goals. The satisfactions arising from these activities are now "purified" from their initial primitive, aggressive, and libidinal goals. The instinctual and aggressive energies, which have been neutralized in the first phase, are displaced to substitute satisfactions. Sublimations, then, may be viewed as derivative activities that take the place of early primitive goals.

How is this substitution or displacement accomplished? Here again the mechanism of identification is of primary importance. Identification, the most primitive form of relationship (as pointed out by Freud), includes at least two major components: the establishment of trust and the mastery of activities (usually preceded by imitation) related to basic ego functions such as feeding, locomotion, and speech. These activities, necessary for the preservation of life and the establishment of relationships that are the prelude to socialization, take place chiefly through the medium of the mother-child relationship. Kris emphasized the importance of the child's identification with the mother's activity in the infant's development of the ego function of initiative and his movement from passivity to activity.[5] To accomplish these tasks the relationship must have stability, and the over-all handling of needs must have consistent patterns of satisfaction. This is the base on which each stage of the process of identification moves forward. In this setting

[4] Hartmann, *ibid.*, and Ernst Kris, "Neutralization and Sublimation: Observations on Young Children," *The Psychoanalytic Study of the Child*, Vol. X (1955), pp. 30–47.
[5] Kris, *ibid.*

the transition from passivity to activity finally takes place. Even when feeding himself the child does so by identification with the mother when feeding him.

The second phase of the process of sublimation clearly bears the imprint of psychosocial functioning. The mother and others close to the child facilitate the development of the child's interests, aptitudes, and talents, and the deployment of his energies to ego-syntonic activities. It is interesting that the combination of talent, available energy, and maternal interest is not always enough; the deployment of energies involves not only activities but relationships to people. Unless the child can achieve further identifications, the synthesis of sublimation may fall short. There must be a blending of the child's aptitudes and talents with the skill and perceptiveness of those figures in his environment who supply a medium for their nurture and development.

Sublimation thus refers to the total process by which libidinal and aggressive energies are neutralized and displaced by substitute ego-syntonic satisfactions.

As has been noted, the process of sublimation is reversible. One factor contributing to reversal of the process is the degree of energy neutralization. When the neutralization is incomplete and some amounts of libido and aggression attach themselves to the activities in which partially neutralized energy is invested, the sublimatory activity is more vulnerable to reversal. It is like a coalition government in which some of the old corrupt elements are sufficiently present to threaten dissolution and, therefore, the restoration of the old regime. Moreover, certain stressful factors that ordinarily lead to regression can contribute to a reversal of the process of sublimation. The stress may be external, such as disruption and disturbances of important relationships, or internal, such as an increase of biological forces as in adolescence, or the weakening of the ego, often characteristic of the aging process.

Clinical Implications

From the viewpoint of casework diagnosis and treatment it is important to know what phase of the total process of sublimation is involved. Is treatment directed to the early phase where energy is neutralized and made available to the ego via the mechanism of identification? Or is it directed to the second phase of sublimation where neutralized energies are deployed to ego-syntonic activities and relationships, again through the mechanism of identification? It is also necessary to consider whether treatment involves working with a partial or incomplete sublimatory process or with a sublimatory process threatened or undermined by reversal. It is obvious that treatment goals and techniques differ according to the individual's stage of development in the process of sublimation; for example, individuals who have not yet achieved sublimation may have an ego disorder characterized by primitive psychosocial development or actual psychosis. Let us now examine the usefulness of this theoretical formulation for casework practice.

Casework with a Disturbance of Displacement

Joan, a sensitive, attractive, eager girl of 19, came to the attention of a social worker in a general hospital at a point where her successful sublimations were about to break down. She was about to enter her third year at a teachers' college where she was specializing in work with young children. She had had an early life of marked deprivation. Her mother had always devaluated her in favor of her sister who was two years older. When Joan was 6, her mother divorced the alcoholic father. Responsibility for the support of the two girls rested with the mother. Both Joan and her sister had to work to supplement the mother's income. Her mother had had many affairs until her recent marriage to a sailor. Joan was protective of her mother and spoke of her romantically as being the only child of weathy parents with every advantage until she married. Currently, Joan pretended her mother was traveling leisurely all over the world with her new husband.

Two years before her mother's marriage Joan had moved in with her sister who was a successful graduate nurse. Despite their early years of intense rivalry, when everyone considered the sister the brighter and more beautiful of the two girls, Joan and her sister got along very well. Apparently the sister's own success and the absence of the mother contributed a great deal toward shifting the sister's relationship to Joan from one of rivalry and devaluation to one of tenderness and encouragement. Her sister had been instrumental in helping Joan select her vocation and had been a continuous source of emotional and financial support.

During her two years at college Joan had demonstrated unusual talent for stimulating and teaching young children. Her

93

teachers spoke highly of her sense of responsibility and creative capacity.

When Joan was about to enter her third year of training, her sister announced her engagement. Joan was told she could no longer live with her sister, who needed a paying roommate to enable her to save for her marriage. Following this news, Joan developed gastric symptoms, anxiety, and inability to concentrate. She decided to give up school and marry a boy friend whom she described as being "under his mother's thumb."

In Joan we see what is often evident in latency: resolution of the oedipal situation, with a consolidation of the personality and sublimation of instinctual energies. These energies are then put at the disposal of the ego and there is a flowering of ego functions into interests, activities, education, and relationships outside the family. Internal problems are temporarily quiescent and the individual is free to devote his activities to external affairs. In Joan's case, this balance was evidently maintained in her adolescence. She had an unawakened quality and apparently had not been subjected to the storms of adolescence.

In the loss of interest in her work, in her engagement, and in the development of her symptoms, we see the dramatic reversal of the processes of sublimation. Regression from sublimation involves a progressive undoing, beginning with the latest accomplishments and moving sequentially to an undermining of its earliest foundations. The regression in Joan involved mainly the second phase of the sublimatory process, although the initial phases of neutralization of energies and primary identifications were also threatened. Joan's successful deployment of neutralized energy in educational and teaching activities was made possible through a combination of her own gifts and aptitudes, her identification with her sister, and her sister's sustaining interest. The withdrawal of the sister's interest and her sending Joan away led to a withdrawal of Joan's interests in education. Furthermore, the sister's engagement altered Joan's image of her sister from that of a professional woman to that of a sexualized woman. Her identification with her sister as a tender, giving woman, whose activities she could emulate, was now undermined. Identification with the engaged sister led to thoughts of her own engagement. Her libidinal energies, hitherto successfully repressed and neutralized—hence available for sublimated activities—were again threatened by restoration to their primitive sexual aims and objects. Her unconscious aggressive feelings toward her mother and her sister, which had been transmuted through the mediation of a tender, non-competitive relationship to her sister, were regressively re-activated toward their primitive hostile, destructive goals. Thus, the whole sublimatory edifice of ego-syntonic growth, which had been so painstakingly erected throughout latency and adolescence, was now threatened with collapse.

A myriad of areas for casework focus is presented. One possible area might be Joan's relationship to her mother, since the mother's marriage is one of the precipitants of her current predicament. Working with this relationship to a primary figure would lead toward an anamnestic blending of present with past. One, however, could question the success of such an approach and its goal of improving her relationship with her mother because the past contains so much deprivation and rejection continued into the present. The affects involved are so repressed by romantic idealization that focus in this area would probably result in the destruction of the facade without the possibility of any resolution of her instinctual feelings.

One might focus on Joan's relationship to her sister, her feelings about her sister's engagement, and, even more significantly, her own response to her sister's putting her out of her home for financial reasons. Such a focus might not ensure the goal of an immediate restoration of her good relationship to her sister, but might well lead to an unquenchable, unmanageable enhancement of her anger and bitterness toward her sister.

Another approach might well be via her relationship to her fiancé and her prospective marriage. Her engagement was not the result of ego growth but a manifestation of the regressive process caused by the disturbance of a primary identification with her sister. This focus would most likely lead to an exacerbation and sexualization rather than a resolution of her difficulties.

A focus on the re-establishment of the sublimatory process seems to offer the optimal course for ego restoration. Her sublimations had been made possible by an identification with her sister as a trustful, giving woman with professional activities. The relationship had been non-competitive and had encouraged the development of her talents through educational experiences and activities. Since regression had involved primarily the second phase of the process of sublimation, the worker could concentrate on helping Joan again direct her energies into the channels of educational activities from which they had been recently withdrawn.

Having made this choice, the worker encouraged Joan to speak of her first two years at school, helping her tell about her courses, her relationship to her teachers, and her experiences in the practicum. This discussion brought forth a good deal of material about the excitement of the learning situation which opened up new vistas about learning and new ideas about children. In talking about children, particularly preschool children, Joan showed a sensitivity and a capacity to give which might have been thought theoretically impossible in the light of her own early deprivation. It soon became obvious that there was little element of rivalry in her relationship to children and it became clear to Joan, in her detailed recounting of her experiences, how much she loved working with children. The worker found herself in the happy position of being able to give Joan a great deal of praise and encouragement on the basis of a rich reality experience of success. Soon Joan asked the worker what she professionally thought of the content and teaching techniques of the school. In this interchange the worker gave freely of her own experience and thinking.

Moving from this content to a plan for living, Joan first dealt with the pros and cons of finding a new home in marriage and perhaps having children of her own. This step led to an increase in anxiety. The next step was to think, not of marriage alone, but of marriage along with a continuation of school. The third step was to defer marriage and think of school alone. Then Joan asked the worker how disappointed her boy friend would be if the marriage were postponed. At this point, by focusing on the possibility of scholarship help and a work home, the worker gave Joan unspoken permission and encouragement to delay her marriage and complete her education.

Casework with a Disturbance of Neutralization *

When John, a slim, 30-year-old, war veteran, silently stood at the door of the worker's office, his rigid expressionless face and hesitant, fearful manner suggested that he probably would

* Case carried by a student worker at Veterans Administration Mental Hygiene Clinic, Boston, Massachusetts.

96

never get beyond the threshold. John had originally been referred to the clinic because of abdominal cramps, diarrhea, morning nausea and vomiting, and nightmares in which either he or someone else was being destroyed. The onset of symptoms had followed his discharge from the air force ten years earlier. At the referral point the worker knew something of John's extraordinary early history, which included many losses through death and many fragmented relationships to mother figures in a series of foster homes. Currently, John was living with a middle-aged couple who worked nights and whom he rarely saw. He himself had been working as a clerk in a large department store during the last ten years.

The worker's initial focus on John's work experience, which appeared to be the one stable area in his life, led to a poignant description of loneliness and yearning for love. In the early interviews John spoke in detail about his symptoms. The worker listened but offered no comments except to find out how much his symptoms interfered with his work. Apparently, despite the magnitude of his symptomatology, his work was his haven and he dealt with his symptoms during work hours either by brief interruptions during which he relieved tension by smoking or by his practice of not speaking to the other workers. An understanding boss, who apologized for John's behavior, assuring John's co-workers he was only nervous, also apparently helped stabilize his performance at work.

The worker's primary interest in John's work and current living arrangements and activities gradually elicited a story that seemed more like the recital of a nightmare than of reality. His story unfolded via two channels: first, his experiences with women and, second, his experiences with death. Initially John stated that women frightened him and tied his tongue. His manner was serious, tense, somewhat hostile, unsmiling, and almost tearful.

The fifth of six children, he went to Scotland at the age of 7, with his 18-month-old brother and his mother, for a year, during which time his mother cared for his dying maternal grandmother. Upon his return to the United States, after his grandmother's death, he and his brother were hospitalized for pneumonia. About to go home, the brother leaped into his mother's arms, had a heart attack, and died. His mother became hysterical, was subsequently hospitalized for a gall-bladder operation and died on the operating table. Three months later John's father died. An older brother died during the Allies' landing in Europe. An older sister died a violent death from burns.

At the age of 8, John was separated from his two older siblings, and lived in a series of foster homes until he entered the

97

air force at 16. He recalled his first foster mother as an old witch who was harsh and domineering and who frightened him. He never liked any of his foster mothers until he found his present one just before entering the air force. Even she would upset him by urging him to bring girls home and asking him questions about marriage. He described how he used to run away, in Tom Sawyer fashion, from his foster homes, because no one cared for him. He used to think that running away would punish his foster mothers.

During the third interview he smiled for the first time. He spoke of his great loneliness and the fact that no one cared for him. He said he had never had a real home. His family never communicated with him and although he now knew where they lived he never saw them.

Any cancellation of appointments because of holidays or illness of the worker resulted in an increase of symptoms. At such times the worker responded by increasing the interviews to twice a week.

After one particularly lonely weekend John spoke of never having a steady girl. "I go with a girl for a while, but when I get to know her, I get scared and stop." "Anyway," he said, "they ask things of me I cannot do—like dancing." He added that girl friends were likely to reject him when they learned about his symptoms; they believed him to be queer. This had happened with three different girls. He would like to find a girl who would understand him, who would care for him, and with whom he could talk. He was afraid, however, of being jilted. In another interview he mentioned that recently he had whistled at work and the other men laughed, saying he must have a new girl friend.

Naively unaware of the blossoming of his feeling for the worker, he said he hoped one day the right girl would come along. At this point the worker told John how glad she was that he was feeling better and that she was sure one day he would find the right girl.

Some months after beginning treatment John revealed that he was spending a great deal of time watching war movies, which inevitably brought on headaches and nightmares. When the worker asked why he always chose war pictures and what he thought they meant to him, he paused and said that perhaps he was punishing himself because so many of his buddies had died and he had lived. The worker helped him to discontinue his visits to these movies, telling him he had done his share in the war admirably and that he should now turn his back on the past and see if he could do as good a job with the future. This discussion marked a climax in treatment which was consolidated by the worker's helping him turn from the past by her increase of interest in the present.

After he was able to shut the door to the past, through the worker's continued emphasis that there need be no more self-punishment or turning back, John seemed to improve. In the course of several months he was elected shop steward, representing forty employees in weekly conferences with union officials. He talked easily with the women and girls at work. He no longer had days when he felt he could speak to no one. He accompanied his fellow workers to lighter movies and joined the employees' bowling club. He reached a rapprochement with his brother and sister, an objective that had been steadily encouraged by the worker. Finally, during one weekend, he had his first date in eight months.

John presents a more difficult problem than Joan in respect to the sublimatory process. Although he had achieved satisfaction in his work, he had not been able to realize other sublimatory activities or to sublimate in his relationships to either men or women. There was thus only a partial success of the second phase of the sublimatory process, due primarily to a failure in the first phase. Since he had apparently been unable to establish primary identifications, his libidinal, aggressive energies were largely unneutralized. Consequently the casework task—unlike that in Joan's case which could focus on the second phase—was primarily directed toward restoration, possibly even the creation, of the conditions that would lead to a satisfactory resolution of the initial phases.

The worker took three major steps in her work with John. First, she dealt with his relationship to women, primarily by listening. The details of his sexual life were not explored, nor were there comments on his aggression toward women. There was no clarification of his behavior or feeling toward women. When John spoke of avoiding women because of their demands, the worker took this as a cue, not to make demands on him as would a mother or a sister or as did the foster mother who asked about marriage. Instead, by creating a situation in which no demands were made, the worker fostered John's feeling of trust in her, thereby helping him to alter his image of women.

Second, the worker focused on John's needs rather than on his symptoms. When he developed symptoms either after a weekend or after the loss of an appointment, she behaved like a loving mother or sister who gives appropriately in response to need. Instead of experiencing rejection, as John had with his girl friends, he experienced being given to. The caseworker often fears that responding to a client's demands will inevitably lead to mobilization of further insatiable demands. It is important, however, to distinguish between neurotic demands and demands that arise from healthy but unmet needs. We know that responding to a child's needs does not lead to a mobilization of demands, but to increased tolerance for frustration. This responding is an essential ingredient in the formation of relationship. The establishment of trust and a response to need enable the individual to establish an identification with the trusted person and thus to move from passivity to activity.

The third thing the worker did was to lighten the intolerable burden of the client's guilt. By working with his guilt toward derivative figures (his buddies who were killed in the war) and by telling John he no longer had to dwell on the past, the worker enabled him to emancipate himself from his masochistic behavior stemming from his feelings about the death of his parents and siblings.

The primary conditions in respect to the mechanism of sublimation were thus fulfilled. Identification was established. It developed in a relationship of trust which met primary needs. The client's ego grew in its capacity for establishing relationships and its energies were increasingly neutralized. They were no longer bound to their primitive aims, objects, and goals but were made increasingly available to the ego. At the same time the ego was freed from its masochistic involvement in primary aggression as a result of John's diminished sense of guilt. We can assume that the gross sexual components of the primitive libidinal energies were also in process of neutralization.

The worker elicited no direct material about John's probable primitive erotic fantasies and practices. To do so would have eroticized the relationship and repeated the unhappy experience with the well-meaning foster mother who inquired about dating and marriage. The worker's silence in this area probably facilitated the maturation of the libidinal organization which often takes place in latency. Through the establishment of a tender, non-seductive

100

relationship to the worker, John's ego was strengthened and his energies increased.

Casework with Constricted Neutralization

So-called "hard-to-reach" families present more complicated problems in the sublimatory process than the cases just cited. Since they are in relatively primitive stages of ego development, their social functioning, relationships to people, and feelings are often quite different from those of the typical neurotic client. Their concept of self-identity is blurred and is closer to that of a small child. When sporadically seen, particularly in family and public welfare agencies, these clients frequently remain uninvolved or precipitously terminate their relationship to the agency. Their contacts occur chiefly during times of crisis. Verbal communication does not consist of an interchange of relationship content or feelings about children and marital partner. The worker's customary language bridge of communication, through a discussion of conflicts and relationships with either current or primary or derivative figures, as in classical child guidance work, is not available. These clients cannot objectify feelings or relationships and in fact are bewildered if the worker communicates in these terms.

Verbal communication with such clients requires the setting of the home rather than that of the office and consists primarily of discussion of what these parents do in the course of the day along with a good deal of participation by the worker in their activities.* Relationships are perceived and understood by the worker through direct observation of behavior in the life situation at home.

In these families one is dealing, not with the regression of the sublimatory process (as with Joan) or with individuals who have achieved some sublimation (as with John), but with people in whom the sublimatory process is barely begun. The initial therapeutic task, then, must be differentiated from the ultimate goal of influencing their child-rearing practices and patterns so that they can get satisfaction from parenthood. The initial task is to bring them

* *Editor's Note:* For further discussion of this issue see Irving Kaufman, "Psychodynamics of Protective Casework," Chapter 11 of this volume.

through the first phases of sublimation whereby the energies are sufficiently neutralized to be available to the ego for deployment in relationships and activities. These mothers and fathers are in a state of rivalry with their children. Their own needs and those of their children merge so closely that they are at first unable to make a proper differentiation. Their need to be given to, their lack of trust, their passivity, their limited capacity for relationships, the disorganized and fragmented states of their egos, and their primitive libidinal and aggressive aims pose many problems for casework. They tend to relate to the worker as a primary rather than a transference figure.

Mrs. B, mother of boys aged 3, 5, and 7, presents an impressive example of what can be accomplished with such a mother.* Although she was Syrian-born and married to a Jew, she defined her religious affiliation as "Protestant-Catholic." Her early life is best described as a gypsy existence in a carnival setting where routine and controls were at a minimum. As an obese adolescent she had little love from her mother, who favored her two older brothers. The oldest, who was "clever" and married to a "lady," had died of a heart attack in his thirties. The second brother owned a garage and was able to travel every winter. Mrs. B had worked as a stitcher with her mother. She had then nursed her for five years, until the mother's death, when Mrs. B was 38. She described her father as indifferent because after the mother's death he expressed no need for her other than wanting her pay check. As a consequence she moved to a rooming house. About this time she met Mr. B in a free, casual setting when she was doing a great deal of sexual acting out. Mr. B had been diagnosed as a schizoid personalty.

She lived in her old family apartment where she had returned after marriage; her father had moved out because of a cardiac condition. The apartment's disorganization, bareness, and filth were incredible. The one room with adequate furniture was closed off; in it were stored her mother's furniture, dishes, and personal clothes. Mrs. B's major activity was feeding the children. She employed no routine and no discipline other than sporadic violent shouting or physical abuse.

When the worker entered this case, Mrs. B was virtually in a state of confusion and nervous collapse. The public school

* This is one of a group of "multi-problem" families being studied currently at the South End Family Program, Boston, Massachusetts. This program is supported by the National Institute of Mental Health under the auspices of the Department of Psychiatry, Masachusetts Memorial Hospitals, Boston.

102

authorities had refused to admit her 5-year-old boy into kindergarten. The boy's bizarre behavior and the questions concerning his intellectual capacity confirmed her image of herself. The experience with the school was a repetition of early relationships involving her mother and herself in which she had been the devaluated one.

Mrs. B expected the worker to rescue her from the evil authorities and find ways of establishing her boy's normality. She naively assumed the worker would take care of everything. The initial period of bewilderment, disappointment, and anger because all was not straightened out, was balanced by the worker's activity in becoming quickly involved in the daily life of the family. The worker, in weekly and for a time bi-weekly home visits, became a part of Mrs. B's life and trials. All details of daily living were brought to the worker's attention—housekeeping, food, and health matters.

Mrs. B's struggle, first to imitate and later to identify with the worker, was seen in several areas. At first she was the personification of role playing. Avidly pursuing information from newspapers and child guidance books, she presented the worker with a number of verbal good-mother images. During the worker's visits she was the mother who sat reading to her children while the pots boiled over. She bought puzzles to develop their minds. She stuffed them with orange juice to provide vitamins. She poured in milk to keep their teeth from falling out. She religiously took the children to the hospital and medical clinics—but faked their health reports. She tried very hard to co-operate and be a good mother and send the boys to nursery school.

In contrast to the picture she presented when the worker visited in the home, it was reported that between visits she abused the boys, screamed violently, and generally mismanaged the home. The apartment was fantastically untidy. Soiled dishes, food, and refuse were often piled up under the stove; children's destroyed toys lay about. Her attempts to be a good mother, which had been prematurely encouraged, finally broke down with several outbursts of temper; she gave orders that the children were to stay out of nursery school and the worker was not to return to the home. When the worker did make a home visit, however, at the regular time, the mother received her, meekly saying she had not thought the worker would want to continue with such a bad mother and housekeeper. Like a small child in a negativistic moment, she had thought she wanted to be alone.

This episode was followed by real attempts by Mrs. B to do what she thought was expected of her. Whereas earlier she could not tolerate having the children in nursery school, she now permitted them to go. She attempted to improve her physical appearance and that of the boys and home. She sewed new clothes for herself. She showed the worker her wardrobe. One day she presented the worker with a tweed skirt saying she had made it. She had not used bright plaids like her own because she knew the worker liked tweeds. Mrs. B commented that her mother had always selected her clothes. She recalled being forced by her mother to buy an unattractive coat when she would have preferred something gayer and younger looking. On one occasion she bought a pair of white gloves and a white purse like the worker's. Later, she expressed a yearning to be a lady like the worker and like her sister-in-law whom she admired.

At first Mrs. B found it difficult to differentiate herself from the worker. She seemed to think that the worker knew everything about her. She talked as if they had had the same experiences and had known the same people. She often wanted close physical contact with the worker. She would cup the worker's face in her hands or hold the worker's hand or button her coat. This need for physical contact appeared more of a pre-oedipal closeness (as between a mother and child) than an erotic attachment to the worker.

Food, particularly feeding the worker, was a central theme in the development of the relationship. In the beginning Mrs. B offered the worker coffee simply because it was there. As the worker became actively involved in the family life, Mrs. B became increasingly insistent that the worker accept food. Finally, Mrs. B declared angrily that unless the worker ate she would be convinced that the worker liked neither Mrs. B nor her housekeeping. The worker steeled herself against the malodorous and unsavory reality of Mrs. B's housekeeping and accepted food. At one point, desperate for a respite from Syrian food, the worker conceived the idea of an exchange of recipes to replace the actual partaking of food.

After almost a year of casework Mrs. B was able to adopt a take-it-or-leave-it attitude about food. Her new attitude was reflected in her use of more limits and planning in feeding the children, in contrast to an earlier massive, undifferentiated presentation of food throughout the day. At about this time, Mrs. B also shifted the worker's visits from the kitchen to the living room where the mother's belongings were.

These events signaled the successful realization of the first phases of the sublimatory process. The achievement of the primary identification with a loving mother, and the establishment of trust led to a gradual shift in her self-image as a mother. The assuagement of her needs by this trusted worker (leading to a reduction of her own need to be cared for) made it possible for her ego to shift from

104

passivity to activity. She was able to devote her energies increasingly to the satisfactions of being a good mother. This change was reflected in her increasing trust in the nursery school teacher and in her pride in her children's accomplishments in school. She no longer feared she would lose her children because outsiders considered her a bad mother.

This attitude was in contrast to her reaction when the worker had prematurely encouraged her to be a good mother. At that time she almost withdrew from treatment because she had been pushed to enter a later phase of the sublimatory process before she had consolidated the earlier phase of identification via trust. In this process her aggression was in part neutralized and her libido moved from a primitive canabalistic orality, seen in her massive feeding, to a higher level of organization. She seems to have started the process of neutralization of the libidinal need to be fed, displacing this need by ego-syntonic activities. She was now able to feed others with some restraint and to perform motherly tasks with less aggression. The further extension and development of her energies in the ego-syntonic activities of motherhood are a continuing treatment goal.

Casework Implications

Successful sublimations lead to enhanced ego functioning in the individual's activities and relationships with others. Ideally one would hope not only for success in both areas but for a concomitant maturation of the libidinal organization, so that the individual might also achieve direct satisfaction of erotic goals. This, of course, does not always happen. Some individuals may achieve their greatest success in sublimated activities, with less achievement in satisfying relationships and no achievement of direct libidinal gratifications. Other individuals may achieve their greatest success in relationships with considerably less success in activities and direct libidinal outlets.

Joan's achievement was in the restoration of her successful sublimation in teaching. Her previously good relationships, except for the current conflictual one with her sister, were unimpaired. The responsibilities and satisfactions of marriage were deferred since her engagement had not represented the maturation of her libidinal organization and readiness for marriage. Instead her engagement was seen as acting out. This situation is commonly seen in the behavior of some teenagers who become involved in sexual activities because of some external precipitant. In Joan's case the external precipitant was her sister's engagement. One could anticipate, however, that, with the consolidation of her sublimations and the passage of time, she would become ready for marriage and the direct satisfactions of motherhood.

John's major sublimatory achievement was in his interpersonal relationships, with concomitant strengthening of his satisfaction in work. There seemed also to be the hope that he might one day be capable of a serious relationship with a women.

Mrs. B's sublimation was of a different order. It involved the activities of motherhood. The setting, the objects, and goals for sublimation were already there; namely, her household and her children. The worker's task was to help Mrs. B develop and utilize her sublimatory capacity.

Conclusion

Social casework in recent years has been preoccupied with two problems. The first is the search for a definition of its own essential nature. There seems to be an increasing consensus that what is distinctive in social casework is the particular way in which social and psychological therapies are blended and synthesized. The second problem is the search for a conceptualization of those treatment goals and techniques that are particularly appropriate to social casework. Although this search has led to many valuable analyses of practice, these analyses often run the risk of oversimplification and fragmentation, thus blurring one's vision of the casework process as a whole. One theoretical difficulty in such attempts is that they tend to follow the model of psychoanalytic and psychotherapeutic methods rather than the model of life and its developmental processes.*

A basic process in the development and growth of the ego is that of sublimation, in its essence psychosocial. Indeed, the sublimatory process, of all the manifestations of ego growth and functioning,

* For further discussion, see Bernard Bandler, "The Concept of Ego-Supportive Psychotherapy," Chapter 2 of this volume.

may have the greatest relevance to social casework. Is not the process of sublimation, in a way, the model in life of the unique synthesis of the psychological and the social?

The casework process has the same movement and direction as the process of sublimation. Both processes start with the individual in the matrix of a relationship, with the child in the matrix of the symbiotic relationship to the mother, with the client in the matrix of the relationship to the worker. Both move from the first phase of the neutralization of instinctual energies by means of the mechanism of identification, to the second phase of the deployment of these neutralized energies into ego-syntonic activities and relationships. It is primarily in the second phase of the casework process that the social and psychological therapies are fused. Here the worker, like those concerned with the child's socialization and education, uses not only his perceptiveness and understanding but his ingenuity and resourcefulness in mobilizing the client and the environment for the client's realization of ego-syntonic satisfactions.

Three cases have been presented to illustrate ways in which an understanding of the sublimatory process can clarify and illuminate the casework process. Further analysis of practice experience is obviously necessary to test the fruitfulness of such an approach. In addition to a more refined theoretical understanding of the sublimatory process itself, use of this approach may sharpen our diagnostic endeavors, and add precision to casework activities, particularly problems of timing, focus, and sequence of treatment goals. Furthermore, the client's current problem may be better understood if it is seen as a phase of his sublimatory development or regression; and casework goals may be defined in terms of the phase of the sublimatory process toward which one is working. Techniques may then be freely employed with the fluidity and flexibility of life toward the optimal achievement of these sublimatory goals.

6. Prospects and Problems in the Study of Ego Functions*

Roger R. Miller

IN A RECENTLY INITIATED project, the Smith College School for Social Work has enlisted master's students in an organized program for the study of ego functions. Through a series of investigations, it is hoped that the project will advance our knowledge of ego operations and increase our understanding of their implications for casework practice. A preliminary report of the project is justified on the grounds that social researchers have not often ventured into this field of inquiry, at least not intentionally. The opportunities for study in this area, as well as the obstacles encountered, occasion some departure from conventional research methodology. The experience in pursuing this project may thus contribute to the current efforts to define the characteristics of the scientific method appropriate for the study of practice problems. Offered here are a review of some of the considerations stimulating and shaping the project, a description of the design, and an illustration of the results obtained during a reconnaissance period of research.

Ego Psychology and Casework Practice

The investigation of ego functions is impelled by the rather curious relationship that now prevails between ego psychological theory and casework practice. Although the aims and techniques of

* In this article the reference numbers refer to the bibliography at the end.

casework have frequently been identified with this line of theory, it is not easy to detect a precise, systematic use of ego psychology in practice. Except in such limited areas as the study of the defenses, connections between ego theory and practice are rarely made explicit. Although superficial descriptions of ego "strength" and "weakness" are ubiquitous, adequate specific descriptions of ego characteristics are rare. In ordinary practice, it is unusual to encounter a record of a treatment course precisely related to carefully drawn distinctions among the ego capacities of the client. The ego orientation of current practice thus appears fragmentary.[20]

The more extensive application of ego psychology to practice is seriously handicapped by certain characteristics of this body of knowledge. To date ego psychology has not attained the status of a true theory—there exists no exposition that orders and relates the thought units comprising ego psychology. Indeed, it is acknowledged that some of the elements from which a theory of ego psychology could be organized have probably not been identified.[1] The constructs, or idea clusters, that constitute the extent of systematization in this area, are of relatively recent origin and have been elaborated in piecemeal and uneven fashion.[13] Only in the broadest terms are the possible functional relationships among these constructs postulated.[14] The components of this system of ideas are remote from behavior and do not contain simple behavioral referents. No assumption can be made that a given psychic process will be manifested only by specific behaviors or that specific behaviors express a single psychic process. Thus, ego psychology may be characterized as an unsystematized, evolving, and highly abstract constellation of concepts.

To utilize a theory with precision requires not only a firm grasp of the idea system but a technology for relating the mental abstractions to practice realities. We do not presently enjoy such a technology. Our literature provides few clues, for example, about the manifestation of the judgment of our clients or their capacity for reality testing. Detailed exposition of clinically important constellations of ego characteristics and the treatment opportunities they contain awaits development.

It is safe to predict that social workers will for some time be engaged in further exploration of the potential of ego psychology as a theoretical base for practice. Not only does much await elucidation, but there are encouraging indications that efforts to relate ego psychology to practice will be rewarding. When thoughtful formulations about ego operations have been used to clarify treatment activities, to illuminate the process of professional education, or to devise novel treatment arrangements, the yield to practice has indeed been impressive.* Continued study of ego functioning can be expected to produce additional knowledge useful for the pursuit of a number of professional objectives.

Ego Psychology and Research Enterprises

In view of the widespread interest in the practice implications of ego operations, it might be supposed that extensive research activities would have been drawn into this area. No such development has occurred in social work research. Of course, the circumstances that have handicapped clinical application also pertain for the investigator; the characteristics of ego psychology make it an inconvenient base for both practice and research. However, investigators from other disciplines have for some time conducted a lively traffic in this area; the objectives, methods, and results of their work provide useful leads for framing further inquiries.

It must be acknowledged initially that the ideas comprising ego psychology have been developed almost entirely by means that fall outside the usual conception of formal research. The case study, including asystematic observation, and allowing the full play of intuition and inspiration supplemented by scholarship, has been the productive avenue toward knowledge in this realm. It is difficult to locate significant elaborations of the theory which derive chiefly from the findings of formal research. There is reason to attribute this circumstance to the poverty of the research rather than to the resistance of the idea system to revisions or extensions.

One instructive line of psychological research is defined by the objective of theory-testing.[18] It is noteworthy that validational studies of dynamic psychology have excited almost no interest among clinicians, who do not share the investigators' skepticism about the

* Among the relevant illustrations of these applications contained in the present volume are the articles by Louise Bandler, Yonata Feldman, and John A. MacLeod.

110

validity of the formulations taken for study. However laudable may be the goal of testing theory, the indifference of clinicians contains a message for the investigator. Some attention must be given to the important concerns of the practitioner if theory-testing is to aid the development of practice. For example, most clinicians do not question the existence of childhood sexuality, but they would welcome additions to knowledge about the course of psychosexual developments, their underlying processes and sequelae.

There are important lessons to be learned from validational research. Validational investigations have commanded little respect on their own merits since they have consisted of tests of inappropriately derived propositions transposed to conform to the requirements of some variant of the experimental model of research. The findings under such conditions have at best an unknown relevance to the theory. This circumstance constitutes a strong case for respecting the requirements of a problem and seeking ways to fit the study method to the problem rather than forcing the problem into a preselected study method.[17]

Like those cited here, many attempts to study dynamic psychology have been handicapped by an apparently irresistible urge to quantify. The pursuit of objective measurement has led either to the study of readily quantifiable behavior, which has at best a tenuous connection to a concept, or to the use of instruments that are optimistically presumed to reflect the concept of interest. To employ a straightforward questionnaire for the study of oedipal wishes is like using a sound truck to stalk deer. Some balance about the place of measurement objectivity in scientific endeavor can be attained by recalling that its purpose is to reduce error. Quantification can, however, obscure as well as reveal. Measurement may defensibly become more formal and objective as knowledge of the significant dimensions of a variable increases. To attach numbers to events can readily produce a sense of mastery when feelings of confusion and uncertainty would be more appropriate and productive.

Between the polar positions defined by experimental studies with objective measurements on the one hand, and the methodologically casual case study on the other, lies a vast field for artful inquiry. Developmental studies illustrate some of the potential of directed, systematic observational methods which, through design flexibility,

111

take full advantage of the observations of the skilled clinician and make imaginative use of objective measuring opportunities.[3, 4, 11] These studies are oriented to the extension of knowledge and show the designers' willingness to use fully toward this end the network of ideas which represent a working conception of the nature of reality. The growing body of clinical research on a variety of problems or clinical processes also suggests some of the potential of research for theory building.[7, 24] It is encouraging to note, too, that the instrumentation developed for more rigorous research in this area shows an increasingly sophisticated relationship to the theory.[10] It therefore seems reasonable to expect research activities, at some level beyond the case study, to become an increasingly important source of knowledge about ego operations.

A Strategy for Further Inquiry

The orientation of the present project was influenced by both the state of knowledge of ego psychology and the course of related research. Additionally, the project sought to accommodate the research capabilities of master's students and to capitalize on the research opportunities of an existing educational system.* The study program adopted was devised to foster independent but cumulative research, through the provision of a general design and the identification of a series of separable study areas.

Aims

The central objective selected for the project was to contribute to the more precise clinical judgment of the components of ego functioning. This focus seemed attractive in view of the central position of clinical study in practice and the problems inherent in judging ego operations. The more adequate appraisal of ego functioning was seen as a vital step in the movement toward developing a more systematic practice theory.

An attempt to use research to advance clinical observation is somewhat unusual. More frequently, investigators have tended either to reject the clinical judge as a data processor in favor of objective

* The Smith College School for Social Work has retained the thesis requirement for master's students in the form of an independent project.

measurements or to use the clinical judge in pursuit of some research objective.[21] The present project falls between these two positions. Although clinical judgment is accepted as a viable source for data, implicit in the study aim is the assumption that clinical judgments in relation to ego functioning have important limitations. It is true that when the clinician is used as a research instrument, provisions are often made to direct and sharpen his performance. Without doubt, such procedures contribute to clinical observation although their contribution is directed by the needs of the research, rather than by clinical problems. Here the performance of the clinical judge, instead of constituting an intervening variable for control, becomes the dependent variable that one hopes ultimately to influence.

Although a multistage study was devised in the hope of enhancing the clinical judgment of ego operations, major emphasis was placed on conceptual clarification. Owing to the poorly organized state of knowledge of ego functions, initial concern was directed toward attaining better mastery of the relevant formulations. Because the literature in this area is scattered, it was anticipated that the location and assembly of relevant theoretical expositions would constitute a service in itself. In addition, efforts at organizing or synthesizing this literature held promise of constituting an important contribution toward the aim of the project. It was expected that progress in devising a technology for using the concepts could be approached as conceptual clarification was achieved. Within this framework, the issues chosen for immediate study included the identification from technical literature of dimensions along which clinical discriminations are required. The logic underlying this strategy was simple: knowledge of a conceptual system constitutes an absolute ceiling on our capacity to take advantage of this system. Increasingly precise knowledge of the theory can therefore be expected to create opportunities to develop more effective clinical observation.

Specification of Ego Functions

Any plan for study of so inclusive a subject as ego functions requires some preliminary delineation of the field. This seemed possible in view of the usual conception of the ego as a functional entity

113

with a variety of tasks. The principal assignments of the ego, such as reality testing and self-observation, offered facets of the construct that could be abstracted for separate study. Such a separation of complexly interrelated parts of course introduces an element of artificiality into the study; none of the components of the ego exists in isolation. Reduction of the construct also delays a study of the interrelationship among its components.[8] In view of the present state of knowledge, however, it seemed essential to reduce the problem to units of more approachable size.

The separation of the construct into its components presented a practical problem. What are the constitutent processes or the principal tasks of the ego? The literature describes a number of ego functions. Freud's own formulation assigned to the ego such tasks as the temporal ordering of mental processes and the testing of their correspondence with reality, the postponement of motor discharge and control over avenues to motility by interposing thought, the coping with instinctual impulses, and achieving the work of sublimation.[5] Although these functional attributes are readily identifiable in current formulations, they have been supplemented and elaborated by subsequent theorists. As might be expected when a number of individuals have delineated such multidimensional abstractions as ego functions, some differences are found in the concepts believed to fall under the construct. The differences, however, appear to be chiefly due to choice about emphasis, and the formulations show compatibility.

The framework selected for the present project drew chiefly from Green's formulation, which was particularly helpful because of the concise preliminary elaboration offered for each of the identified components.[6] Green's formulation, amplified by content drawn from other sources, was taken as a workable preliminary delineation of elements within the construct of ego.[1, 23] The concepts identified were: judgment, intellective capacity, frustration tolerance, self-concept, motility, insight, reality testing, and object relationship. Subsequently, this preliminary delineation was expanded to include sublimation and the defenses.

It is recognized that the components thus identified may not be comparable in level of abstraction so that one function identified here may subsume all or part of another. Since a categorical scheme

114

that may not be exhaustive or mutually exclusive is anathema to methodologists, it would be well to note that no assumption is made here about the capacity of this formulation to order all the constituents of the construct. Instead this scheme was expected to identify a series of focal points for study; the utility of this limited use of the formulation is at least open to exploration.

Study Sequence

To facilitate study in the component areas identified for the research, a cumulative sequence of study phases was developed. As previously indicated, the program of study was to be based on and derived from a review of relevant literature aimed at locating, organizing, and summarizing the current conceptual formulation of a given ego function. The design emphasized the identification and abstraction of dimensions along which clinical distinctions were regarded as important.

It was planned that the survey of literature be followed by an experience survey to tap the observations of skilled clinicians about clinically useful distinctions concerning ego functioning. It was hoped that discussions with practitioners would supplement and check inferences drawn from literature about important diagnostic differentiations in each study area.

The general design also identified the subsequent possibility of studying some of the diagnostic implications of the more precisely identified dimensions of ego functioning as well as the possibility of working toward formal measurement of these components. These relatively remote goals for the study were not elaborated in the general design and it was expected that the problems in each component area might direct the study into unique issues at that stage.

In summary, then, the general design sketched out a sequence of progressive study intended to contribute to increasing precision in clinical judgment about selected components of ego functioning. This plan, which encouraged diversified study effort rather than concentrating the studies in a restricted area, had the advantage of providing potential investigators with leeway for the expression of choice. Because there seemed no clear basis for the selection of one or two among equally attractive (or equally intimidating) focal points for study, the inclusive plan elected here was regarded as appropriate. It was hoped, of course, that preliminary experience would clarify the differences in the workability and productivity of studies in several areas. At such a point, a narrowing of the focus of the project could more rationally be achieved.

The reader will have noted that in design this project departs from customary strategy for social work research. The project is lodged in psychodynamic theory and a major effort is placed on conceptual clarification. The collection and interpretation of data occupy a less prominent place in this program of study than is usually the case. Data collecting begins at a methodologically casual level and more formal measurement is contemplated only as a potential subsequent eventuality. Rather than identifying a definite and attainable objective, the design sketches out a direction for inquiry and provides for the subsequent elaboration of the design. For these reasons it might be argued that the enterprise is not "research" at all. Indeed, if research were defined by methods such as sampling and formal measurement, this would be true. This project, however, is cast within the conception of research as a quest for knowledge by whatever methods seem best suited to produce it. In these terms research is defined by its product; the present design constitutes an estimate of a strategy likely to yield knowledge in a particular substantive area. To the extent that the methods employed here succeed in producing verifiable, generalized knowledge they have a place among the approaches appropriate for study of our professional concerns.

Initial Experience

Since it was decided to initiate the project on a modest scale, no active recruiting of research participants was done. The availability of the design stimulated a number of research efforts, however, and the work of student volunteers has accomplished some reconnaissance of the study area. The preliminary experience with the project has been enlightening.

The general design has been used by students in two different ways. Some found in the plan a springboard for the development of studies which, though interesting in their own right, departed from the central purpose of the project. The work of other students expressed the intent of the project. Ten individual projects, completed to date, constitute study efforts within the domain identified by the design and these provide some basis for appraisal of the approach.* These studies are concerned with sublimation, motility, insight, reality testing, object relationships, and the defenses.

Somewhat unexpectedly, several of the investigations falling outside the scope of the project contributed to the appraisal of the design. This was found to be the case with several projects generated by the identification of self-concept as a dimension of ego functioning. Without exception, the designs of these theses were influenced importantly by the numerous and readily available measuring devices related to self-concept. The psychological literature abounds with techniques for obtaining self-reports—adjective check lists, rating scales, sentence completion tests, and narrative response tests. The ease with which such reports could be collected and the extensive precedent for their use in the research literature tended to draw studies away from the issues relevant to the present project.

Devices for collecting self-descriptions, developed to tap a social definition of the self, yielded data that seemed quite remote from a dynamic sense of self.[19] Major problems arose in attempting to interpret data obtained through the use of "common sense" measuring devices. What does it mean, for example, when an isolated individual describes himself as "popular"? Some elements of self-description appeared to reflect either unconscious processes such as reaction formation, denial, or displacement, or conscious processes such as suppression and distortion. In the absence of provisions that would allow for an untangling of these threads, the quality of the data for the present project had seriously to be questioned. To the extent that the information obtained through objective measurements requires interpretation, the problem of conceptual clarification remains. Although it may be argued that ad hoc measurement efforts contribute to the elaboration of a concept, the studies of self-concept do not appear to illustrate this pos-

* Grateful acknowledgment is extended to Mary Bonime (1959), Donna Church (1962), Sybil Cohen, Evelyn Hiller (1961), Charlotte Holena (1961), Judith Jhirad (1961), Emily Leshan (1962), Roberta Ruliffson (1962), Carolyn Tunnock (1961), and Mimi Wannamaker (1959), on whose work this part of the paper is based. Miss Cohen's report is published in *Smith College Studies in Social Work*, Vol. XXXIII, No. 2 (February, 1963). Abstracts of the other reports may be found in the October issues of the *Studies*, in the years indicated.

sibility. Thus, there may be no alternative to the demanding task of locating and utilizing all available sources of knowledge to elaborate a concept prior to efforts at measurement.

Use of the Literature

The literature relevant to the aims of this project presented a number of problems. Although most of the identified components of ego functioning enjoy an extensive literature, so uneven is the treatment of these topics that the exposition of certain components was actually too limited for the purposes of the project. Such functions as self-observing capacity and motility have apparently not attracted the repeated and extensive consideration given to, say, object relationship capacity and reality testing. Unevenness was also found in the extent to which the literature has been organized. Summary review articles are available on reality testing and formulations about insight have undergone some synthesis.[15, 25] The defenses have attracted a discrete literature as has, to a considerably less extent, sublimation. In contrast, the literature relevant to object relationships seemed widely scattered and lodged for the most part in the exposition of a variety of different technical processes. The terminology currently in use made some of the literature elusive. For example, a common term may be used by different authors to denote separate processes; this was conspicuously the case in the literature referring to self-concept. Conversely, almost identical concepts were found to carry different labels. Some of the technical vocabulary for the development of the concept of motility, for example, appeared in a literature on kinesics and parakinesics.[2]

Even when identified, the literature proved of mixed value for pursuit of the projects undertaken thus far. Some of their presentations were so general and simplified as to be valueless. More frequently the literature was found to be framed in so highly technical a network of ideas as to intimidate the reader. The discussions of the defenses, motility, and insight contained some suggestions about clinical appraisal. Discussions of sublimation and object relationship, on the other hand, presented fewer clear and immediate implications for clinical appraisal.

The unevenness in the relevant literature had an immediate influence on the course of the individual studies. The pace at which

118

the research could be pursued differed importantly among the components of ego functioning identified. The review and organization of the literature constituted a major undertaking in certain areas; consequently the studies related to sublimation and object relationship capacity represent attempts to survey the literature. Although library study in itself may yield only a modest contribution toward the ultimate goals of the project, it provides the foundation needed for further work in these areas. The obstacles to management of this literature were such that the review of literature constituted a demanding unit of work. The beginning consideration of clinical relevance of the resulting formulations appeared to constitute an appropriate second unit for study. On the other hand, motility, which is less voluminously treated, is supported by detailed literature regarding clinical manifestations. Consequently, theses in this area were paced more quickly and entailed some study of clinical appraisal. In seven of the ten projects some attempt was made to move beyond a survey and organization of the literature.

Survey of Experience

It had been hoped that inferences about clinical judgments derived from the literature could be checked against and supplemented by the observations of practitioners. Attempts to utilize this source of knowledge were not uniformly rewarding; the experience with this step led to some re-formulation of procedure. It was found that when student investigators had familiarized themselves with the theoretical elaboration of the content areas, their conception of the subject was richer and more detailed than that held by many clinicians. Efforts to tap the experience of practitioners were handicapped by problems in communicating the precise issue for discussion and in confining the discussion to a delineated area. It became obvious that clinical experience should be used selectively. For help in mastering the technical exposition of a concept, it seemed advisable to approach the most theoretically sophisticated practitioners. It seems likely that the knowledge of other practitioners, which may be rich at the operational level, can be utilized helpfully for other phases of the project. When the problems are reduced to specific clinical discriminations, the skills of a wider group of practitioners may become a valuable resource for the study.

Application in Clinical Study

It was anticipated that the progress in organizing the theoretical literature would suggest potential perspectives for the study of practice. Such a development would raise two questions: (1) Are these perspectives usable within the range of opportunities presented by the usual clinical study? (2) Do they contribute importantly to clinical understanding? The strategy followed here was to address the first of these questions with the expectation that progress in working out a way to use the idea system would facilitate an appraisal of its value. That is, the focus for this phase of study was on the development of a technology for connecting abstractions to behavior. Attention was given to such questions as the relevant evidence required for theoretically identified clinical discriminations and the conditions of study which would be likely to yield such evidence.

In only three of the areas thus far investigated has the study proceeded as far as a beginning consideration of connections with practice. An illustration from this group of theses may help to clarify the course the project has taken and provide a glimpse of what lies ahead.

The Study of Insight [9]

Initially conceived as "one's ability or the degree of ability to view his functioning and/or dysfunctioning as related to himself and in alignment with reality," insight was seen to denote the capacity an individual shows to view his own functioning from a perspective that corresponds to the conception that other informed persons have of it. In the development of the study, the identification of relevant literature was made difficult by the fact that the term insight is used in three discrete senses: as a goal in treatment; to denote a level or form of treatment; and, finally, as a characteristic of human functioning.[26] Early attempts to secure help from clinicians in locating the appropriate literature were confounded by the multiple usages of the term. In order to make communication about the concept possible, it was found necessary to re-name it. When the focus of the study was identified as "self-observing capacity," the term became stabilized. Some relevant literature was located concerning the topic of introspective capacity, conceived as the ego's capacity to split into an observing and an experiencing part.[5] Other resources were found in discussions of the concept of consciousness in the exposition of processes underlying thought.[12] Little headway was made in locating a literature describing the genetic development of self-observing capacity, and the energistic bases of self-observation remained obscure. A number of global ideas about self-observation were located but the literature with precise definitions was limited. The psychological measuring development was not a conspicuous help in the effort at clarification.[16] The student was driven to abstracting the formulations of interest chiefly from clinical literature; in this literature the manifestations and some dimensions of self-observing capacity were detectable.[22]

From the review of literature the student developed a two-dimensional model of certain elements of self-observation. One dimension concerned the level at which self-observation occurs, distinguishing awareness (consciousness of an abstract thought or feeling) from full recognition in which localization of present with previous experience occurs. The second dimension identified by the student concerned the content included in self-observation. Distinctions were drawn among observations (1) restricted to internal processes (for example, affects, defenses, derivatives of instinctual impulses); (2) broadened to include behavior as a manifestation or interdependent function of internal life; or (3) encompassing the recognition of responsive patterns as appropriate or inappropriate, as customary or atypical responses. Some conceptions about identity were also introduced to denote the content to which self-observation may be directed.

The student was able to check her model of some elements of self-observing operations against the knowledge and experience of several senior clinicians. By submitting in advance her attempted formulation and related questions, she received helpful consultation. In addition to sketching some tenable formulation of the process underlying self-observation, and some of the forces within the patient and the interview situation which might influence performance in this area, the consultation with clinicians also enriched the formulation of connections between the concept and behavioral referents. Distinctions between cognitive and affective

121

functioning in regard to self-observation were made. The interesting suggestion was advanced that self-observation may also be studied temporally. It was pointed out that a clinically important difference exists between introspective ability which functions only after the fact and such ability as may be available immediately or may anticipate future events. Finally, it is noteworthy that questions were raised about the possibility of making other than qualitative statements about so complex a function as self-observing capacity.

The student's formulation of elements of self-observation was recast to accommodate certain of the suggestions of her consultants and a revised scheme was organized. This formulation calls attention to the explicitness with which self-observing capacity is manifested in several self-observational areas (internal processes, behavior as an interdependent function of internal processes, and characteristics and appropriateness of response patterns). The chart below illustrates a portion of this scheme.

DIRECTNESS OF MANIFESTATIONS OF SELF-OBSERVING IN
SELECTED OBSERVATIONAL AREAS

Observational Areas	Implied	Indirect	Direct
1. Internal life	shows displaced awareness or recognition of feeling state	recognizes or shows awareness of some of own behavior denoting feeling state	explicitly verbalizes recognition or awareness of feeling
a. affects	"There was lots of confusion"	"I found myself yelling"	"I was angry"

Since high level constructs are remote from behavior, it is probably inappropriate to ask whether the student succeeded in identifying *the* most relevant dimensions of the concept. It is probably more appropriate to ask whether such a specification holds any promise for application—whether it is usable and useful. Unfortunately, neither of these questions can be answered satisfactorily at present. The student was able to initiate a study of a small sample of cases in these terms. Through this effort at application, the reliability of which was not checked, there were indications that judgments in this area could be made and it seemed clear that a

122

study of cases in these terms illuminated this aspect of a client's functioning more fully than does a customary case study. There seemed little doubt that this student made more thorough and precise observations of her clients' functioning in terms of self-observation than was possible prior to the study. No attempt was made to check the utility of these observations, although a presumptive case for their value could be advanced.

This preliminary check did suggest that meaningful differences in the self-observational capacity of individuals were identified by this scheme. Clients selected on the basis of impressionistically distinguishable levels of insight were found on study to show identifiable and cumulative differences in performance. This experience suggests that a basic condition for the development of reliable and precise judgments may obtain; the possibility of working toward increasingly refined judgments in this realm appears open for exploration.

Discussion

In the present project an attempt was made to accommodate the complexity of the study issue by selecting methods apparently suitable to it. While only minimal simplification of the problem was introduced in order to facilitate study, the methods chosen were informal and largely non-objective. The rationale for this strategy lies in the belief that any method that effectively extends knowledge of an issue is defensible. If this is accepted, then judgments about the study approach used here would entail a consideration of the results of the research. Since there is reason to believe that many professional issues offer a comparable range of choice between methodological rigor and theoretical richness, a critical appraisal of the study strategy in terms of its results is in order.

But it must be acknowledged that an appraisal of the study method is not a simple matter. The "findings" from this project show neither the definitiveness nor the concreteness of some other study styles. At best, truth is approached rather than established, and the course is a slow one. As previously indicated, in only a few of the areas investigated has the study progressed far enough to allow some consideration of the product.

Of greater importance for the study of the method, however, is the fact that results may reflect not only the efficacy of the research approach but the efficacy of some of the components of the theory as well. Preliminary experience with exploration in areas thus far included suggests that great variability may exist among these concepts in their relevance to practice. For example, excursions into the area of motility suggest that it is a complex rather than a unitary concept whose import for practice may vary according to the patient group under study. A preliminary check against some cases suggests that, when motility patterns and verbal communications are reasonably integrated, specific study of motility may add little to the clinical picture. This impression may be related to the fact that motility, unlike many of the components identified for study, is regarded as an ego apparatus of primary autonomy, existing in the undifferentiated phase and serving a pervasive function in development. Observations about motility may thus contribute, for many subjects, more to their general characterization than to the location of specific systemic distinctions.

It also seems possible that important clinical implications of a more sophisticated grasp of ego operations may lie in the intra-individual distinctions among such components of functioning. That is, the value of these concepts for clinicians may be found in their sensitizing the practitioner to the relative rather than the absolute capacities of the client—to islands of strength as well as areas of malfunctioning. This possibility can only be studied at a later stage in the research.

Further work on the project may be expected to clarify the potentialities and limitation of the study approach used here. The experience to date has been most encouraging; the components identified for study appear to constitute workable focal points for inquiry, and the plan for study apparently serves to facilitate engagement with significant dimensions of the problem. The description of a plausible study method is offered in the hope of stimulating further inquiry in this challenging realm by any method. From such experience clarity may be achieved about the effectiveness of a range of study approaches to practice theory.

Bibliography

1. Beres, David, "Ego Deviations and the Concept of Schizophrenia," *Psychoanalytic Study of the Child*, Vol. XI (1956), pp. 164–235.

2. Birdwhistell, Ray L., "Paralanguage 25 Years After Sapir," *Lectures on Experimental Psychiatry*, Henry W. Brosin (ed.), University of Pittsburgh Press, 1961.

3. Erikson, Erik H., *Childhood and Society*, W. W. Norton and Company, New York, 1950.

4. Escalona, Sybille K., and others, *Early Phases of Personality Development: A Non-normative Study of Infant Behavior*, Child Development Publications, Evanston, Ill., 1953.

5. Freud, Sigmund, *The Ego and the Id*, Hogarth Press, London, 1927, p. 81 ff.

6. Green, Sidney L., "Psychoanalytic Contributions to Casework Treatment of Marital Problems," *Journal of Social Casework*, Vol. XXXV, No. 10 (1954), pp. 419–423.

7. Grunebaum, Margaret Galdston, "A Study of Learning Problems of Children: Casework Implications," *Social Casework*, Vol. XLII, No. 9 (1961), pp. 461–468.

8. Hartmann, Heinz, "Comments on the Psychoanalytic Theory of the Ego," *Psychoanalytic Study of the Child*, Vol. V (1950), pp. 74–96.

9. Jhirad, Judith, "Clinical Assessment of Self-Observing Capacity," Unpublished Master's Thesis, Smith College School for Social Work, 1961.

10. Metz, J. Richard, "A Method for Measuring Aspects of Ego Strength," *Journal of Projective Technique*, Vol. 25, No. 4 (1961), pp. 457–470.

11. Piaget, Jean, *The Construction of Reality in the Child*, Margaret Cook (tr.) Basic Books, New York, 1954.

12. Rapaport, David, *The Organization and Pathology of Thought*, Columbia University Press, New York, 1951.

13. ———, "A Historical Survey of Psychoanalytic Ego Psychology," *Psychological Issues*, Vol. 1, No. 1 (1959), pp. 5–17.

14. ———, *The Structure of Psychoanalytic Theory: A Synthesizing Attempt*, International Universities Press, New York, 1960.

15. Richfield, Jerome, "An Analysis of the Concept of Insight," *The Psychoanalytic Quarterly*, Vol. XXIII, No. 3 (1954), p. 403.

16. Sargent, Helen, "An Experimental Application of Projective Principles to a Paper and Pencil Personality Test," *Psychological Monographs*, Vol. 57, No. 5 (1944).

17. ———, "Intrapsychic Change: Methodological Problems in Psychotherapy Research," *Psychiatry*, Vol. XXIV, No. 2 (1961), pp. 93–109.

18. Sears, Robert R., *Survey of Objective Studies of Psychoanalytic Concepts*, Social Science Research Council, New York, 1943.

19. Spiegel, Leo A., "The Self and Perception," *Psychoanalytic Study of the Child*, Vol. XIV (1959), pp. 81–109.

20. Stamm, Isabel L., "Ego Psychology in the Emerging Theoretical Base of Casework," *Issues in American Social Work*, Alfred J. Kahn (ed.), Columbia University Press, New York, 1959, pp. 80–109.

21. *Use of Judgments as Data in Social Work Research*, Proceedings of a Conference held by the Research Section, NASW, June, 1958. National Association of Social Workers, New York, 1959.

22. Waldhorn, Herbert, "Assessment of Analysability: Technical and Theoretical Observations," *The Psychoanalytic Quarterly*, Vol. XXIX, No. 4 (1960), pp. 478–506.

23. Wallerstein, Robert S., and Roberts, Louis L., "The Psychotherapy Research Project of the Menninger Foundation: Chapter IV, Concepts," *Bulletin of the Menninger Clinic*, Vol. 20, No. 5 (1956), pp. 239–262.

24. Warren, Effie, "Some Social Class Dimensions in Family Casework," *Smith College Studies in Social Work*, Vol. XXXIII, No. 1 (1962), pp. 1–18.

25. Weinstein, Avery B., "Reality Sense and Reality Testing," *Behavioral Science*, Vol. III, No. 3 (1958), pp. 228–261.

26. Zilboorg, Gregory, "The Emotional Problem and Therapeutic Role of Insight," *The Psychoanalytic Quarterly*, Vol. XXI, No. 1 (1952), pp. 1–24.

Part III

Practice Applications

7. Family Interaction: Some Problems and Implications for Casework*

Frances H. Scherz

SOCIAL CASEWORK FROM ITS beginnings as a method of treatment has been concerned with understanding people and helping them to manage problems in interpersonal relationships. Recently new insights into the nature of the interwoven strands of individual and family health, individual and family pathology, and the intermeshing of individual and family dynamics with sociocultural forces, have led to new ways of integrating this knowledge more effectively into the existing framework of the casework method. Some of these insights stem from casework practice, some from cross-fertilization between casework and psychiatry, some from a new look at the contributions of the social sciences to social work.

These recent developments have pointed to our need to understand family interaction more fully in order to increase our ability to help individuals and families who are experiencing difficulties in personal and social functioning. Since it is axiomatic that individual and family are parts of one interactional field and that both can be helped effectively only if they are understood in the context of their manifold, complicated dealings with each other, it is understandable that there is a growing point of view that all casework, regardless of the setting in which it is practiced, should be family

* Presented at a meeting of the Smith College School for Social Work Alumnae Association, Chicago, November 16, 1959.

129

focused. It is in order, then, to examine family interaction patterns that enhance or impede individual and family functioning. This is not to say that casework does not take into account individual needs and dynamics, as well as social and somatic factors and extra-familial interpersonal relationships, in arriving at treatment decisions. Indeed, these factors always must be considered in terms of their meaning for and influence on family interaction, as well as in the interests of the individual.

This paper will describe some common elements in family interaction and their implications for casework diagnosis and treatment, some techniques in working with interactional factors, and some problems in integrating concepts of family interaction into present casework practice. The term "family interaction" will be used to designate the interchanges, communications, and ways of relating between family members and within the family group that are characteristic in our culture and unique to a particular family unit. Family interaction thus refers to the unique day-to-day patterns of family behavior and management, patterns of response to stress and problems, and patterns of agreement and disagreement in values and standards which are of major significance to family equilibrium and disequilibrium.

Social Perspectives on Family Interaction

One of the problems we face in more effective integration of cultural aspects into concepts of family interaction, as well as into our present over-all framework of casework practice, is the limited use we make of the knowledge we have gained from our experience. Although we know a good deal about the impact of social and cultural change on family structure, and about the developmental tasks associated with age, sex, marital status, employment phase of life, and the like, we have not made adequate use of this knowledge in working with individuals and families. In a like vein, we know that individual and family values and standards affect the nature of family interaction. How a family feels and operates in such matters as money, education, choice of living arrangements, relationships with members of the family who are not in the immediate household, and relationships with the community, is to a considerable extent influenced by prevailing cultural values and standards

130

in the segment of the community with which the family is identified, in its relationship to the larger community, and by built-in attitudes that derive from the family culture in which the individual members were reared. Yet, somehow, these cultural imports have not received their rightful due in the immediate problems with which we deal. We gather cultural data as part of the social study process but then fail to make sufficient dynamic use of them in the formulation of the total material. The same criticism holds true for treatment. One reason for this may be, as Dr. John Spiegel [1] points out in relation to psychotherapy, that some cultural value orientations are learned in childhood only through their indirect impact on conscious behavior and are, therefore, "behavior without awareness." We, as well as the people we help, can only describe and formulate them in fragmentary terms. At the same time, however, cultural values can be expected to exert strong influences on the behavior and attitudes of individuals and families and, therefore, require as much casework consideration as the more clearly psychological processes.

There are several reasons why the need for better integration in this area is perhaps more evident at present than some time ago. One is that focus on the family and, therefore, focus on family interaction, requires a broadening of our diagnostic base to include, more fully, all the impacts on family living. For example, conflict between 14-year-old Betty and her mother over the wearing of high heels may be largely a result of problematic aspects in their relationship, or of differing cultural values that are generationally based, or because the family lives in a neighborhood where a particular prevailing pattern is significant in peer relationships and family living. When there is conflict between family members over social values and goals, the weighing of this factor in the full diagnostic picture may determine the method and goal of treatment. In some cases the treatment decision may be to ameliorate or remold the culturally based behavior and attitudes that interfere with adequate functioning. For example, Richard, 17, was referred by Boys' Court after he was caught acting as a

[1] John P. Spiegel, "Some Cultural Aspects of Transference and Countertransference," *Science and Psychoanalysis, Volume II. Individual and Familial Dynamics,* Jules H. Masserman (ed.), Grune and Stratton, New York, 1959, pp. 160–182.

receiver and disburser of stolen goods. A full study showed that personal disturbance, while present, was less significant than a family and neighborhood value standard that prized the making of a "fast buck." A therapeutic effort was made to break into a family culture pattern that created difficulties for Richard; to work with him in such a way that his goal, which was respected, could be achieved in more socially acceptable ways than the one he had used, without destroying his relationship with his family.

A second reason why fuller integration of social and cultural concepts is desirable seems to stem from ego psychology. We have become more aware of the tasks that the ego is charged with throughout the life of an individual and of how the family influences individual ego development and, in turn, how family development is influenced by the individual. We assess a person's ego capacity in performance of sequential life tasks by testing his capacity to balance gratification needs and reality demands. In a sense, when we describe a family's ability and vulnerability in relation to stress and problems, we are describing its collective ego capacity. In the evaluations we make we note that differential response to stress is related to cultural value orientations. Similarly, in treatment, dynamic inclusion of these factors helps us to use these values in working with existing and potential strengths in the individual and family. Such focus, I believe, offers the possibility of broadening the present scope of casework treatment. For example, Mr. and Mrs. B, who fought about practically everything throughout their marriage, were in accord in one crucial area—Mr. B's choice of vocation. The status values of both were reflected in their agreement that Mr. B should teach in a university setting. Casework treatment, it was believed, would achieve little in modifying certain attitudes that created the marital conflict, but perhaps some stabilization could be brought about by utilizing their shared values. Mr. B was on the verge of a breakdown because he faced qualifying for a doctoral degree and looking for his first job, while his situation was exacerbated by Mrs. B's interference with his studies. The main treatment focus was to give Mr. B support in his academic strivings. Mrs. B's concern was enlisted in helping her to minimize her destructive attacks on her husband so that he could concentrate on a goal satisfactory to both.

When the caseworker includes specific cultural material in the data about a family, it may act as a desirable check on some of his own culturally based attitudes that might interfere with sound casework decisions. Making judgments in this area may pose particular problems for the caseworker. Somehow it is easier and less threatening to make casework decisions in the psychological area. Some of our difficulty may be due to the fact that the scope and variety of cultural value orientations are so vast that we are overwhelmed by the task of knowing what to look for. The social scientists can be of assistance to us in this aspect. Dr. Wheelis has pointed out, in *The Quest for Identity,* that we have so many choices in the making of assessments and decisions that our own sense of cultural identity tends to become blurred and uncertain.[2] Living as we do in an era of such drastic and constant change in value standards, with individual and family roles in a state of unprecedented flux, we, as individuals, suffer from cultural lag in making sufficiently quick shifts to meet the demands made on us.

Perhaps because social workers usually represent middle-class values, we are not well attuned or too sympathetic to values that seem somewhat alien to ours. For example, in the Jewish Family and Community Service of Chicago we sometimes struggle with our feelings about a request for a homemaker (a service that is a form of financial assistance when a family cannot pay for it) from a suburban family which has a heavy mortgage on the house and debts for a variety of appliances, has one or two cars, and provides private dancing classes for the children. Or we may disapprove, even if not overtly, of the family on marginal income which deprives itself of essentials in order to possess a car or a television set. The clash in values is not always as clear cut as in these illustrations. It is often expressed in subtle transference and countertransference reactions that may impede the therapeutic process.

Patterns of Communication in Families

In casework diagnosis and treatment, we seek to understand the specific area of crucial breakdown in family interaction, the particular stresses to which the family is vulnerable, the specific areas both

[2] Allen Wheelis, *The Quest for Identity,* W. W. Norton and Company, New York, 1958.

133

of conflictive and of adequate functioning, as well as the wish and ability of the various family members to work on the problem, and the manner and means by which the family has dealt with similar problems in the past. The pervasive family climate for support of, or interference with, treatment efforts also needs to be considered. Cause and effect connections among these factors as well as individual diagnostic assessment should lead to an evaluation of whether the disequilibrium is centered primarily in disturbances in family interaction or in an individual. It is, of course, understood that there is always some spilling over of one to the other and that emphasis and degree must be our main considerations. Focus on the family during exploration may, therefore, require involvement of various family members to further our understanding of individual and family. Techniques for this will be presented later.

When problems of interaction are to be the main focus of treatment, it is usually necessary to involve the significant family members and, when it is not possible to do so, to limit the treatment goal. Sometimes it is necessary to work with interactional factors in order to stabilize family functioning as a forerunner either to casework treatment of individual disturbance or as preparation for psychiatric treatment. The reverse may also be true, that is, treatment efforts may be directed toward supporting, clarifying, or modifying individual behavior and attitudes prior to efforts to restore or alter patterns of family interaction. Or there may be a combination of both methods. For example, a mother may be helped by educational techniques to manage her child better while the child is in treatment, when, as is commonly found, this is all the energy that the mother has available. Perhaps later she can invest in an examination of her personal problems.

One of the main problems in obtaining appropriate data of family interaction is in understanding the patterns of communication in families. By communication, I mean the kinds of interchanges—verbal, behavioral, and attitudinal, both in conscious expressions and in those derived from the unconscious—that are in harmony with the realistic and affective needs of all members of the family. One of the most frequent complaints made by people who seek help is the feeling of being misunderstood because of lack of, or breakdown in, communication among family members or with others in the larger environment. We find that appropriate communication may never have existed or may have obtained in some areas of intrafamilial relationships and not in other significant ones. It may have broken down in all respects or may still be intact in some. People may describe a failure in some crucial area or in the day-to-day events of family living.

Patterns of communication may be similar or different for different family members or may be pervasive in the family unit. We are familiar, in casework, with verbalization that is primarily attack or defense, is provocative or reactive to it; in short, that is used to meet the neurotic needs of one individual or the interlocking, destructive, neurotic needs of various family members. Nonverbalization may be used for the same purposes. Withdrawal into silence is often felt by the other person as provocative or hostile. Sometimes verbalization is used as pseudocommunication, as in families who talk along parallel lines while each individual is preoccupied with his own needs. Or some people verbalize about superficial matters but do not really communicate with each other out of fear that doing so would foster closer relationships than could be tolerated. Speech or its lack may be used to ward off anxiety or as an effort to contain intra-psychic conflicts. In some families communication is primarily through verbalization; in others little verbalization is required for understanding. Culturally also there are differences in verbal communication in degrees of volubility, intensity, and colorfulness. Hollingshead and Redlich suggest there may be differences in the use of communication patterns by class structure as well.[3] Age, stage of development, intelligence, and education are factors. Old people, for example, often starved for verbal communication, may talk at length about the past in a discussion of the present, in a way that suggests senility but is not necessarily a sign of it. The latency-age child is not noted for his verbal communication with adults.

Certainly a great deal of communication is expressed in appearance, behavior, and body attitude. (My daughter, at 12, said, "Don't look at me in that tone of voice" when I thought I was being fore-

[3] August B. Hollingshead and Frederick C. Redlich, *Social Class and Mental Illness, A Community Study,* John Wiley and Sons, New York, 1958.

135

bearing by not scolding her.) Characteristic ways of using facial expression, body posture, and gestures reveal character traits, modes of adaptation and defense. Some individuals use motor or muscular means of communication primarily. The infantile character, for example, tends to use impulsive kinesthetic action as a means of discharging tension in place of more mature communication. Neurotic symptoms are often used as a means of communicating needs that are not acceptable or only partially acceptable to the person himself. Cultural differences are also expressed in certain characteristic non-verbal modes of communication.

The caseworker's problem is to understand what it is the person in a variety of ways is trying to express and to find ways that will facilitate communication. Each individual as well as each family is unique in patterns of communication. At the same time, we do know that people of different personality types, in different psychiatric classifications, from different cultural groups, and at various stages of development, tend to use patterns of communication that offer a broad guide to understanding the meaning of the communication. The verboseness of the compulsive talker, the particular distortions of the hysteric, the exaggerations of the adolescent, the reticence or volubility of people from different cultural backgrounds, can be understood in the context of specific individual dynamics. Similarly, patterns of communication within a family must be understood in cultural and dynamic psychological terms. The unique flavor of each family requires that the caseworker make no prejudgments about values, strengths, and problems until he understands the prevailing mode of family communication, its strengths and interferences in family operation.

This is more easily said than done. The complexity of the methods of communication and their rapid shifts, the different levels of communication, conscious and unconscious, as well as our insufficient and fragmented knowledge about family group process, contribute to problems in understanding family communication patterns. Semantic difficulties as well as differences in cultural orientation between caseworkers and some of the people they serve are contributing factors. There are other aspects of practice that may stand in the way of appropriate communication in casework. Confusion, for example, about the technical difference between attacking a defense and helping the person to express fears that interfere with his telling the problem may hold us back from the spontaneous natural questions and responses that are the essence of appropriate communication. We may fear that we shall "lose" a case if we raise questions that we think may hurt the person; for example, asking a parent why he has lived with a problem for a long time before seeking help. The good intent to support troubled people becomes confused at times with failing to help them face their problems as realistically as they can, or fearing to ask them to undertake difficult tasks in treatment.

Perhaps it is also somewhat uncomfortable for us to face the fact that caseworkers also communicate on different levels; that people often sense, quite accurately, the meaning of our non-verbal communications and that these may conflict with what we are saying. While the caseworker has a professional responsibility to maintain disciplined control of his own attitudes and behavior, he has an equal responsibility to use his own unique modes of communication freely and spontaneously, and to learn his particular strengths and limitations with different people. We know that we influence people consciously by attitudes that are the results of our own life experience, including professional development. Sometimes, in an effort to be objective, we try to suppress personal, cultural, and professional attitudes that might better be expressed and dealt with accordingly. I am not advocating license of expression, but rather responsible liberty to communicate freely. For example, Mrs. K was astonished and resentful when the caseworker cautioned her against continuing to sleep with her 11-year-old son and was completely unaccepting of this advice. Although it is true that this sleeping arrangement is not desirable and we do have responsibility for influencing child-rearing practices, this bit of advice had little meaning or value for this particular family. Professional concern and personal feeling were at variance here with the cultural and psychologic dynamics of the K family. There are occasions when it is better for the caseworker to express his feelings and then deal with the consequences, rather than attempting to suppress and handle them by labeling the person as resistive to treatment.

In cases involving problems of family interaction, major treatment decisions may relate to whether to restore, interrupt, or modify family communication patterns. In any treatment situation, whether we are working primarily with derivatives of internalized problems of one person or primarily with interaction factors, we are always concerned with problems of communication in the family. In other words, it is largely a matter of emphasis and degree as to whether major treatment focus is on individual psychological problems or on specific interactional aspects that are interfering with the individual's and family's self-management. Although the caseworker has responsibility for treatment planning, he must learn, through communication between himself and the family, what they need and can tolerate in treatment. It is, for example, not by accident that people choose for conscious or unconsious reasons one type of help rather than another. Certain mothers have serious personal problems of which they are unaware and of which they cannot bear direct examination; they therefore seek help for themselves through the child's problem in a particular setting. Or a person who the caseworker believes needs psychiatric help is not motivated for it but may be helped with some part of the difficulty in a social agency. Or, as we have indicated earlier, a family may need stabilization before other treatment measures elsewhere can be undertaken.

Techniques for Studying Family Interaction

There are, to be sure, diagnostic clues that aid in determining emphasis, timing, and setting in treatment planning. The extent and nature of a person's current destructive, repetitive behavior resulting from unresolved developmental problems of the past, the kind and amount of regression in meeting daily life demands, the amount of energy available for making day-to-day decisions, and the capacity to invest in treatment are some of the clues that may point to treatment emphasis on individual psychological aspects of his functioning. The specific cause and nature of stress, the kind of problem that results, and the ability to respond to different adaptational demands exacerbated or created by the problem are factors that influence the type and setting of treatment. Of vital significance are the correlation and assessment of these factors with the needs of the total family unit; with its capacity to support and tolerate changes anticipated in treatment as well as projected treatment outcome for both individual and family, before the specific treatment decisions are made. It is not uncommon, for example, in marital conflicts to work primarily with interactional factors, despite diagnostic assessment that places the main problem in individual personality factors; such treatment continues until it becomes possible for the partners to bear closer scrutiny of the personality difficulties that have contributed to the discord, or until it is evident that they cannot do so.

It is obvious that focus on the family in casework diagnosis and treatment involves flexible dealings with various family members throughout the period of treatment. There is no doubt that individual interviews are basic in the therapeutic relationship, and at the same time we can add greatly to our knowledge of family group interaction by the use of joint or multiple interviews in home and office. We have always used these in casework, but our newer insights, stemming from our awareness of the need to broaden the base of casework diagnosis and treatment, have led to a reappraisal of their value.

For the purposes of adding to and clarifying diagnosis, the home visit can be an invaluable aid to the caseworker in seeing family interaction at firsthand. Mrs. W, in an initial office interview, complained bitterly that her 3-year-old son was driving her to distraction because he clung to her incessantly. In the home the caseworker observed that Bobby played for short periods of time by himself before approaching his mother. Each time, before he could touch her, she took a cookie from a nearby box, stuffed it into his mouth, and pushed him away without a word. From this observation the distortions in her verbal communication in the office became clear.

The home visit can also be used to heighten or lower anxiety about a problem, to stimulate positively or to remove obstacles to motivation for help, and to clarify the problem when the person is too frightened, angry, or defensive to communicate appropriately. When the caseworker showed Mrs. J that she could understand what 4-year-old Jean was saying and that she thought the child was using her toys as a 4-year-old should, the mother, who had been insisting she had a totally damaged child, relaxed sufficiently to begin to talk about her shame and guilt. Similarly, it was only when the caseworker saw how a seemingly psychotic mother dominated the household from her wheel-chair, while her husband stood submissively by, that he could fully appreciate the despair felt by the 18-year-old son and could understand that the boy's account in the office was not exaggerated. When Mr. P complained that his wife's housekeeping standards were a main source of marital friction, Mrs. P verified this by automatically wiping the ash trays each time they were used. The caseworker's on-the-spot observations helped to offset some of Mrs. P's denials about the existence of a problem.

Often the home visit helps the caseworker get a clearer picture of the pervasive climate, of characteristic patterns of communication, points of stress, and of cultural values and standards. Some families, for cultural reasons, are more comfortable discussing a problem in the home environment; some for personal or cultural reasons are fearful of coming to an office until they have developed some sense of trust and comfort with the caseworker. In my experience, many Italian families did not feel a relationship had been positively established until I shared a meal in their home. The use of a home and its meaning to the family are often reflected in its furnishings, its state of organization or disorganization.

Home visits may be useful also in the course of treatment. The tempo of treatment may be heightened when certain processes of family interaction, in areas of conflict or agreement, can be dealt with in the home rather than in an office. In the course of treatment, Mr. and Mrs. L were locked in combat over differing points of view about George. Mrs. L was sure Mr. L was too demanding; he was equally sure Mrs. L was too permissive. The same material had been discussed individually and jointly in the office, but a real gain in understanding came to both of them during a home visit; Mrs. L could see how she permitted George to wreck the family dinner and Mr. L could see how his perfectionistic demands on George when he was running an elaborate electric train made George feel he could do nothing to please his father. Gomberg, in a paper on family diagnosis, illustrated the use of a home visit at termination of treatment for the purpose of consolidating and celebrating treatment gains.[4] Appropriate timing is, of course, a

[4] M. Robert Gomberg, "Family Diagnosis—Trends in Theory and Practice," *Social Casework*, Vol. XXXIX, Nos. 2–3 (1958), pp. 73–83.

matter of casework judgment, but I believe that in many more cases than it is used at present a home visit early in exploration would be both time-saving and clarifying for diagnosis, and such a visit later in treatment would also be useful.

The use of joint or multiple interviews in the office offers the possibility of some of the same values as home visits for diagnosis and treatment in family-focused casework. A sensitive worker, during a flexible joint interview at intake, may be able to remove obstacles to motivation for help. Mrs. G, for example, brought her 9-year-old son to the initial interview. She came under duress, angry that the school had insisted on referring her because Sam smelled bad in the classroom. Mrs. G admitted this but insisted that Sam deliberately failed to control his bowels. The caseworker's calm discussion, giving recognition to the fact that this situation made life hard for both the mother and Sam, seemed to have some effect. Mrs. G, after speculating about this suggestion, realized the boy had feeling about his problem and she could concede that perhaps the soiling was not done just to spite her.

Joint interviews are at best complicated to manage. In using them early in a case for diagnostic clues to interaction, the caseworker must sense, for example, when to intervene between combative marital partners in order to clarify the nature of the problem, or to indicate areas for further exploration, or to help the partners take responsibility so that they may know what they will be working on in continuing contact. He may need to help the more passive marital partner—or in a parent-child situation, the child—to express feelings about the material that is being presented. He may need to point out the destructive use of a defense derivative. For example, Dan and his parents were seen shortly after his release from a mental hospital. The parents projected all blame for a return of regressive behavior on Dan and the hospital. Some specific bits of interaction showing how projection was being used were discussed in order to create a different base for participation in ongoing service. If the caseworker cannot control an interview that seems to him to be harmful or wasteful, he may, of course, decide to terminate it. These illustrations indicate the nature of the caseworker's activity in joint interviews. The caseworker cannot be a passive observer, nor can he back away from dealing with painful or explosive material. He must become an intrinsic part of the interactional process. The examples also indicate some of the varied and flexible uses of joint interviews at intake or early in a case. Some people may need to be encouraged or discouraged from wanting individual or joint interviews. In some situations the caseworker may make either type of interview a condition of continuation. The client's comfort as well as the caseworker's and the purpose and timing of different types of interviews are important considerations. In the Jewish Family and Community Service we are inviting clients to make a choice of individual or joint interviews at intake. We have also found it useful to have joint interviews with key members of a family after the social study is completed in order to clarify their understanding and their agreement to participate in the proposed treatment plan.

During casework treatment also, when the goal and method are those of stabilization, modification, or enhancement of family interaction, a flexible use of joint interviews may be indicated, timed and spaced according to the needs of the situation. They may be used to enable the caseworker to move directly into areas of conflict in order to help the individuals first to perceive and then to modify interfering behavior and attitudes, or to broaden their perspectives of each other's needs, or to learn new ways of behaving and communicating. Some people can learn from educational treatment techniques, such as by appropriately expressed approval and disapproval from the caseworker, to communicate with other family members in constructive ways they have never known. Some need the support of the caseworker to express, in the presence of other family members, feelings they consider dangerous, to learn that such expression does not necessarily destroy themselves or the other person. When treatment is stalemated or slowed because people are too fearful, defensive, or resistive to try out in the life situation what has been considered in the individual interviews, they may be enabled to do some testing in a joint interview.

Areas of constructive agreement and other conflict-free areas in a family may be used fruitfully in joint interviews to strengthen and increase the strivings toward better family equilibrium. In such instances, healthy patterns of communication can be highlighted in the interests of motivation toward reaching similar goals in areas

142

of conflict. Joint interviews may also be used to assess and consolidate gains in treatment, to direct the treatment efforts into new areas, and at termination.

Certainly, the joint interview is not a valid technique when family members have no wish or ability to move toward amelioration of a problem in the interests of the family unit, or when the therapeutic intent is to separate family members or to loosen family intra-relationships. Similarly, joint interviews may not be indicated when the focus of treatment is on helping an individual to examine and sort out connections between specific past events and present problems, or to deal with specific personal psychological problems.

Inevitably, joint interviews in treatment, both in the home and in the office, present particular problems for the caseworker. His own conscious problems of empathy and identification are heavily taxed in this type of interview. The type of activity required may not suit his personality; sometimes this is evidenced in the extremes of passive participation or undue authoritative intervention. The fear of being drawn in as a referee is one that is commonly expressed and is indeed difficult to avoid. Communication with more than one person is difficult. Transference and countertransference phenomena may be heightened; on the other hand, transference manifestations may be lessened. For example, fantasies that may interfere with or sabotage treatment can sometimes be dispelled or minimized in joint interviews. Some people who strongly deny their need for gratification of dependency can sometimes better tolerate treatment if there is dilution in joint interviews with other family members. Others, who bring into the casework relationship strong dependency needs for which they are seeking gratification, cannot tolerate sharing an interview or a caseworker. A mother who needs to be in firm control of her own and a child's life may develop fewer transference problems if she can see, from time to time, what is transpiring between the caseworker and the child. It is obvious there is no mechanical guide that can provide one answer to cover these differential considerations.

Although the caseworker may know only some aspects of his countertransference reactions, he needs to be alert to changes in behavior and attitudes on the part of all the individuals involved, including himself, which appear to be different from the usual patterns of communication and from the predicted course of treatment. These may indicate some shift in the therapeutic relationship which may have transference and countertransference implications and which may require examination and action. He also needs to be alert to any sense of uneasiness or discomfort on his own part and to seek help if he cannot identify its nature or source.

Summary

Despite the problems raised in this paper and the lack of tested material through research, I believe that the empirically based descriptive data we are accumulating are highly useful to us in our day-to-day practice. We are beginning to learn to describe the pervasive climate, the unique over-all interactional patterns in a family, as different in many instances from the patterns of interaction between family members, and to understand their implications for treatment potential and method. We are able to describe patterns of communication that are crucial in family functioning. This aids us in determining whether treatment should be focused primarily on interactional factors or on individual dysfunction, as well as helping us to determine who in the family should be included in treatment. Knowledge derived from the social sciences can help us to delineate broad areas of social and cultural impact on the family, and to use these as an aid in dynamic exploration of the particulars of a family unit. We shall continue to add to our store of knowledge in the interests of effective service, to seek in the future, as we have in the past, better answers to old and new questions and problems.

8. Brief Ego-Oriented Casework with Families in Crisis*

Howard J. Parad

THE UNBALANCED EQUATION of too many clients and too few trained workers to help them makes vital the search for new ways of offering more effective casework services. While thoughtful professional workers are properly skeptical of panaceas, they are increasingly receptive to the developments in theory and practice offered by a wide variety of professional efforts to seek at least partial solutions. One such project, a multidiscipline study by the Family Guidance Center of the Harvard School of Public Health of how families cope with commonly encountered stress situations, provided the experience on which much of this paper is based.[1]

Use of Crisis Theory

This paper will discuss the rationale and technique of a brief, ego-oriented, family casework approach utilizing crisis theory. The

* Presented at the Annette Garrett Memorial Institute, sponsored by the Michigan Chapter of the Smith College School for Social Work Alumnae Association, Detroit, Michigan, November 3, 1961. Part of this material was also presented at the Sixth Annual Metta Bean Lecture sponsored by the Wisconsin Anti-Tuberculosis Association, Milwaukee, May 8, 1962.

[1] This project is briefly described in Howard J. Parad and Gerald Caplan, "A Framework for Studying Families in Crisis," *Social Work*, Vol. 5, No. 3 (1960), p. 4.

application of crisis theory has been found appropriate in preventive casework intervention where the emphasis is on reaching out to families who might otherwise not be seen by a social worker; it has also seemed applicable to many cases routinely seen by social workers. Crisis theory offers an additional tool to the medical social worker who deals with the crisis of illness, to the court worker who deals with the crisis of an antisocial act, and to the family, child welfare, or psychiatric worker who constantly deals with crises in personal and family functioning. It is presented, not as a substitute for traditional psychodynamic ego assessment, but as a supplementary tool in diagnosis and treatment. I offer no utopian solutions nor do I advocate a cultist movement. I do hope, however, to encourage a better perspective on the possibilities of applying short-term casework services to a range of casework programs.

Definition of Crisis

Since its earliest beginnings social work has regarded helping people in stressful situations as its proper domain. Mindful that many of the clients under care (whether as a result of voluntary application for help or agency out-reaching efforts) are in crisis situations, let us first summarize the main postulates of crisis theory.

Simply stated, a crisis consists of a hazardous circumstance or stress that constitutes a threat for individuals and families whose psychological organization makes the stressful event meaningful in terms of two broad criteria: (1) the stress threatens important life goals such as health, security, or affectional ties, and (2) the threat posed by the stress appears impossible of immediate solution and overtaxes the immediate resources available to the ego.[2] Therefore, by definition, a crisis state generates high anxiety and tension. Obviously, the entire normal life cycle is replete with such potentially hazardous events and tension points as the birth of a baby, illness, death, and various types of role transitions, such as change of job or entry into school. A person or family is in crisis when

[2] *Ibid.*, p. 5.

146

its interior equilibrium is off balance, thus making it vulnerable to further breakdown.

During a crisis, the person is challenged to produce a "novel" solution to his present problem which may well invoke a new use of the ego's standard battery of coping efforts. Familiar clinical observations will be recalled, indicating that some persons are weakened by adversity while others who are exposed to the same stimulus rise to the occasion, strengthened by the experience of ego mastery to cope effectively with subsequent life problems. Fromm-Reichman, for example, observes that many patients, after successful experience with traumatic stress in wartime Britain, strengthened their ability to endure the emotional hazards of later air raids because of the opportunity for previous abreaction of anxiety and explicit detailed discussion of traumatic experiences, thus avoiding unhealthy suppression and repression and permitting the integration of the traumatic experience into the ego's adaptive capacities.[3] In this way the traumatic experience is prevented from becoming pathogenic and the ego is spared the hazard of facing subsequent crises with "immature emotional equipment."

In relating the organism to the reality principle, the ego, in response to the stressful stimuli, is faced with the important tasks of perception, mediation, integration, mastery, and control.[*] The stages through which the ego performs these tasks are in many ways similar to those documented by Lindemann in his classic study of the crisis of bereavement: shock in reaction to the initial impact, mobilization of communication efforts with the self and others, recovery of defenses, and problem resolution.[4] Three common clinical types of response to stress have been identified: (1) *threat* to instinctual needs, experienced as anxiety; (2) *loss* or deprivation of a loved object, as depression; and (3) *challenge,* as an opportunity to mobilize ego strengths and reach a higher level of mental health and social functioning.[5]

[3] Dexter M. Bullard (ed.), *Psychoanalysis and Psychotherapy*, (Selected Papers of Frieda Fromm-Reichman), University of Chicago Press, Chicago, 1959, p. 56.
[*] See Chapter 3 of this volume.
[4] Eric Lindemann, "Symptomatology and Management of Acute Grief," *American Journal of Psychiatry*, Vol. 101, No. 2 (1944), pp. 141–148.
[5] Lydia Rapoport, "The State of Crisis: Some Theoretical Considerations," *Social Service Review*, Vol. XXVI, No. 2 (1962), p. 213.

Each stress reaction is affected by earlier modes of resolving stressful situations and will in turn affect subsequent efforts at coping with future life stresses. There is, then, an important link between various stressful life experiences which are, again in the words of Fromm-Reichman, "tied up by the mutual bond of the initial traumata." [6] Crises typically reactivate unresolved old problems, and, although causing great anxiety and suffering, provide fresh opportunities for dealing with unresolved, traumatic issues previously hidden in the preconscious and unconscious parts of the mental apparatus. The far-reaching implications of this approach, while perhaps receiving more emphasis at present, were recognized many years ago by W. I. Thomas: "Often in personal and social development crisis is a catalyst disturbing old habits, invoking new responses, and becoming a major factor in charting new developments." [7]

We now turn our attention to the casework implications of this over-all concept of crisis.

Casework Implications

Our first question is: When and to whom should brief services be offered? Any clinician immediately recognizes the difficulty of specifying precisely applicable diagnostic criteria for brief casework since so many variables—including problem perception, client capacity and motivation, agency function, and worker skill—are intertwined. Moreover, it is generally known that at intake virtually any case may be theoretically regarded as short-term or long-term and that treatment arrangements are as often influenced by expediency as by design. At this stage of our knowledge, the basic criterion for this type of short-term activity is that the crisis must be a recently developed one exhibiting immediacy and urgency as contrasted with a chronic state of disequilibrium. But in the last analysis the client's response to the worker's early supportive and interpretive efforts offers the best practical clinical clue. In a sense, then, because of the paucity of definitive research, we are

6 Bullard, *op. cit.*, p. 58.
7 Quoted in *Symposium on Preventive and Social Psychiatry*, Walter Reed Army Medical Center, Washington, D.C., 1957, p. 158.

in the embarrassing position of having to say: What works, works!

If the caseworker is to play the role of a true enabler who helps "chart" new developments, proper timing cannot be over-emphasized. Speaking informally on the basic strategy of short-term interventive efforts, Caplan emphasized the supreme importance of timing: "If you press at the right time you don't have to do it for very long and you don't have to do it very hard . . . at crisis time things boil up and you have an opportunity which you never had before and which you will never have again." [8] A recent study of precipitating stress as a focus in treatment at the Langley Porter Neuropsychiatric Institute cites three reasons for early intervention: (1) the actual facts concerning the stress configuration are less likely to be distorted; (2) the more active the conflict, the more amenable it is to treatment; (3) before a new equilibrium has been set, secondary gain gratification is avoided, thereby intensifying the patient's motivation for help.[9]

Entering the complicated field of forces in the crisis situation, the caseworker ideally begins on the spot, while the problem is being experienced and worked through before his eyes. He is at once participant, observer, and agent of change in the unfolding drama. The caseworker mediates between the precipitating stress and the underlying problems it evokes, thereby attempting to engage and mobilize the client's untapped ego forces and those within his "current ego span" (to use Dr. Babcock's phrase) as well as the larger forces in the relevant family and social environment. To deal constructively and adaptively with the tasks imposed by the impact of crisis, the worker encourages the development of new coping patterns. This involves identification of the individual's reaction system, which is woven of elements of dependence and independence, passivity and aggression, and changes over time with the dynamic interplay between the person and the threatening event. Hence, in assessing the early reactions to a stressful situation, the caseworker must have a sound understanding of the range of normal and abnormal, adaptive and maladaptive reactions to

[8] Lecture on "The Role of the Social Worker in Preventive Psychiatry," Harvard School of Public Health, Boston, July 2, 1954.
[9] Betty L. Kalis and others, "Precipitating Stress as a Focus in Psychotherapy," A.M.A. *Archives of General Psychiatry*, Vol. V, No. 3 (1961), p. 225.

stress. Such an understanding implies some sort of clinical prediction of what would happen without the intervention of casework service.[10]

Simultaneous activity on two fronts is required: precisely articulated diagnostic formulations and immediate therapeutic contact. Thus, diagnosis and treatment are two sides of the same coin. Formulations of differences in levels of ego functioning, understanding of variations in intensity of the accompanying emotional constellations, taking into account the circumscribing influence of the prevailing reality demands, and setting flexible goals appropriate for the client's emotionally relevant problem—to accomplish all these within the framework of a limited number of interviews is indeed a task requiring a skilled clinician and obviously is not to be belittled as a professional task appropriate only for those not capable of intensive long-term treatment efforts! In short, the time-honored methods normally used in casework are employed in this kind of approach. They combine differential techniques of support (in Bandler's terms "repressive," "expressive," or "progressive"—depending on the diagnostic cues),* on-the-spot clarification and use of environmental aides in the context of an out-reaching empathic relationship.

Treatment Considerations

In the consideration of the techniques of forming a relationship in short-term casework, any implication of a mechanistic approach must be carefully avoided, for the art of relationship is as important here as in any kind of casework practice. As in any case-

---

[10] See Fritz Redl, "Strategy and Techniques of the Life Space Interview," *American Journal of Orthopsychiatry*, Vol. XXIX, No. 1 (1959), pp. 1–18. The mediating role thus assumed, in significant respects comparable to the life-space approach used by Redl, attempts to tip the client's problem-solving efforts in the direction of mentally healthy adaptive solutions. See also David Kaplan's unpublished doctoral dissertation, "Predicting Outcome from Situational Stress on the Basis of Individual Problem-Solving Processes," University of Minnesota, December, 1960, which offers the alarming observation that as many as 40 per cent of the cases known to one municipal hospital are characterized by rather pronounced early maladaptive responses on the part of mothers of premature babies.

* For an elaboration of this point of view see Chapter 2 of this volume.

work situation a relationship is not built *in vacuo,* but develops as specific human needs for support and relief from tension are met by an intuitively understanding, clinically competent person. Ideally, we should take as our model such life processes as growth, restitution, and trial and error, rather than a specific therapeutic model. Although the techniques are similar to those used in all good casework, a number of features deserve special mention.

The first task, especially if the client has not formally requested help, usually involves an attempt at developing fuller conscious awareness of the problem on the part of the client. In practice, this means promoting the first stage of ego mastery, namely, the development of an adequate recognition response to the objective meaning of stress. For example, in casework with a patient who finds it difficult to accept the reality of an illness such as tuberculosis, such recognition becomes a most important goal. Often the lack of cognitive awareness springs from deep anxiety, superficially disguised as "not knowing" or "not caring." Family Guidance Center experiences were replete with examples of families unable initially to understand the special needs and perils surrounding the birth of a premature baby. Denial of certain aspects of reality, often apparent at the very beginning in the ego's definition of stress, must be dealt with in the context of a positive controlled transference. However, the worker's approach is typically more active and confronting than passive or reflective. And although some regression is inevitable, it is discouraged rather than encouraged, so that the transference does not follow the classical casework adaptations of the psychoanalytical model of planned regression employed in insight treatment.

Another persistent theme is the worker's demonstration of confidence in the client's ability to deal with the problem as well as the implicit offering of hope as a kind of maturational dynamic to counteract the ubiquitous feelings of helplessness and hopelessness often associated with the first impact of stress. The worker's demonstration of confidence does not mean simply vibrating sympathetically to the client's plight; rather it implies an early engagement of his ego in constructive efforts on his own behalf. At this point we are attempting to avert such phenomena as undue

151

regression, unhealthy suppression and repression, excessive use of denial, and crippling guilt turned against the self. Obviously, some suppression and some denial are not only necessary but healthy signs of economic ego functioning. Since the crucial question is one of balance, the worker must use clinical knowledge to decide whether defenses are being used pathologically. We know, of course, that all defenses have their proper place in healthy adaptation; here we safeguard against the development of defenses into pathogenic mechanisms.

If we were to plot a curve on a graph representing the intensity of the client's tension level in reaction to the crisis experience, we could depict a similar curve representing the intensity and frequency of the worker's efforts during the crisis situation. In practice, therefore, the caseworker begins by making a quick contact, fostering a warm, reality-oriented relationship at the point of crisis. In response to the client's needs, the worker's use of emotional and environmental support changes in intensity and frequency through the use of carefully-timed, in-person office and home interviews, telephone calls, and such vital concrete social resources as homemaker service, nursery school, and medical aid. As the crisis tension mounts to a peak, the client's ego adaptive efforts reach what Sarvis calls an "integrative crest," often characterized by sudden and dramatic changes.[11] This type of mechanism is frequently seen in fathers who, previously occupying a back seat in the affairs of the family, suddenly rise to positions of leadership in response to the crisis challenge. In such cases we also see, concomitantly, the beginning of a more effective kind of role allocation to other members of the family. To understand and promote the processes necessary to healthy role allocation, reciprocal support, and less fearful confrontation of hidden but emotionally potent problems, the worker must obviously deal with the family as a group as well as with the individual family members.*

The general goal, as we have indicated, is to achieve "an adaptive integration" out of the disruptive experience, thereby enabling

[11] Mary A. Sarvis, and others, "A Concept of Ego-Oriented Psychotherapy," *Psychiatry*, Vol. XXII, No. 3 (1959), p. 284.
* For further discussion of family interaction see the paper by Frances H. Scherz, Chapter 7 of this volume.

the client to use his ego resources more effectively.[12]   Two types
of approaches are involved: (1) reducing the impact of stress by
immediate or emergency emotional-environmental first aid, and
(2) strengthening the person in his ego-adaptive and integrative
efforts by what Redl describes as "clinical exploitation of life events"
through on-the-spot interpretations and clarifications.[13]   The two
are obviously interwoven, and the tactical decision as to which will
be used in any given situation calls for the clinician's best judgment.
In decisions of this sort there is obviously no substitute for clinical
judgment and experience.

Case Example: The B Family *

Mrs. B, the shocked mother of premature twin girls, commented in the seventh of twelve interviews that she had reached,
in her own words, "the crisis peak."   Gripped with panic she
said, "Either the situation will give or we will break!"   The
younger children were still in pajamas, although it was already
after lunch.   She had recently had a most upsetting quarrel with
her husband to whom she had been denying sex relations.   Her
youngest son, who was suffering from extreme jealousy of the
twins, had wandered away from the house and had been taken
to a police station by a neighbor.   The twins' continued colic
had deprived Mrs. B of even a few hours of sleep, and her
fatigue was understandably uppermost in her mind—"I've never
been so weak or tired in all my life.   Next week you'll see me
at State Hospital."
In this interview I first gave Mrs. B an opportunity to discuss
her many fears and then I focused quite actively on her fear
that her aggression might lead her to an act of annihilation,
mentioning specifically her anger against the "extra twin" and
her husband.   She quickly associated the babies' crying with
her husband's sexual interest, saying that she could not respond
at all to him sexually since all she could think of was that inter-
course produces crying babies.   However, in discussing this
further she realized that her husband had been deprived of sexual
gratification for several months and had been looking forward
to the resumption of normal marital relations following the
birth of the babies.   Mrs. B was strongly urged to begin to admit

[12] *Ibid.*, p. 277.
[13] Fritz Redl, *op. cit.*, pp. 8–10.
* Although multiple interviewing was used with the children as well as
with the parents, this case presentation focuses on work with the mother because
of space limitations.

that it was obviously harder to care for two babies than it would have been for the one she had originally expected.

Her pervasive helplessness had reminded her of her mother's death (when she was 7 years old) and her father's subsequent remarriage. Her early experiences and the trauma she suffered at this time flashed before her as if they had all happened yesterday. She poured out in an agonized, tearful way her guilt about not having gone to her father's funeral, and on surface impression seemed about to enter a psychotic-like episode.

Treatment efforts focused on relieving some of Mrs. B's guilt and pointing out its unrealistic quality, and on using a number of concrete environmental supports to which she had previously reacted with great resistance because of her own fears of helplessness. She was able, with considerable support, to initiate help from relatives in making plans for the babies' christening. She permitted herself to accept gifts of clothing from her friends. Her husband was helped to secure supplementary financial assistance since he had been temporarily laid off from his job because of a strike at the plant.

Since, in her previous visits to the well-baby clinic, Mrs. B had presented an impassive facade to the examining physician, she was actively encouraged to bring her questions to the doctor and was accompanied by me to the well-baby clinic, where I remained throughout the examination. She was encouraged by the physician to feed the babies when they were hungry, without worrying about overfeeding, and was urged to strengthen their formula, suggestions that seemed to have a great deal of psychological significance to her. The net effect of this examination, along with reinforcing discussion, was to reassure her that she had not in fact annihilated the babies. She seemed able to respond with much less hostility to her stepmother's advice that they arrange a rotating system for feeding the babies instead of trying to feed both at once.

Mr. and Mrs. B were soon able to resume satisfactory sexual relationships. Mrs. B was helped to acknowledge her youngest son's jealousy which was discussed in joint interviews with her and Mr. B, whose supportive efforts were appreciated. The meaning of her son's wandering off was discussed as a reaction to the new babies. As the routine in the family began to settle down to a normal pattern, she was able to take the child with her to church and on shopping expeditions, and one day even took him on a private outing. The father satisfied the child's needs by taking him on his lap along with the twins, saying, "I have a big lap; there is room for you, too."

Regular visits and active support from the public health nurse completed the picture, along with the use of an efficient, but not too motherly, homemaker who permitted Mrs. B to get some rest and throw off the fatigue that had helped to contribute to her deranged appearance.[14]

Case Analysis

Our efforts over a period of twelve interviews were focused on linking up the present situational crisis with previous unresolved problems which erupted under the impact of what Mrs. B herself referred to as a "crisis." She was helped first to develop an adequate recognition response to the problems involved in having twins, and then to confront her own problems in a way that gave her a better perspective on her relationships with her mother and father, allowing her to cope with previous unresolved problems in an ego-syntonic manner. Anticipatory guidance was extensively used in preparing her for subsequent relationship adjustments among the children and with her husband. The success of these efforts was borne out in a number of follow-up visits over a period of several months. Emotional first aid and discussion of previous issues stirred up by the crisis were co-ordinated with specific environmental aids.

To argue that the environmental support was of greater importance than the psychological aid would ignore the psychosocial nature of this kind of intervention. Treatment procedures for both the inner and the outer stresses proceed simultaneously and are dynamically dovetailed for maximum therapeutic benefit. Ventilation, abreaction, and the clarification of the associative links obviously played an important part in the successful result. Encouraging this family to separate themes interwoven from previous life situations—from a guilt-laden past to a confused present—helped its members to gain a more realistic awareness of what had been an intensely dreaded future. Past, present, and future characteristically merged into a single perception, particularly at the crisis peak. The key issue concerning the mother's guilt about her hostility toward the extra baby was extracted, her current feelings of helplessness were linked with her old feelings concerning the loss of her parents, and then the illogical connections were modified

14 See Howard J. Parad, "Preventive Casework: Problems and Implications," *Social Welfare Forum*, Columbia University Press, New York, 1961, pp. 185–188, for an analysis of the preventive component in this case.

155

through discussion and abreaction of the associated affects. Thus, the central, emotionally relevant issues were selected from a welter of other feelings, observations, and experiences. The focus was on the current stress configuration, that is, the stressful event and the conflicts related to it. Previous life history data were elicited spontaneously and used selectively.

The worker must be willing to risk direct confrontation and interpretation of issues if circular negative reactions are to give way to a more benign pattern of family interaction.

Case Example: The C Family

In trying to help Mrs. C, an intelligent, somewhat excitable 34-year-old woman reacting with unusual tension to the stress of mild, bilateral club-footedness in her 3-week-old daughter, I observed the mother to be constantly hovering over the child, despite positive medical reassurance about the child's prognosis. In response to active confrontation, Mrs. C brought out instances of marked friction with her husband and indicated they were on the verge of separation. Except for a heated discussion about a possible divorce, they had been engaged in a war of silence. Her husband, who also suffered from a marked orthopedic handicap, was very attached to his parents. He had infuriated his wife by visiting them, thereby not being available when the baby was born. Mrs. C's perception of the stress revealed that she somehow felt at fault for having given birth to a less than perfect baby. "I have been punished for wrongdoing." Subsequent discussion of her "wrongdoing" indicated guilt about premarital sex relations, a nagging guilt that had been stirred up by the birth of the baby with a mild congenital anomaly. "God is punishing me for my sins." Since she had been unable to discuss this feeling with her husband, she was actively encouraged to verbalize her feelings. Mr. C had also fantasied himself responsible for the child's defect and felt that his "sperm was defective."

Formerly paralyzed by guilt and anger toward each other, the C's war of silence was broken by the wife's reopening of communication with her husband at my suggestion. Joint interviews provided opportunities to air a number of disagreements about the care of the child, and husband and wife were encouraged to discuss their fears with each other. The risks involved in giving each other the silent treatment were pointed out. Mrs. C's guilt was relieved when I observed that, while she might imagine that previous activities had caused the defect in the baby, she was being hard on herself. Techniques of universalization,

156

emphasizing that many mothers who had babies with anomalies felt this way, served to bolster her feelings of confidence about not being a bad person. Avenues of communication continued to widen, and Mr. C was gradually helped to see the importance of paying more attention to his wife. Both Mr. and Mrs. C were able to emancipate themselves somewhat from their dependent relationships with their respective parents. Follow-up reports confirmed that family and baby were doing well.

Case Analysis

Whereas Mrs. B had an under-recognition response, Mrs. C's response was highly overexaggerated. Mrs. C's ego ideal was mirrored in her baby. Since she fantasied her as a ballerina, she was encouraged to bring out her own feelings of frustration as a child and to begin to think of her baby as a person in her own right, thus minimizing her need to live vicariously through the baby. The precipitating stress, a mild bilateral club-footedness, had stirred up a good deal of unconscious castration anxiety in both husband and wife; this was handled in the interviews as a preconscious derivative fear of mutilation, displaced on the baby. Intense emotions of anger and guilt were aroused, as each blamed himself and the other as the cause of the baby's defect. Guilt associated with previous life experiences was stirred up and was considerably relieved through careful, detailed discussion. In this case the therapeutic goal was threefold: improvement of the husband-wife relationship by encouraging better communication and direct expression of feelings of guilt, anger, and helplessness; fostering continued efforts at emancipation from dominating, possessive, parental ties; and stimulation of more accurate perception and satisfaction of the baby's needs and respect for her as a developing personality in her own right—not as an extension of a narcissistic parental self-image.

The C case is an example of a family that was actually strengthened in the course of its exposure to a stressful situation. The new equilibrium was better than the old. So successful were the parents' coping efforts that their marriage took on a richer significance and they were able to deal in a more mature way with subsequent vicissitudes without debilitating failures in communication. This result would have been impossible had the worker not been flexible

157

in making home visits, keeping in touch through home calls, and arranging both single and joint interviews in the office and in the home.

Use of the "unlinking technique" prevented the development of a disordered mother-child relationship.[15] The goal of confining the mother's conflict so that it would be segmented off and not be acted out vicariously in the life of the baby was realized over a period of three months. This technique, variously called "child-centered treatment of the mother," "focused casework," or "segmental therapy," obviously involves carefully limited goals; it has been successfully used in preventive work and in early treatment of mothers who have attempted abortions.[16]

Cases of Chronic Disequilibrium

Obviously, not all outcomes were as successful as the brief examples we have presented. In a number of situations the underlying pathology was so persistent that brief casework, while producing some alleviation of symptoms, was insufficient, and efforts were made at referral for long-term treatment. In a few of these cases carried along experimental lines, widely spaced interviews were used to encourage mobilization of ego efforts in families hitherto passively resigned to a fate of long-term dependency and disability. Techniques of accompaniment often helped to stimulate their faltering motivation for help.

In dealing with a Negro mother, Mrs. D, who obviously feared authority figures, we found that all efforts of outside social and health agencies seemed to be greeted by a smiling mask, which made any sort of meaningful help impossible. When Mrs. D's premature baby was born, she seemed unable to follow medical and nursing advice. Although eligible for an increase in her public assistance allowance, Mrs. D did not qualify because of her inability to produce a birth certificate for the child. The public welfare worker speculated that Mrs. D refused to submit the required birth certificate because the baby was conceived out of

15 Gerald Caplan, "The Role of the Social Worker in Preventive Psychiatry," *Medical Social Work*, Vol. IV, No. 4 (1955), p. 151.
16 Gerald Caplan, "The Disturbance of the Mother-Child Relationship by Unsuccessful Attempts at Abortion," *Mental Hygiene*, Vol. XXXVIII, No. 1 (1954), pp. 67–80.

wedlock. Since I felt there was no real evidence of extra-marital sexual activity, I told Mrs. D that I felt she was making things unduly troublesome for herself and suggested that there were other factors involved, which we did not understand, in her refusal to get the birth certificate. Without attempting to probe, I offered to accompany her to the registry of births, to which offer she responded with alacrity. The explanation was dramatically revealed when we passed, on our way to the office where births are recorded, another municipal office where the death of a previous child had been recorded. This was a stillborn baby about whose death Mrs. D had enormous guilt which had never been discussed. Quite emotionally she brought out some of these feelings and was able to say she could not bear the thought of going to this building again to get a birth certificate.

Although no pretense is made that this kind of technique and the related discussion of one issue—no matter how central or emotionally relevant—would solve the multiple problems of this family, this experience was a corrective, educational one for Mrs. D and helped appreciably to improve her relationships with other health and welfare agencies. Techniques of accompaniment, while expensive in time and involving a great deal of adaptation on the part of the worker, may be used successfully in many other situations when diagnostically indicated. Clearly, they are not to be used in a "gimmicky" sense, any more than home visits or family interviews have special magic. The worker must be willing to leave the sanctity of his office and enter actively into the client's life when this technique is diagnostically indicated and geared to specific casework goals.

I should like to discuss briefly three issues related to this type of approach: (1) motivation and its operational definition; (2) the perennial riddle of whether a change in outward behavior reflects a change in ego patterns; and (3) the proper place of this type of interventive work in a spectrum of casework services.

The Problem of Motivation

Too often we tend to by-pass certain cases in our daily practice, stereotyping them as characterized by "too many reality problems" or "too crisis-ridden" or "too messy." Such labels are often a transparent kind of professional rationalization for failure to act in critical situations. And too often we substitute the language of motivation theory for our earlier epithet of "unco-operative client." Although the difference between needing and wanting help is admittedly crucial in short-term casework where issues must be faced squarely and time responsibly used, the problem of helping people who need help to want help is equally crucial and hence worthy of our best clinical efforts.

In the preface to a recent study Grinker points up "the need for increasing the number and strength of boosters towards treatment by external social forces and the responsibility of the clinic for increasing the motivational strength by satisfying more of the family's needs." [17] In this view of motivation, active effort on the part of the therapist is clearly implied. "Effective motivation involves the integration of the need for help in all family needs." [18] Therefore, motivation cannot be assessed in a mechanistic, unilateral sense. It frequently develops even when resistance initially appears very high, if the family needs are satisfied in a reasonable way, and the emotional crises of its members are properly understood and not placed in a social vacuum. The worker's therapeutic zeal and the intensity of his countertransference investment are of greater than usual importance in this kind of activity. The assessment of motivation and treatability is a transactional interplay, not only of what the client wants and how much he wants it, but also of what the worker wants and how much he wants it. Thus, the worker's commitment to an early and tangible result frequently communicates itself to the family. As latent strengths are identified and fostered, the drive toward help is intensified.

The Problem of Assessing Change

The controversial question inevitably arises: Are we relieving symptoms and not treating underlying emotional causes? Of necessity many problems are untouched since our efforts are beamed to selected, emotionally relevant issues. Although this approach focuses on conscious and preconscious derivatives rather than on the core pathology, is this altogether different from long-term intensive treatment in which some issues are worked on and others

[17] Philip Lichtenberg and others, *Motivation for Child Psychiatry Treatment,* Russell and Russell, New York, 1960, p. xii.
[18] *Ibid.,* p. 218.

160

ignored? Even psychoanalysis does not pretend to deal with all issues; it has been often said that the main purpose of analysis is to enable people to face the vicissitudes of life in a mature way, not to provide a talisman for all life's problems. In the kind of activity described here it is artificial to differentiate between outward changes in functioning, based on environmental manipulation, and changes in ego-adaptation patterns based on internal shifts in the defenses, since the two go hand in hand. Typically, alterations in social functioning reflect improvement in such basic ego functions as perception, judgment, control, and mastery.

Although it is possible that some life crises may pass with improvement in functioning but no change in adaptive patterns, the opposite is probably more frequently true. We know that in ordinary human experience people become stronger through successful mastery of crisis situations without making clinical headlines. However, as recently pointed out by Hollis, supportive casework *can* change the quality of the ego's adaptive patterns.[19] Whether previous adaptive patterns are restored through re-establishment of a former equilibrium, whether the life-situation remains the same (which in a pure scientific sense is impossible although clinically it may seem to be the same), or whether the functioning of the family improves, the focused use of both emotional and environmental support is indicated in virtually all crisis situations calling for outside intervention. For purposes of analysis, cases may be arranged along a continuum, extending from those in which techniques of clarification predominate (resulting in the ego's increased awareness of hidden motivation in its behavior) to those in which environmental support is the main dynamic of change. However, this spread in techniques and emphasis is fundamentally no different from ordinary casework practice, regardless of the setting.

The Place of Short-Term Casework

Our third question, in itself requiring a separate paper, is: What is the proper place of short-term, crisis-oriented casework in the

19 Florence Hollis, "Analysis of Casework Treatment Methods and Their Relationship to Personality Change," *Smith College Studies in Social Work*, Vol. XXXII, No. 2 (1962), pp. 103–105. The formulations outlined in the article are elaborated in Dr. Hollis' forthcoming book, *Casework: A Psychosocial Therapy*, Random House, New York, 1963.

total range of traditional casework services? Happily, brief services are attracting increased attention in our professional literature, partly because the shortage of skilled mental-health manpower has forced many agencies and clinics to initiate short-term treatment arrangements and partly because of the widespread concern with lost cases or unplanned terminations. Although some observers may continue to draw invidious distinctions between brief and long-term services, a number of studies confirm the fact that in many treatment programs the overwhelming majority of applicants receive fewer than ten interviews. For example, a recent comparison of brief and long-term cases in a family agency serving a predominantly middle-class clientele revealed that only 14 per cent of a total of 118 cases received more than ten interviews.[20] A similar study of 232 psychiatric clinics found that 64 per cent of the patients were seen for fewer than five interviews.[21] Such surveys have forced a reappraisal of the relevance of certain types of intensive long-term treatment approaches, as well as the adaptation of brief-service approaches, as a more realistic response to the client's need for help.

Although some study efforts have resulted in brief-service approaches as a matter of necessity—dictated by the exigencies of manpower and finances—many progressive agencies and clinics have developed brief therapeutic services as a matter of choice. Carefully avoiding any pretense of miracle cures, these new adaptations are nonetheless impressive. For example, the Langley Porter Neuropsychiatric Institute in San Francisco and the Jewish Board of Guardians in New York have been experimenting with short-term casework services as the treatment of choice designed to deal effectively with the stressful event and the conflict it engenders.[22] Using a broad concept of crisis as a stress-conflict configuration, the Langley Porter study operates on the "assumption that every appli-

---

[20] Bernice Boehm, "Characterististics of Brief Service and Long-Term Cases," Family and Children's Service (unpublished report), Minneapolis, Minn., April 1961, p. 1.

[21] Luther E. Woodward, "Increasing Social Work Effectiveness in Meeting Mental Health Needs," *Social Work*, Vol. 5, No. 3 (1960), p. 65.

[22] Betty L. Kalis, and others, *op. cit.*, and Elise Fell, "Short-Term Treatment in a Child Guidance Clinic," *Journal of Jewish Communal Service*, Vol. XXXVI, No. 2 (Winter, 1959), pp. 144–49.

cation reflects a kind of subjective crisis," [23] while the Jewish Board of Guardians' experiment is systematically designed to help with crises in parent-child relationships through a series of twelve interviews over a three-month period. Still another example is provided by the Buffalo Psychiatric Clinic which for several years has been effectively employing brief casework services, made available as close as possible to the point of crisis impact.[24]

Leaving aside the theoretical and operational emphases which naturally vary from program to program, we observe in these projects a common reliance on the kinds of formulations outlined in this paper: avoidance of waiting periods, quick diagnostic assessment, immediate engagement of the client's ego capacities, direct confrontation and examination of the key emotional issues, an awareness of the type of learning possible during periods of high emotional tension, and a disciplined variety of therapeutic optimism. Crises should not be viewed as signs of defeat but as developments to be expected. Hallowitz and Cutter have noted: "When crises occur, such as an antisocial act on the part of the child, effort is made to take therapeutic advantage of the family's heightened anxiety." [25] Also characteristic of most of these new programs is the practice of offering support and continued interest in routine follow-up interviews, as well as an open-door policy welcoming back clients who require additional periods of either brief or long-term help. The latter offer, however, is infrequently accepted as clients seem to regard their own improved day-to-day living as the best form of therapy.

Conclusion

The thesis, then, of this paper is that the crisis concept and a more precise application of the time-honored as well as newer techniques of family-focused brief casework can greatly enhance the social re-

[23] Betty L. Kalis, "Restoring Emotional Balance as a Goal in Psychotherapy," presented at the Fifteenth Annual Psychiatric Social Work Institute, San Francisco, April 20, 1961.

[24] David Hallowitz and Albert V. Cutter, "The Family Unit Approach in Therapy: Uses, Process, and Dynamics," *Casework Papers, 1961*, Family Service Association of America, New York, pp. 44–57.

[25] *Ibid.*, p. 51.

163

sponsibility and social contribution of casework. Again I wish to stress that I am proposing neither the abolition of intensive long-term services nor a sophomoric use of the adaptations of crisis theory that would lead to a type of pseudo-omniscient, ubiquitous, frenetic casework. Many changes in the organization and distribution of social services as well as in administrative procedures are suggested by the type of approach advocated here. For example, the virtual elimination of most waiting lists, the avoidance of prolonged diagnostic investigations that leave the worker with all the information and the client with all the problems, and the reappraisal of the uneconomic aspects of the traditional ortho-psychiatric team are but a few of the problems pressing for solution if our model of brief services is to become a palpable social reality.[26] Thus, instead of wailing about the prevalence of brief-service contacts as signs of professional failure, I suggest we re-examine our practice to see how, in the light of crisis theory and modern forms of preventive intervention, we can make services more constructive. Such an objective reappraisal involves professional soul-searching, research-oriented experimentation, and a renewed emphasis on the quality rather than the quantity of service rendered.

In the last analysis, our troubled clients and patients care less about how "long" or "deep" their treatment is than they do about its relevance and usefulness in helping them in their everyday living relationships.

[26] See, for example, Ruth C. Oakey, "Meeting the Problems of Intake in Child Guidance and Marital Counseling," *Mental Hygiene*, Vol. 45, No. 1 (1961), p. 54.

9. Some Criteria for the Modification of Treatment Arrangements *

John A. MacLeod

A CURIOUS SITUATION exists in most psychiatric clinics and social agencies. Applications are rising, numerous patients and clients are benefiting, and community acceptance of mental health services continues to improve. But of the people coming to agencies and clinics for help, large numbers somewhat abruptly, and often inexplicably, fail to follow the recommended treatment programs. Since these terminations are not planned, they must be regarded as treatment failures.

The Problem

The ubiquitous problem of unplanned terminations is being increasingly documented. For example, a recent study of 232 outpatient clinics indicated that almost two-thirds of the patients attended fewer than five treatment sessions.[1] It is estimated that 25 to 50 per cent of clients and patients recommended for treatment actually attend five sessions or fewer. It is unlikely that maximum benefit can be derived from such a small number of treatment visits

* Presented in the Monday Night Lecture Series, Smith College School for Social Work, Northampton, Massachusetts, July 17, 1961.
[1] Luther E. Woodward, "Increasing Social Effectiveness in Meeting Mental Health Needs," *Social Work*, Vol. 5, No. 3 (1960), p. 65.

although they may aid the patients in surmounting a few crises. Moreover, the patients * most likely to withdraw from treatment seem to be those with the most urgent and serious problems—those who usually have an impressive need for a continuing contact with a professional agency. Studies at the Central Clinic in Cincinnati have confirmed that the patients with diagnoses of psychosis and severe personality disorders are most likely to withdraw from treatment prematurely. The clinical diagnosis alone, however, does not distinguish the group on whom our attention is focused.

The problem of numerous drop-outs raises several questions. Do these persons fail to return because of the inappropriateness of the treatment recommendations and arrangements? What is the nature of our usual treatment arrangements and what do these arrangements require of our clients and patients? These and similar questions are being considered by many agencies, clinics, and hospitals throughout the country.[2] Various treatment approaches are being tried experimentally. This paper describes the "sub-clinic" or Wednesday Afternoon Clinic which was evolved as an approach to the problem of drop-outs at the Central Clinic of Cincinnati. We are searching for an answer to a basic question: What are the criteria for modifying the treatment arrangements when, as seems evident, a variety of treatment approaches is necessary?

The Basic Model

The term "treatment arrangements" refers to the nature, content, frequency, duration, and locale of interviews, and whether the same professional person continues to work with the client or patient. In most agencies these arrangements fall into a standard pattern: routinely planned weekly interviews in an office, usually lasting about an hour, taken up with "talk," most of which is expected to be done by the client or patient. Almost invariably every visit is with the same professional person. This once-a-week, 50-minute, face-to-face arrangement for talking has come to be the basic model

* *Editor's Note:* Although the term "patient" is mainly used, the observations offered here apply also to clients of non-medical services.

[2] See, for example, Agnes Ritchie, "Multiple Impact Therapy: An Experiment," *Social Work*, Vol. 5, No. 3 (1960), pp. 16–21.

because it has so frequently proved useful in conducting psycho-therapy and casework.

My thesis is that we must develop variations of this basic model so that we can respond more flexibly to the many people coming to our agencies. Social workers often have taken the lead in such explorations. Since originally much of social work was done in the field, social workers can recognize that it may not be possible for an individual to come to an agency and therefore that the worker may need to make home visits. Home visits are considered desirable not only because of the inability of clients to come to the agency but because of a conviction that a visit will enable the worker to gain a deeper understanding of the person's environment, thus enabling him to be of more significant help to the individual.[3] Social workers have long recognized, also, that many individuals are unable to modify their unacceptable behavior, and the workers therefore have pioneered many efforts to manipulate and change the environment of the sick individual rather than to attempt modification of deviant behavior or neurotic and psychotic defenses. Moreover, social work is now experiencing a heightened interest in multiple interviewing in an effort to increase the effectiveness of casework practice.[*]

The Influence of Treatment Arrangements

With the exception of the personality and skill of the therapist, no factor plays a greater role in the treatment process than does the structure of the treatment arrangements. The frequency and duration of interviews, for instance, have a critical influence on the meaningfulness and intensity of the worker-client or doctor-patient relationship. On the character of this relationship rests the outcome of any treatment. The usual arrangement of a weekly interview with a continuing therapist fosters the development of an intense relationship and may stimulate excessively dependent and regressive behavior. With many patients such an arrangement is

[3] Jane E. Paterson and Florence E. Cyr, "The Use of the Home Visit in Present-day Social Work," *Social Casework*, Vol. XLI, No. 4 (1960), pp. 184–191, and Emily C. Faucett, "Multiple-Client Interviewing: A Means of Assessing Family Processes," *Social Casework*, Vol. XLIII, No. 3 (1962), pp. 114–120.
[*] See Frances H. Scherz, Chapter 7 of this volume.

the most effective, but with many others it is of questionable value —even when handled skilfully.

Diagnostic Criteria

From our clinical experience we already know that we cannot gain sufficient information from a clinical diagnosis, a review of the symptoms or presenting behavior problems, or even the conduct of an individual in a diagnostic interview, to be sure that the individual has the requisite capacity and motivation to participate in the traditional type of treatment. As Eissler has pointed out, "Symptoms and behavior do not necessarily betray the true structure of the ego organization." [4] Therefore a detailed and on-going examination of the ego functions required by the traditional treatment model is needed.

What are these requirements? First, we all recognize that a certain amount of ego integration is required for the individual to so conduct his life that he is able to come to an agency for a regular weekly appointment. Yet we often embark on an exploratory treatment program of the usual variety without sufficient evidence that the individual will be able to attend regular appointments. The difficulty may not be due entirely to the patient's inability to proceed with his life affairs in an organized way. The failure to keep appointments may be the result of the ego's struggle with a level of anxiety which leads the person to avoid any new experiences or relationships. When the ego is under stress and experiencing anxiety it is often conservative in its approach to new experiences, even avoiding them if at all possible. In this connection, it is interesting to note the frequency with which a number of people change their addresses or move out of town as they begin to get help from an agency. Although transiency may well be related to the patient's emotional problems, such moves may result specifically from the threat to the patient of initiating the new relationship associated with the treatment experience.

We are often called upon to deal with the tardiness of a patient, which we hope he can abandon as the treatment program progresses.

4 K. R. Eissler, "The Effect of the Structure of the Ego on Psychoanalytic Technique," *Journal of the American Psychoanalytic Association*, Vol. 1 (1953), pp. 104–143.

However, patients are often unable to give up this defensive technique; their egos find it impossible to deal realistically with the treatment experience and therefore they dilute or avoid the threatening situation. Certainly if a patient is chronically late for appointments he will be a difficult person to help.

Frequently we overlook the necessity that a person be able to talk in a reasonably well-organized and somewhat introspective fashion if he is to be helped by the treatment approach that we are discussing. Constructive conversation calls for a certain degree of intelligence on his part and, more important, the belief that talk is meaningful. Many people coming for help are from lower socioeconomic groups where the idea that it is helpful—or even possible—to discuss one's feelings with others is novel and strange. It is not uncommon for a patient to refuse to pay for clinic visits because he thinks he should not pay for "just talk."

The need of many patients to have an immediate response from the helping person is another factor in determining capacity for treatment. To indulge in talk means that "real" gratification has to be postponed. Frequently this postponement of immediate demands for concrete help (for example, medicine or money) is more than the patient's ego can tolerate. An illustration of this need for real gratification is found in the patient's frequent parting question, "Aren't you going to *do* something?"

Our recognition of the need to postpone gratification leads to another observation: the patient finds it is necessary to postpone "action" if he is to be helped through our basic mode of treatment. For instance, if the patient becomes angry, it is not possible for him to fight in the interview; and if he wants to receive something from the worker it is not possible for him to steal. We recognize that such postponement of action, with the tension and anxiety it entails, is often beyond the patient's threshold of tolerance.

Obviously, it is of basic importance that the patient be able to sustain a relationship with a therapist during the treatment experience. For a number of reasons many individuals find it either difficult or impossible to develop object relationships with people in their current environment. The patient may be too anxious about the repetition of an early traumatic experience with a parent and may therefore avoid any possibility of developing new object rela-

169

tionships. The reasons behind such avoidance are not usually within the realm of the patient's awareness. Or the individual may never have had an opportunity to form healthy object relationships and, as a result, may have been always preoccupied to an unhealthy degree with his inner fantasy life. Caught in this vicious circle, he may be uninterested in developing new object relationships.

Then, too, we commonly encounter patients who, despite their initial eagerness, are unable to develop a new object relationship. For in these situations the therapist is dealt with as though he were an old object—without appropriate awareness of this fact on the part of the patient. The following is an example of such a problem. An experienced social worker came to me for consultation regarding what was mistakenly perceived by her as a "countertransference problem." The worker was becoming, in her own thinking, inappropriately angry at the request of her client for a close personal relationship with her. Very early in the treatment experience the client would bring in religious tracts, place them on the worker's desk, and want to use the treatment time for a discussion of religious life. Repeatedly the client expressed disappointment over the infrequent appointments and the lack of an opportunity to see the worker outside the professional atmosphere of the agency. The client would call the worker to ask her to her home for Sunday dinner or for other social engagements. It was clear from the case material that the client did not see the worker as a professional person but actually was dealing with her as she had with her mother, who was at that time afflicted with a terminal illness. The client was not able to conform to the usual treatment arrangements because she was not able to see the caseworker as a professional person.

Finally, if the patient is able to enter into the treatment relationship and talk freely during the appointments, he must at the same time be able to stand to one side and observe what is going on. Such self-observation on the part of the ego makes it possible for the individual to consider more constructive ways of handling problems. Thus he does more than relive the old problems that have brought him for help; he also has the opportunity to make some new starts or to abandon archaic techniques.

170

In summary, the ego functions necessary for successful participation in traditional treatment include the patient's capacity to attend interviews regularly without being unduly tardy; to tolerate considerable tension and anxiety because of the delayed gratification and the usual necessity not to have a concrete response from the helper or agency; to delay action; to use "talk"; to form a new and healthy object relationship; to define the professional person as such rather than as an old object in his life; and, probably most important, to develop sufficient ability for self-observation, while involving himself in the treatment experience. These appear to be rather high demands upon our applicants; indeed when we review them we are surprised that so many sick persons are able to meet these traditional criteria to an extent that enables them to profit from treatment.

The Problem of Clinical Assessment

In many situations it is clear that the usual treatment structure will not do. For instance, if we see an individual who arrives for the appointment half an hour late, informs us that he is currently maintaining contact with half a dozen physicians or agencies, requests that we call the landlord to have the plumbing fixed, calls us by the wrong name, and sits looking at us for long periods waiting for us to speak, then we know that some variations of the traditional treatment model will be required. However, most of our clinical experiences are much less clear-cut than this type of encounter.

Accurate early assessment of a patient's capacity to use psychiatric or casework help is exceedingly difficult, and leads to the prevailing —and often abused—recommendation for "an exploratory period" or "a trial of treatment." At times we are critical of our failure to be more definitive in the initial planning of a treatment program but more often we recognize the limitations of our observations, knowledge, and techniques. In our clinic, after postulating an initial formulation and tentative plan of treatment, we interest ourselves in the nature of the patient's handling of the treatment experience. For example, when we have evidence that the patient will be unable to profit from our usual treatment approach, varia-

171

tions are initiated to enable the patient to maintain contact with the agency and obtain the necessary help.

We must not overlook the absolute necessity for the professional worker's continuing self-assessment of his participation in the development of the treatment. It is absolutely crucial to the worker's professional development that he be concerned with and aware of the influence of his own personality on the progress of any treatment. *In other words, modification of treatment arrangements should not be used as an easy escape to avoid facing countertransference problems.*

Given our present stage of knowledge and skill, it must be admitted that the patient's actual response to the on-going treatment process often provides the best indication of whether he can benefit from the treatment experience. Occasionally we see a reasonably capable individual develop into a demanding, chronically dissatisfied patient who is angry with the worker but unable to give up the treatment relationship. Because of frustration and anxiety associated with the treatment encounter, these patients have regressed to such an early dependent level of adaptation that they are unable to give up the non-satisfying therapist. This usually means that an unsatisfactory relationship with an important parent has been reactivated without the possibility that it can be used in a therapeutic way. Although such a transference problem may be worked through in the usual mode of treatment, variation in the mode of treatment itself may be indicated.

Some Possible Variations

Treatment arrangements can be varied by (1) changing the frequency of the interviews, (2) altering the duration of the interviews, (3) modifying the activities and routines of the interviews, (4) arranging for the patient to see different therapists. In other words, those patients who are unable to use the basic mode of treatment should be allowed to use agency service on a more flexible basis, with greater or less frequency of visits, involving briefer interviews, perhaps at irregular intervals. The therapist's activity during interviews should be much more direct, with less verbal participation expected of the patient; and, possibly, a number of different therapists should work with one patient.

172

Such treatment modifications can be carried out only with difficulty in the usual agency for reasons that are easily seen: Almost
all agencies work on the basis of a one-hour interview, and any
other arrangement is rather awkward and difficult; offices may be
shared and the sharing schedule usually works best on an hourly
basis; the clinical and staff conferences are scheduled on the hour
and usually last for one or two hours; patients and clients have
become accustomed to calling their workers at the hourly intervals
during the day when they expect their therapist to be available.
When a large caseload is carried it is awkward to have one or two
patients who are seen for fifteen-minute or half-hour interviews at
irregular times since this conflicts with the regular weekly scheduling
of the rest of the caseload.

A Supportive-Care Program

The staff in Central Clinic recognized that a large number of
patients were unable to participate successfully in our typical treatment arrangements. A group of these patients was placed in a
special sub-clinic where the suggested variations could be carried
out more effectively. I believe the following experiences demonstrate that when the criteria for the modification of treatment arrangements are observed, more appropriate treatment arrangements
are possible and patients are likely to gain more from their contacts
with clinics and agencies.[5]

The central idea of the sub-clinic was that a substantial number
of patients could be helped if the psychotherapy were so arranged
that they would be encouraged to relate to a group of doctors and
to a clinic rather than to one psychiatrist. The sub-clinic was
designed primarily for supportive psychotherapy, that is, psychotherapy directed toward restoration of intrapsychic equilibrium
rather than toward personality growth and maturation.[6] The pa-

[5] This sub-clinic, also called the Wednesday Afternoon Clinic, has been re-
ported in a paper by John A. MacLeod and Francine Middelman, "Wednesday
Afternoon Clinic: A Supportive Care Program," *Archives of General Psychiatry*,
Vol. 6, January, 1961, pp. 56–65.

[6] Maurice Levine, "Principles of Psychiatric Treatment," in *Dynamic Psychiatry*,
Franz Alexander, and Helen Ross (eds.), University of Chicago Press, Chicago,
1952, pp. 307–366. Also see Bernard Bandler, "The Concept of Ego-Supportive
Psychotherapy" in the present volume. (Editor's note.)

tients comprising the clinic group were rather seriously disturbed, had limited ego development, and generally were encountering environmental pressures that continually threatened to disrupt their tenuous intrapsychic balance. Almost invariably family relationships had been quite chaotic, with multiple traumatic experiences and little opportunity for healthy identification. The patients came from lower socioeconomic groups where introspection and communication of certain kinds of feelings are often discouraged. Patients who had received previous treatment had had difficulty developing relationships with their therapists. Our typical treatment goals in these cases were to maintain the borderline status quo; such goals might include the prevention of hospitalization, the maintenance of a poor but continuing job, or the reduction of chronic and disabling symptoms.

As to clinic structure, it was decided that in view of the patients' limited ego development and limited capacity for adaptation, the content of the therapy and the pattern of treatment arrangements should be as close as possible to the patients' expectations. The clinic had to make more than the usual effort to meet the patients' needs and expectations rather than expect the patient to adapt to the clinic's model of psychotherapy.

Under the new plan, we try to meet the patients' needs through brief sessions of approximately fifteen minutes, in which the therapists are relatively out-going, active, and direct, giving the patient little opportunity for regression or for the development of an intensive relationship. In the patient's eyes the therapist remains clearly the doctor, the giver of advice and medication. It is possible for patients to come in more or less frequently and on short notice. There is little or no waiting following the recommendation for therapy. Finally, in view of the patients' difficulties in working with a continuing therapist, they have the opportunity to see a number of different therapists. Basic to the planning of this new service is the recognition of the importance of encouraging this group of patients to maintain contact with the clinic over a considerable period of time or even for an indefinite period of time.

In practice, the clinic meets for one hour each week. During this time 35 or 40 patients are scheduled to be seen by 10 or 11 doctors. Usually a patient sees a different doctor on successive visits. Among the administrative techniques providing for continuity of the treatment plan is a meeting of the group of doctors in the clinic for an hour after the patients are seen. The patients' progress is then discussed and treatment programs are scrutinized. Repeatedly stressed, even for a brief interview, is the importance of combining therapeutic understanding and skill in order to serve the patient with optimal effectiveness. During its three years of operation, the enthusiasm and professional investment of the doctors have been remarkably strong. The number of active patients in the clinic, at any given time, has ranged to over 200. The patients in this sub-clinic are slightly older than those in the usual form of individual therapy, and there is a somewhat higher percentage of women. Using occupation and educational achievement as criteria, we should classify most of them as lower class. And almost all of them have clinical diagnoses suggesting severe psychopathology.

A comparison of these patients with a group of similar patients, seen prior to the initiation of this clinic, reveals the following findings: The patients in the new sub-clinic have made substantially more visits over a considerably longer period of time than the comparison group. For instance, 11 of a group of 20 sub-clinic patients maintained contact with the clinic for more than six months whereas only one of the comparison group of 20 patients maintained contact with the clinic for more than six months. In addition, a striking difference was noticed in the improvement in the patients of the sub-clinic (15 out of 20) as compared to the comparison group of patients (2 out of 20). The above comparison is only an initial attempt to validate impressions of the sub-clinic's work. Statistically validated impressions will require the inclusion of a research design in the sub-clinic's future operation.

Summary and Evaluation

In summary, the Central Clinic felt challenged to provide a treatment approach that would enable a group of seriously disturbed patients to maintain sufficient contact with a psychiatric center to profit from a dynamically oriented psychotherapy. We developed a supportive-care program emphasizing patients' relating to a number of significant people, and requiring a minimal amount of adaptation by the patients. In addition to observing that patients have generally benefited from this treatment experience, we have been impressed with the considerable reduction in therapeutic time lost because of the patients' failure to appear for appointments. In evaluating the program, we believe the most controversial aspect is the pattern of treatment arrangement whereby patients see different doctors rather than continuing with one doctor. Yet it has been shown that the patient group discussed is not able to benefit from individual therapy with the usual arrangements, and apparently can benefit from therapy where the arrangements encourage opportunity to relate to a number of therapeutically oriented people, thereby providing a continuing relationship with the clinic rather than with one individual. The therapist remains responsible for so conducting the interview that the patient has maximum opportunity for a therapeutic experience even though the doctor and patient meet but once for fifteen minutes.

Conclusions

Many of the patients applying to clinics and social agencies fail to make use of the treatment opportunities offered them. These early drop-outs apparently lack the necessary ego integration to enable them to participate in the usual type of treatment. The assessment of the patient's ego strength—a typical feature of the dynamic and genetic formulation—should be specifically tied in with an assessment of the patient's capacity to make use of the usual treatment arrangements. The extent of the demand these arrangements make frequently has gone unrecognized. It seems evident that we must provide modifications of the treatment arrangements now in use in most professional agencies if we are to offer maximum therapeutic facilities to many different kinds of patients.

10. A Group Approach to Clients with Ego Defects*

S. Michael Turner

WITHIN THE RANGE of character disorders we often find the person whose inadequate ego functioning brings him into repeated or long-term contact with social agencies because he cannot successfully meet his own basic needs. The chronicity and multiplicity of his problems may be expressed on an environmental or an emotional level, or both. His family, of which he may be the key member, often patterns its characteristics to complement his own characteristics. The children, for example, may assume parental responsibility not only to siblings, but also to their own parents, or they may be infantilized to bolster the sagging egos of their parents. When the parents' dependency needs predominate over those of their children, we can be reasonably sure that the children's later development will be characterized by an impoverishment in their ability to find gratification outside a narrowly circumscribed area of object relationships and accomplishments. When such persons seek help with their problems one is at once struck by this quality of impoverishment. Whether the individual presents himself as a passive and submissive, or as an arrogant and independent, client, one can almost immediately sense the underlying void in his personality and in his search for gratification of his dependency needs.[1]

This search for gratification assumes either a pattern character-

* Presented at the Biennial Meeting of the Family Service Association of America, New York, November 14, 1961. The paper is based on the author's experience as District Director, Family Service Association of Greater Boston.

[1] Beatrice Simcox Reiner and Irving Kaufman, *Character Disorders in Parents of Delinquents,* Family Service Association of America, New York, 1959.

ized by repeated, unproductive, aggressive contacts with a great number of agencies over a prolonged period, or a prolonged passively dependent but equally unproductive treatment relationship with a single agency. This presentation will deal with a group of clients whose helplessness, isolation, and poverty of achievement suggest treatment difficulties that are indeed serious but are perhaps more subtle and less publicized than those of their more aggressive counterparts.

The clients in this particular group were young, unattached men who had been severely damaged by the unconscious exploitation inherent in their distorted relationships with their parents. Their difficulties had been recognized early and they had received great amounts of psychiatric and casework help. In five cases, for example, a total of forty-eight years of psychiatric and casework help had been invested. Relationships with meaningful figures in their environment continued on an infantile, mutually dependent basis. All of them had severe ego defects, lacked feelings of adequacy, and repeatedly acted out their early parental conflicts with authority figures, such as teachers and employers. Their most important relationships usually had been with their psychiatrists and caseworkers and life without some kind of treatment seemed to them unthinkable.

Casework with these men had become a discouraging prospect indeed. The caseworker's investment in each case proved to be emotionally and physically enervating because of the client's extremely slow movement as well as his repetitious need to over-personalize the treatment relationship. Such clients present a problem common to social agencies, and one may speculate on why the traditional one-to-one method does not meet their needs. The treatment situation had become to these men an end in itself rather than a means to an end. It provided a source of satisfaction for infantile needs. The fear of separation from this satisfying but far from satisfactory relationship seemed to account for the clients' resistance to the caseworkers' attempts to develop their capacities for more realistic ego-satisfying relationships and accomplishments.

These speculations suggested the appropriateness of group treatment.[2] A group has many "plus" qualities. Casework skills adapted

2 *Ibid.*, p. 174.

178

to group leadership might well be more effective with these clients than individual treatment had proved.[3] I undertook the leadership of a group of men with the problems described as part of an experimental group therapy program of the Family Service Association of Greater Boston.[4] In the organization of this group, five members were chosen from my own caseload and three were referred by other workers in the agency. All the men were single, ranging in age from 22 to 36. All but two were high-school graduates; one had taken many college courses and one was a college graduate. All members had had some work experience, but almost all were periodically unemployed. Six members stayed with the group—which met weekly—until its termination three years later.

The purpose of the group was explained to the prospective members as a means of helping them to "get along better with others." In addition to providing material for the assessment of individual members, the group offered: (1) a setting in which infantile needs could not predominate; (2) a corrective experience with authority and sibling figures; and (3) a laboratory or workshop for reality experiences in relating to others, with the protection and guidance of a leader. The goals for the individuals within the group were also threefold: (1) greater comfort in relationships with authority; (2) improvement of self-image; and (3) more productive and satisfying peer relationships.

The Initial Phase

The on-going life experiences of the members provided the primary focus. Since treatment had assumed such an important role in their lives, the most significant among these experiences was the shift from individual treatment to the group setting. We know that, in the intake interview with individual clients, it is extremely important for the worker to explore the way the client feels about coming for help, and the attempts he has made in the past to resolve

[3] Doris Menzer, Lillian S. Irvine, and Elvin V. Semrad, "The Role of the Social Worker in Group Therapy," *Journal of Psychiatric Social Work*, Vol. XX, No. 4 (1951), pp. 158–166.
[4] For an account of group therapy with mothers with character disorders, see Saul Scheidlinger and Marjorie Pyrke, "Group Therapy of Women with Severe Dependency Problems," *American Journal of Orthopsychiatry*, Vol. XXXI, No. 4 (1961), pp. 776–785.

179

problems, and to communicate the worker's understanding of his feelings about these attempts. In the group, too, this was essential. The plus quality in the group was that this process of exploration and clarification facilitated the formation of the members' relationships not only toward the leader, but more particularly toward each other.

In this initial phase of group treatment the leader must be prepared to deal with great resistance to change. This was especially true with individuals who had protected themselves against intrusions from the outside and found the group situation threatening for this reason. The leader had to proceed slowly and painstakingly and communicate his acceptance of each member to the group. This was a difficult assignment because it was natural for these clients to want to relate in a one-to-one way to the leader. Conversely, it was inevitable that there were some clients in the group with whom the leader could identify more easily than with others. Awareness of these phenomena and conscious self-discipline helped the leader maintain a position of impartiality.

A climate of feeling was created in which the group members could learn to trust the leader and each other. This trust provided the vehicle which enabled the members to overcome their fears and proceed with the treatment. The leader set this vehicle in motion by enabling the members to share in each other's experiences, relating to equivalent feelings in all the members. Awareness of the universal feelings that were being expressed was essential, although the content of the discussion might vary on the surface from member to member. Each member had an underlying fear of the group setting, coupled with a fear of losing the protection of his therapist. Rapport was established among the individual members and between them and the leader by his relating to these common underlying feelings, thus making their dilemmas available for recognition, examination, and resolution.

The following illustrations highlight the material in the group's beginning work in the diminution of infantile behavior and toward increasingly appropriate response to the reality situation.

Bert, who was 22, early in life had undergone considerable surgical treatment, incapacitating him for several years. He had been regarded by his parents as a cripple, even though his condition had improved so markedly as to become almost unnoticeable. Caught in a web of distorted dependence on his parents, his struggle to grow up became a struggle for life almost greater than he could cope with. His world had become one of reverie where living people did not exist and only animals, birds, and images of remote places and events had meaning. In individual interviews, these reveries and fantasies preoccupied him almost totally but, from the very first session in the group, he began talking about realistic situations involving finding a job and having more satisfactory relationships with girls. In others, too, there was a marked contrast to their individual sessions, almost as though in a peer group situation the mask of infancy had been dropped.

Another demonstration of this phenomenon on the group level occurred in the following way: Refreshments were introduced in the first session on the assumption that this would ease the transition from the individual to the group situation and because it was deemed appropriate in view of the clients' fixation at the oral stage of development. By the second or third session, however, the group members made it very clear that they did not wish to be fed by insisting that dues be charged to cover the cost of refreshments. Simultaneously, this decision gave them freedom to choose the kind of refreshments they wanted.

These events were undoubtedly the immediate concrete evidence of the struggle for recognition. The more subtle and difficult challenges inherent in the working out of their struggles, in dealing with figures of authority and in getting along with each other's differences, were yet to come. At first the men felt comfortable only in sharing their experiences at work, in social situations, or at home. It was a period of becoming acquainted and of trying to stabilize their environment sufficiently.

The group members gave each other advice and suggestions about specific problems. Within a remarkably short time, most of the members had obtained steady employment or made vocational plans and it was at this time that one of the members was able to clarify for himself and the group that their purpose would be to "see ourselves as others see us." This definition lent added meaning to the frequent discussions about the various situations in which the men found themselves, until it was no longer enough for a member to gripe about a relative, teacher, or employer. More thorough explanations were demanded and the process of mutual exploration was furthered.

Since it was anticipated that the change from the one-to-one method to the group would be a trying one for the members, it was agreed that individual contact would be continued in the initial phase of the project. It was difficult to predict whether the men could adjust to the group situation, and it was of considerable help to the leader to be able to check their reactions with their workers, since in the beginning they were quite hesitant in expressing any reactions to the group itself. This arrangement had a serious disadvantage in that members could use it to avoid working in the group, bringing their serious concerns to their individual workers. However, for these men, who were so afraid of getting their feet wet, the advantage of holding on to the individual treatment outweighed the disadvantage.

Transitional Phase

As the members began to share observations about their previous psychiatric and casework treatment, simultaneously struggling with the transition from the one-to-one to the group therapy milieu, they began to resist the more intensive direction in treatment. Indicative of this was their difficulty in trusting each other and the leader.

When one of the members asked, "What would happen if I should meet my worker at a public meeting or social gathering?" he was describing the group's struggle with the transition from individual to group treatment. This struggle was revealed even more clearly in the group's testing of leadership, which continued throughout the first year. At first each session began with a long, difficult silence, punctuated by sighs and occasional questionings about where the group had left off last week. In subsequent meetings, this was followed by questioning the confidentiality of their sessions, the minutes that the leader kept, and whether group members talked to others outside about the people they had met in the group. Finally, the group itself made several attempts at keeping records to enable it to begin working more quickly.

In the beginning of the second year the question of the leader's taking a long vacation evoked a great deal of discussion about the effect on the group of his absence. Also discussed was the question of whether the group should continue meeting without a leader. Feelings of hostility were freely expressed and opened the way for the members to discuss their fears. One said that without a leader he was afraid that others in the group would dominate and not give him a chance to speak up. This person had frequently dominated others and the group was quick in pointing out his projection. They resolved to assume responsible leadership for themselves and decided to continue meeting during the summer.

The early signs of resistance and defensiveness diminished as the group began to feel more comfortable with each other and with the leader. It was time to begin setting the stage for the working phase of the group. The content of the discussions still related primarily to the on-going life experiences outside the group, and the leader's goal at this stage—to help members stabilize their environment—was being achieved.

The members were now able to relate their difficulties in the educational and employment situations to the personal problems that had precipitated their need for therapy. At this point a member's description of an unfair boss was no longer accepted at face value. Members began to question each other about what *they* might have done to provoke their employers or fellow employees, and how they could prevent such conflicts in the future.

Bert, for instance, had a very difficult time in finding suitable employment. It seemed no job ever satisfied his need for recognition and self-confidence. He registered in a night course to advance his employment potential. Halfway through, he wanted to quit school in discouragement. The group strongly supported his continuing and he was able to finish with passing grades. However, he was still unable to approach jobs with confidence and he continued to bemoan his fate. The group was irritated and one member was able to take responsibility in helping Bert by asking some pointed questions. What, he asked, did Bert think was the effect on the group of the way in which Bert presented his problems? Bert reflected, and said that he really made it impossible for the group to respond except in a belittling way and that this was the only way that it had ever been possible for him to obtain any kind of response from his immediate family. He was then helped to see that he was confusing the group with his family and that it was because of his prolonged conditioning that he was eliciting such a negative response from the group.

Bert himself was able to develop this insight further and began to reflect about his expectations from work; he finally concluded that jobs were not satisfying to him because he was continually expecting that a job could offset all the negative feelings he had harbored within himself over the years.

As their everyday functioning improved, the group's resistance to more intensive treatment was revived. Members began to question the purpose of the group, signaling their hesitancy in proceeding further. It seemed clear that the group members would be unable to invest more if they continued to receive concurrent individual treatment. Natural points of terminating individual treatment, such as a worker's leaving the agency or transfer to another district within the agency were utilized. Provision for individual conferences with the group leader were made on an "as needed" basis, the focus being to enable members to bring their concerns back to the group.

During the period following the decision to terminate individual treatment, the group again considered itself as a laboratory "to see ourselves as others see us." The members became less preoccupied with their everyday vocational adjustment or the *modus operandi* of the group. They now turned their attention to more active participation and examination of their own interactions and interrelationships. At this point, one of the group brought in as a new member a friend whose level of achievement was considered more mature than that of the group members. It was this member who ultimately became the prime force in stimulating the group in the working phase of treatment.

The Working Phase

The group began to travel an unfamiliar road. As long as it was possible to discuss concrete issues the members were not at a loss for words. Now, out of their anxiety, they began testing each other and, of course, the leader. Was the leader one of them, or was he an autocratic boss? Could they really trust each other, or would they walk over each other, exploit each other? Such questions abounded and had to be handled in the group. As the leader I had to be not only with the group but ahead of it (for that is implicit in sound leadership), and help its members relate to the universal, underlying feelings of fear and change. A member's reluctance to pay the fee was an example of this. When a fee was first discussed in the group, it was related to the wish for greater investment, not to the question of the fee as such.

The personality of the leader figured very prominently during this stage. As a defense, a client often endows his therapist with omnipotent qualities. As long as the therapist is seen as an all-knowing, powerful person, the client can avoid taking responsibility for himself. Therefore, it was important that the leader recognize the group's reaction and, at the same time, take stock of himself during this crucial period. At one point when I was under severe personal stress, my leadership of the group was affected adversely. As a result the group members believed that *they* were making mistakes, that *they* were not working hard enough. It was, therefore, important that I share with them what had happened to me and how this had affected my leadership, so that they could understand and proceed without feelings of guilt and anxiety.

As the group moved into the main working phase, the activity of the leader diminished noticeably. The members used material and content from the group situation itself. How did what one member said or did in the group affect another member in the group? Why were other members unable to accept the explanation offered to them so that they could modify some of their thinking? Why was it necessary for one member to act like Mr. Know-It-All, another like Mr. Pessimist, another to be ingratiating at all cost, and still another to rebuff all closeness and understanding? Such questions were the tools by which the group's work was carried out. The themes worked on during this interactional phase of treatment concerned the illusions and misconceptions that members had about themselves and, consequently, about each other.

Marvin, age 23, had been an autistic child and continued to function on a very primitive level, although he was able to hold jobs, albeit for very brief periods of time. The group, while accepting his severe limitations, repeatedly helped him to test reality, especially in his relationships to authority figures. The pattern of repeating his ambivalent relationship with his father and mother became very clear in the group, and examples of this behavior were offered to him over and over again, so that eventually he could separate some of his distortions from the current reality and function better in relation to employers.

A more detailed picture of the group during this working phase of treatment can be seen in the following description of the conscious use of the interaction through which group members clarified and resolved their resistance to treatment.

Andy, 27, was very obese and looked older than his real age. He appeared highly disturbed and expressed feelings of being persecuted and downtrodden. Graduation from college had failed to eradicate his poor self-image. An only child, whose mother had died ten years previously, he came from a rural area where his father eked out a meager existence. After two years of individual treatment, Andy was still a very solitary and isolated individual who needed to prove to himself repeatedly that the world was a hostile place and that any attempts on his part to gain recognition were doomed. Efforts to work through some of these difficulties in individual treatment only aroused intense anger and a redoubling of his defenses. It was felt that he might make greater gains in the group situation. He readily agreed and became one of the charter members.

In the group setting Andy initially proceeded on the assumption that no one else's troubles in life had been as great as his. He had ready solutions for other members' problems. The group quickly sensed that Andy was merely expounding, attempting to settle everyone else's difficulties without looking at his own. The group, it seemed, was violating in every way his mode of operating; whereas Andy, in the past, had been able to bluster his way through almost any opposition, he now found a more formidable adversary. The group questioned his vacillating and his choice of employment, his setting very high goals for himself on the one hand, yet continuing to work at a menial job on the other. He defended himself, saying that, if he left his job it would be like "being cast adrift," and the group took an extremely active part in exploring with him what he meant by this. They were direct, but they were kind, too, and, most important, they were very much like him. Through this influence came his growing awareness that his own feelings of inadequacy were playing a large part in his staying on a menial job. He tried ineffectively several times to leave the job. The group members finally told him that his trouble was that he was in error about himself in thinking that this job was good enough for him. Quite precipitously he left the job and took a better paying one, although it was just as menial. He continued, however, to represent a stumbling block to the group, and members next began to question him in other areas. They wanted to move ahead but they showed that they were trying to pull Andy along with them.

Discussion of fee payment had been initiated by one of the members, who felt it was a tangible way of investing more in the group and would stimulate more meaningful participation by all the members. Andy spoke up in a voice half-challenging and half-resigned, saying if everyone agreed to pay a fee, it would mean that he would have to leave the group since he could not go into debt. Actually, he was making as much money as anyone in the group. When this fact was pointed out, he replied that if members paid fees, everyone would expect to get more out of the group and it would be bedlam, with everyone trying to dominate. Andy fretted about why so much time was spent in discussing his problems. Again he was challenged, several members saying there were only one or two occasions when, in talking about his family relations, he had really talked about his problems; money and debts were only his symptoms. Under pressure, Andy was willing to pay a fee, but the group felt that the issue was really whether he wanted to belong, whether he had ever really joined the group on anyone's terms except his own, whether, in other words, he had ever really tried to get along with the others.

Andy did not appear for the next two sessions and the group understood that, behind the excuses he made for his absence, he had not really been able to solve his problems with the group and that perhaps they would have to continue without him to do the work they had outlined. Upon his return, the group accepted his unwillingness to pay a fee and stated that each member would pay part of his fee for the time being. To Andy, this was a tangible demonstration of concern about his problems and willingness to accept him without loss of face so that he could continue to come.

Three weeks later Andy appeared, dressed for the first time in a business suit and tie, looking quite respectable and announcing that he had obtained a job in an accounting office. He now wanted to pay his own fee and insisted on paying up for those sessions in which the group had paid his share.

Another member who had most closely identified with me as leader examined his need to do so in the group, and felt, as a result of his having appointed himself the natural leader in the group, he had in effect put on a mask that he could not take off even when he wanted to. He pointed out occasions when he had expressed considerable emotion about himself, which the group had patently ignored. Furthermore, when I came to terms with my own tendency to use this member as an assistant to myself and clarified this with the group, he was freed immensely by the clarification of his status as a group member, and was able to proceed in working on his own problems.

This important phase in the group treatment, focused on the interaction of members, was a prolonged and intensive one. The relationship that had developed among the members was based on a more mature, empathic feeling than the earlier relationship, which was primarily a feeling of all being in the same boat. As their feeling of closeness grew, the leader directed the focus toward carrying this new found ability into more satisfying and appropriate relationships outside the group. This, in turn, inevitably led to the terminating phase of treatment.

Terminal Phase

The terminal phase of the group began about halfway through the third year when the members were showing signs that they were becoming more involved in social and recreational activities outside the group. One member was reinstated in the college from which he had been dismissed prior to joining the group, and this meant his moving out of town. Another member became interested in amateur theatricals and found that this made him unavailable for group meetings. A third left the squalid room he had occupied for several years to move to the suburbs where he could be nearer friends, relatives, and a better job. Members were becoming interested in trying out their wings, and termination was suggested by the leader.

The reaction to the introduction of this topic was generally a constructive one, although, as one might expect, there was initial avoidance of the topic and temporary regressions occurred. As the group overcame its reluctance to face this issue, members became able to consider the idea of termination versus interruption. Several members felt they preferred termination to interruption, because they would never rise to the occasion of actually trying their wings if there were a possibility of the group's being reborn. They did not, however, preclude the idea of joining other treatment groups for different purposes, groups perhaps including women as well as men.

Members discussed whether they wanted to meet socially after the formal termination, and this suggestion was ruled out on the

188

basis of the majority sentiment that to continue social group association would be to defeat the basic purpose of the treatment group. They expressed their conviction that the group was not set up to supply them with a substitute experience, but to encourage them to discover why they were unable to form their own social relationships with their own acquaintances and friends.

Although it may be impossible for the group or leader to tie up all the loose ends, this final phase, as ideally in all treatment, offered an opportunity for further growth. The group now reviewed its history and its objectives, and decided on its manner of terminating. The leader had to be alert to signs of regression and able to identify the members' inevitable feelings of loss and fear about what life would be like without either individual or group treatment. The sustaining force at this point stemmed from the new and more profitable social associations of the members, their improved employment status and, most of all, their newly found confidence.

Conclusion

This paper has described group treatment of a number of unattached men with defective ego functioning. Prior to their participation in group treatment, these men had had prolonged and rather unproductive psychiatric or casework treatment, characterized by excessive dependence on their therapists.

As selected by relatively simple criteria, the group seemed to offer meager potential for effective group treatment. It should be pointed out that no amount of careful selection could have ruled out the two members who dropped out of the group precipitously in the first two months. The first of these, a man who had been seen for a long period in individual casework because of severe feelings of inferiority resulting in chronic unemployment, attended a few group meetings and participated quite appropriately. He obtained a position involving extensive travel and was therefore unable to attend further meetings. The other man, who had been previously hospitalized during psychotic episodes, needed further hospitalization when he suffered several severe stresses in his environment, despite the fact that he had been one of the most outgoing, socially active members of the group. When one of the members reached out to a friend and the group included the latter as a member, the value of a more heterogeneous group was demonstrated.

What factors enabled this group of frightened, hostile, unsuccessful men to respond to the group treatment method?

The group offered these clients an enriching experience while reducing the over-stimulation of dependency needs which is a typical phenomenon of the passive character disorder personality in individual treatment. In other words, the group was used as a method of *weaning*. It goes without saying that, like parents, caseworkers may have ambivalent feelings about letting those who depend on them become weaned, and the leader always must keep in mind that weaning is a process of growth, not rejection.

The emphasis throughout was on the ego strengths, those areas in which the ego was able to cope successfully, rather than on the weaknesses. Moreover, the group ego is stronger than the sum of its individual parts and thus lends its strength to the individual members. Belonging to the group was in itself a form of achievement. This achievement was as significant as the relearning process that accompanied it.

Although the work pace in the initial phases was slow, there was an almost immediate focusing on reality at a more adult level than had previously been reached in individual treatment. The anxiety created by the intense personal relationship of individual casework was diminished as each individual's relationship with the leader was diluted through the process of group sharing, thus encouraging the abandonment of infantile preoccupations. As in all treatment groups, the main working phase focused on the interchange between members—how they affected each other, how they acted toward each other, what their unexpressed feelings were, the forces that interfered with their working, and the forces that promoted their working together. It was in the stimulation and examination of this interchange that the treatment and the helping process took place.

11. Psychodynamics of Protective Casework *

Irving Kaufman

PROTECTIVE CASEWORK OCCURS in the context of a special form of parent-child-community relationships. Protective services are occasioned by pathology that represents a simultaneous threat to the child and to the community itself. While the community sets the standards for acceptable, desirable, and necessary parent-child behavior, the caseworker offering protective services, as a member and representative of the community, must present these values and standards to the client in a therapeutically meaningful way. Therefore, the symptomatology with which the caseworker deals has to be considered not only in terms of intra-psychic conflict and of parent-child pathology, but also in terms of the relationship of the disturbed family to the community. Since these diverse points of reference present a challenge to the integrative capacity of the caseworker, some observations on the multiple roles of the caseworker in this field of forces may be helpful. A formulation of the function of the worker, stemming from the nature of the problems most commonly encountered in protective casework, will be followed by a discussion of the treatment implications for work with certain of these parents and children.

* This article, based on the author's experience as a psychiatric consultant to the Massachusetts Society for the Prevention of Cruelty to Children, is an extension and reformulation of an earlier paper, "The Contribution of Protective Services," *Child Welfare*, Vol. XXXVI, No. 2 (1957), pp. 8–13.

The Pathology of the Parent

One of the characteristics of protective casework is that, with very few exceptions, the caseworker initiates the service. There are sound dynamic principles involved in this procedure. The service is directed to clients whose disturbances manifest themselves not only in gross symptomatology but also in an inability to initiate and take responsibility for the continuity of treatment. Indeed, the most conspicuous feature about protective casework is the degree of ego pathology in the parents. Their pathological functioning, obvious to every observer, is expressed in both the parent-child relationship and in their lack of control over their own impulses.

Among the most frequently recurring, interrelated manifestations of pathology in the parents is regression or fixation at infantile levels of functioning. Many of these parents are disorderly, disorganized, dependent, hostile, and demanding. They tend to operate on the pleasure principle. Their primitive level of functioning is also reflected in poor reality testing. Unable to learn by experience, they cannot plan for themselves and their children. Immediate gratification of their own impulses dominates their behavior. For example, a mother who does not feel like shopping may not do so and seems unable to anticipate that there will be no breakfast for the family or to be concerned about it. Poor reality testing includes an inability to view the child as a child and to meet his physical and emotional needs. In some cases, actual psychoses in the parents are found. They lack the normal methods that most people use to cope with the stresses of living. Their object relationships, though often intense, are on a primitive plane, most frequently that of hostile dependence. They behave as though motivated by the concept, "What can I get?" Their oral fixation shows itself in many ways, including alcoholism and depressions. Such persons tend to act out their impulses through promiscuity and other forms of anti-social behavior.

A Topographical Model for Protective Services

These parents live in a community which determines the standards of acceptable behavior for parents and children and defines appropriate interaction between them. It is well to recognize that such standards are fluid and dynamic and vary tremendously from place to place and from time to time. In a sense, however, the community functions as does the superego of an individual, with its standards, values, moral code, ideals of behavior, and conscience. A protective agency is an extension of the community and a special representative of it. Such an agency must also make superego evaluations; protective casework is thus judgmental, for example, in determining the adequacy of parent-child functioning. However, this is only part of the protective agency's role. A more accurate simile might be that the agency's role is like that of the ego, which, in psychoanalytic thinking, includes the superego. The agency must do the reality testing; it must also evaluate the strengths and weaknesses in a given situation, and, finally, it must determine the necessary course of action. If the function of the agency is comparable to the role of the ego and superego in an individual, then it would seem appropriate to compare the client's behavior to the id impulses. These id manifestations have broken loose in the community, to the detriment of the client and of his child.

If we consider the agency and the client as a unit in which id, ego, and superego co-exist as they do in an individual, then the agency, as the ego of the client, must judge the pathology according to the standards of the community and its culture. It must not only convey these facts to the client but also help him to absorb and integrate them so that he is able to modify his pathology. The agency tries to achieve this aim by offering the client a new ego ideal and, even more importantly, by alleviating the parent's own feeling of deprivation through its accepting, mothering role. Only then can the parent achieve a community-syntonic behavior pattern. Is it necessary to add that the agency's task is not an easy one?

Diagnostic Groupings

There are two major groupings in the classical neglect and abuse patterns seen in protective casework. In practice these may be found to co-exist in the same family.

Disturbances in some parents are manifest as an *absence* of adequate parental functioning and are expressed by neglect, abandonment, or inadequate control and management of the child. This inability to fulfil an acceptable parental role may result from organic

193

brain damage, feeble-mindedness, incapacitating physical illness, psychoses, or lack of adequate emotional development in the parents. Treatment of this group of cases will be dealt with later in this paper.

In a second major grouping of cases the parents show the presence of a special kind of unhealthy interaction with a child—that is, the child has a special *pathological* meaning to the parents, or the parents use the child to act out their own conflicts. Sometimes the parent places the child in the parental role because of his own infantile needs. The parent may identify a child with a rejected part of himself or with another rejected family member. The child then bears the brunt of the displaced feelings. Sometimes the parent feels a special hostility toward a child because the birth of the child or some other event in his life is particularly associated with a traumatic event for the parent. For example, when a mother dies in childbirth, the child may be treated with hostility because of his association with the death of the mother.

In some cases the parent himself was abandoned or abused and mistreated. Often such a parent will attempt to resolve his own anxiety through the ego mechanism of identification with the aggressor and the repetition compulsion. He will then repeat the pattern by abandoning or abusing his own child. The parent, in his attempt to work out his own conflicting wishes about delinquent behavior through the child, may stimulate the child to act out his delinquent wishes and then punish him for doing so. In some situations a parent acts out directly or symbolically his sexual and aggressive wishes through the child, as illustrated by the following example:

A family, consisting of a mother, 29, her 8-year-old son, and the maternal grandmother, 62, came to the attention of a protective agency through a report that the mother left the child all day while she stayed out with drinking companions. The grandmother's complaints that the responsibility for the child was left to her seemed well-founded. There was continual debate about the rearing of the child. The mother wanted to rear him as an independent person and gave him very little attention or affection although she attended to his physical needs. The grandmother resented the mother's callous treatment of the boy and said that the mother was no good and should be confined to an institution. During her adolescence, a child guidance clinic had recommended

194

that the mother "needed protection from herself and her impulses, and society needed protection from her." The mother was aware of the feelings of the maternal grandmother. She had expressed her dislike of authority from any source, bragged about her various escapades with the law, and felt she would try to get away with things whenever possible. She repeatedly mentioned her strong attachment to her father and her dislike of her mother, saying she was bad because of the maternal grandmother.

For ten years the mother had been involved with a man who could never marry her because his wife refused to divorce him. The child was attached to this man and unrealistically regarded him as his father. The mother feared losing her lover because of her wild temper; she was on a year's probation for damaging his car while in a rage. She had threatened him with physical harm and had made suicide attempts.

From limited observation, the child was found to be quite anxious and openly rebellious toward both mother and grandmother.

Study of the family suggested that the grandmother identified the mother with the bad part of herself and the mother reacted by pathologically acting out the bad self of the grandmother. She did not know how to get the affection that she craved. She had been aggressive and destructive in her behavior toward her lover, smashing his car and conceiving the boy illegitimately to spite him. Her devices for getting attention by bad behavior were infantile. She saw this married, middle-aged man who had become a pseudo-father to her primarily in the role of protector. In this relationship she was reliving the earlier father-daughter role, repeating the process of taking this man away from his wife as she, symbolically at least, took her father away from her mother.

In her relationship with her mother there appeared to be mutual rejection and a hostile dependence. The grandmother "knew" the mother would be bad because she wanted her to be. She thought of herself as completely good and the mother as completely bad. She identified the mother with the bad part of herself and was punishing that part of herself through her rejection and criticism of the mother. By remaining in a situation which on a conscious level was uncomfortable for them both, these women were meeting each other's neurotic needs.

This mother was too involved with her own problems to be able to meet the emotional needs of her child. Her fantasies about making him independent referred to her own needs and did not take the child into consideration. Her callous attitude toward the boy reflected the way she had been treated and, in this sense, represented an identification with the aggressor. In addition, while still involved in her struggle with her mother and search for a father-figure, she tended to treat her child as an incestuous product; as a result she had confused and distorted attitudes toward him.

For this group of cases, in which the pathology is based on the special symbolic meaning of the child, the treatment takes a form familiar to all clinicians. However, the client who demonstrates a lack of parental functioning requires a special restitutional type of treatment. As we have said, clinical features of both groupings are often apparent in the same cases. Moreover, many of the techniques of treatment are similar.

Treatment of the Inadequate Parent

Many of the parents in this group are extremely infantile. The caseworker who goes into the home has the opportunity to help these parents work out a routine of living. The caseworker thus assumes the role of autonomous ego for these parents. He adopts a kindly but firm, supportive, parental role. He helps the parent to work out day-by-day activities, suggesting both areas of gratification and necessary limits. We often find that, as these parents receive such attention, they are better able to function as parents to their children and as citizens of their community.

The actual casework technique—confronting the parents with the concept that behavior such as abuse and neglect of children creates a community reaction—has a dynamic significance of its own because a part of the parent is also identified with the child. Although almost all of the parents express a certain amount of resentment and hostility at the idea of being questioned and criticized, it is amazing to see how many indicate quite directly their relief and gratitude for the help given to them.

A most extreme example of a parent's cry for help is illustrated in a case in which a telephone call was received reporting abuse of a child. When the caseworker discussed the call with the mother, the latter revealed that she herself had called the agency because she was in despair about her ability to control her hostile outbursts

196

toward the child and because of her own unresolved needs. A review of the source of referrals of the cases seen at one protective agency revealed that an impressive number of referrals actually came from children's parents.[1] Even the referrals from the spouse who was out of the home were assumed to be that parent's way of asking for help; hence we have concluded that the complaining parent should also be included in any treatment plan. In many instances, part of the absent parent's wish was to establish or re-establish an adequately functioning family unit.

However, when the caseworker passes through the initial phase of the parent's hostility and achieves his acceptance of the need for therapy, this does not mean that all then goes along smoothly. There usually are many regressions and resurgences of hostility and acting out during the course of treatment. The worker's capacity to deal with hostility in a non-vindictive way and to continue to offer his help represents one of the most important aspects of treatment. Part of the ambivalence of these clients about being involved in a treatment relationship is based on their lack of trust and the fear that they will again be hurt. The resistance to change is related to the basic depression which these people are handling in their relationship with the child; this depression is based on the absence of a satisfactory parent-child experience in their lives. Since these parents are acting out the pathological parent-child reactions they have experienced, it is understandable that they also want to interrupt the traumatic relationship they are repeating with their child and replace it with a different kind of interaction. The worker's frustration in working with such severely disturbed clients can be balanced by the gratification of seeing definite and concrete changes in the parents and their management of the home.

Before a caseworker can serve as an effective auxiliary ego to an inadequate parent, several conditions must be met. The parent must somehow be engaged in a meaningful way; that is, the caseworker must become a reality to the parent. The worker must represent a continuing, stable, and predictable force to the parent. Further, to serve as an effective ego the worker must demonstrate effectiveness in those areas that are important to the parent. As

[1] Unpublished report, Massachusetts Society for the Prevention of Cruelty to Children, Boston, May, 1962.

we know, the ego becomes "visible" when actively engaged in coping efforts. Hence the worker must make his presence felt by activity. The treatment required by most of these parents and their children can be accomplished only by going out to them. Bewildered by the disruptive forces that have swept over them, many of these parents need the protection and reality framework supplied by the caseworker's firm, clear, and consistent stand, in order to begin functioning realistically.

It is not possible to overemphasize both the importance and the dynamic significance of the worker's provision of auxiliary ego strength. People who are severely depressed are not ready in the early stages of contact to deal with such questions as their relationship to their own parents, sibling rivalry, and oedipal conflicts. The definitive casework technique indicated with such parents includes going into the home and reviewing in considerable detail the reality plans of the day. What time do they wake up? What do they and their children have for breakfast? What time do the children leave for school? This procedure does not mean that the parents do not know the answers to the reality questions. They know intellectually what time to wake up. They are, however, emotionally unable to cope with the problems because of their own disturbances. The caseworker is supplying his ego and super-ego to the parent until the parent can incorporate the concept that someone cares, and can develop the psychic strength to deal with the underlying depression.

Some therapists feel that talking about the budget or a trip to the dentist is not "dynamic" and therefore is of "a lower professional status." However, if the therapy is to be meaningful to the orally-fixated, acting-out, depressed patients of the type described here, it must be geared through communication that is understandable to them. Therefore, any one who wishes to help the patient, whether his training be in psychoanalysis, casework, or psychology, will have to relate to the patient in the way that enables a therapeutically meaningful type of communication to develop. The workers' concern about the technique of therapy is analogous to the anxiety some people feel about modifications in technique used in therapy with children. In working with children, therapists found that play techniques were necessary as the media for communication. We now know that playing with toys does not in itself cure the child, but unless the therapist is willing to relate to and work with the child in a way that has meaning to the child, he may not be able to reach him.

Following the initial period of relating to the basic reality problems, there is a long period of testing out. Often cases are terminated just before or during this phase. Obviously, an auxiliary ego that abdicates its functions offers little help to the parent; instead the worker may, by withdrawing, heighten the parent's sense of vulnerability and his destructive self-defeating management efforts. If, however, the parent can be supported through this testing-out phase, he will be ready for the more familiar techniques used in working out depressions. Such clients with severe character disorders are generally long-term cases with many set-backs and regressions.

For another group of parents who show failure in adequate parental functioning, but whose fixations are at anal-sadistic or possibly at oedipal levels, treatment involves the more usual verbal discussion of the client's problems. The treatment process in these cases is often much shorter. The particularly arduous problems encountered in initiating and maintaining therapy with the orally regressed client are illustrated in the following case.

The family, known to the agency for three years, consisted of the mother, 40, and her three children, Mary, 19, Nora, 15, and Olive, 7. The husband, who had been living separately, had died. Two older children, a girl of 21 and a 19-year-old boy, had also died within the past six years. This family was first referred to the protective agency because of the mother's heavy drinking and the children's truanting from school. The mother was receiving Aid to Dependent Children and the family was also known to the probation officer. Study of the home at that time indicated a neglect complaint was not warranted.

At a later date a neighbor informed the worker that the mother had been drinking heavily for two weeks and was in a very bad state. While the mother was out at night, the girls had boys in the house with whom they went down to the cellar. The probation officer accompanied the caseworker to the home where they found the mother very sick, hands trembling, extremely dirty and disheveled, crawling out from under the bed. The bedroom was filthy—the bare mattress soaking wet, bottles lying under the bed, and rags strewn about the room. Unpleasant odors permeated the house. Unsuccessful efforts were made to get the mother to the hospital for treatment. Conditions in the home improved somewhat when Mary left school to help care for the younger children.

Three months later the mother was arrested for drunkenness. She was given a suspended sentence and six months' probation, during which she improved.

Within the year a new complaint was made: the mother was deteriorating and the children were not receiving any care. Mary had to stay at home to prevent the mother's harming herself or the children. She again refused hospitalization for psychiatric help. She soiled herself and her bed and threw lighted cigarettes at the wall. The home was again found in a chaotic, filthy condition.

Study revealed considerable deterioration in the mother's functioning. On the advice of the court psychiatrist, the mother was committed to the state hospital for observation. The children were placed with a maternal aunt, and the case was continued for a later court hearing. The state hospital reported that the mother was not committable. She was diagnosed as having a manic-depressive psychosis, depressed type; her condition was considered the result of chronic excessive drinking. The mother was found guilty of neglect and placed on probation for one year. The children were allowed to return home. While under close supervision, the mother ceased drinking for almost an entire year, the home conditions improved, and the children received more adequate care.

The case was reopened by the agency because of a complaint from the court that the mother was again drinking heavily. She was seen panhandling on the streets and in taverns. Home conditions and the children's school attendance were again very poor. The children lacked supervision.

The caseworker started to work with the family and was able to help the mother discontinue drinking, improve physical conditions in the home, and supervise her children better. Following the caseworker's contact, the mother went on only one brief drinking spree. She was very accepting of the caseworker and looked forward to his visits. She took more active interest in her apartment, illustrated by the purchasing of new furniture for the living room, painting and whitewashing the kitchen, putting curtains on the windows and giving the entire apartment a more consistent type of care. The mother also showed an interest in her own appearance by having a permanent, using cosmetics, and making plans to be fitted for false teeth. Mary, recently married, was living in the apartment below her mother's. Though the mother depended heavily on Mary, Mary's marriage did not precipitate her into another drinking spree. Nora was attending high school and seemed to be taking more active interest in school now that she had a more secure home life.

This case demonstrates clearly that when a protective supervisory figure acting as an auxiliary ego was in the picture, the mother was able to function more adequately and give more to her children. Each time the case was closed or the protective work of either of the agencies was interrupted, the mother regressed to drinking and neglecting her home and children. The basic depression underlying her disturbed behavior and her potential capacity for more adequate functioning were also clearly demonstrated.

Treatment of the Children

Since the abusive treatment of the child by the parents is usually the reason agency activity is initiated, the child is a central part of the entire process from the very beginning. He needs, first, to be helped to understand what is going on and then to deal with his own feelings. Another basic consideration is that the child is entitled to help in his own right.

Disturbed parents obviously constitute poor models for identification and, as such, create seriously distorted concepts in the minds of their children. Unless children can use their own parents as models, there is no reason to expect that they will understand how to be parents themselves. In the absence of some form of preventive intervention, it is unlikely that these children will locate and identify with appropriate parental figures. Since deviant behavior involving abuse, neglect, and instinctual acting out is in contrast with the cultural ideal of loving, protective, parental care, the lives of these children are constantly at variance with the reality demands of the community. Their own reality orientation, in this sense, is disturbed as well as their concept of how parents should function.

The pathological behavior in the parents produces disturbances in the children's control of their instinctual drives. The children suffer both from the poor example provided by these parents and from the lack of incentive to give up immediate gratification. Unfortunately, the community often rejects these children and treats them as unwanted elements. The community response, which shows intolerance for lack of instinctual control, leaves the children at a loss as to how they should act. Thus they are subjected to unpleasant pressures from inside and outside the home.

The caseworker has an opportunity to be of considerable help to these children by representing the forces of social reality and the necessary disapproval of pathological elements in the parent-child relationship. He acts as an agent of the community which is expressing both its disapproval of the behavior of the parents and the desire to rehabilitate the parents and children. Within this framework he represents the new good parent who will set limits and foster more suitable avenues for the expression of the emotional and instinctual needs of the parents and children.

While the caseworker is the representative of the community, which may look upon the behavior of the parents and the resulting activities of the children in moralistic terms, he is also a professional person who regards these people as sick and in need of help. He must define his professional position to the parents, the children, and to the community. He must see that the children are provided with the necessities of life, protected from physical abuse and the hostility of the community, as well as given an opportunity for normal emotional development. Often the first need in protective help to children is for a stable environment where the physical and emotional needs of the children can be met. Efforts to meet this need may include casework treatment of the parents and children, arrangements for placement, or hospitalization. The protective worker encounters these clients at points of major crisis in their lives, the management of which may be decisive for their future. The skill required by the professional personnel who do such work must not be underestimated.

Sometimes, when there is great pressure for action and the child is placed outside his home, one gets a sharp reminder of the need to work through the underlying parent-child relationship conflict as much as possible. Some children who are placed in a setting where they receive good care run back to their own parents even though they were abused and neglected by them. When such a placement problem occurs, it tends to identify the agency as opposed to the parents. Since the child typically introjects his parents, with all their behavior patterns, as part of himself, criticism of the parent is felt by the child as an attack on him. If, from

202

the beginning, the worker's role is not defined in terms of his interest in the welfare of the whole family, there is a tendency to solidify the pathological aspect of the parent-child interaction. This interferes with the ability of parent or child to deal with the basic emotional disturbances that are producing the symptomatology.

Like their parents, children sometimes show relief and even pleasure when the worker steps in and interrupts the pathological process in the family. When children are fully aware of the existence of pathology in the home and want help, they frequently appear entirely accepting of this help on initial encounter. The ambivalence generally is expressed later. Even in an initial contact, however, some management of attitudes and feelings of the children about the pathology can be undertaken. It is neither possible nor desirable to deny the existence of problems. The worker in effect, then, clarifies verbally or non-verbally, with the children as well as the parents, that the disturbed behavior is unhealthy and undesirable. Children commonly know that in some way this is true.

Children who are caught in such disturbed situations have to deal with their guilt, their fear and anxiety, and their hostility. Much of the fear and anxiety is based on the reality threats, and the hostility is related, among other things, to the sense of deprivation. Some of the guilt arises from the feeling these children often express as to whether all the trouble is caused by their having been bad. It is often phrased, "Am I to blame? Is this why mother and father don't love me?" Many of these children express their guilt through the need for punishment and the attempt to gain reassurance and forgiveness in this way. Another source of guilt springs from the hostility that the parents stimulate in these children. Neglect, abuse, and deprivation make these children angry. The anger, in turn, frightens them and then they often feel that the parents neglect them because of the "bad" hostility in the child. Such a vicious circle often has no solution outside of therapy.

In relating to the child, the worker finds himself in a particularly difficult role. If he discusses with the child the disturbance in his parents, he has to deal with the emotion this arouses in the child—anxiety, hostility, and depression. The child often views the worker simultaneously as the bearer of bad tidings, object of hostility, and substitute parent. Of course, the exact way in which this complicated problem can be handled varies with the special circumstances of the given situation as well as with the worker's experience in dealing with emotional disturbances in children. The child must be allowed to express his hostility and at the same time be protected from becoming drowned in a sea of guilt or self-pity. The worker lets the child know that he can be liked, even with all of his "bad" feelings, and that the necessary controls do not represent punishment.

The child who is expressing his hostility about his parents may at the same time feel he, too, is bad because he comes from them and is like them. The only hope of overcoming this difficulty with or without insight therapy lies in the long sustained relationship with an adequate parent figure, permitting the child to build up a new ego ideal. This includes learning that he can select those qualities from his parents which are to his advantage and incorporate other qualities from other sources. It may be helpful if the worker can convey the idea that the parents are not bad, but are sick and need help; they do not know how to be good parents because they did not have good parents themselves and the worker is trying to help them in every possible way.

A child's reaction to the disturbance in the home frequently includes denial and pseudo-maturity. It is particularly disconcerting to see a child who has handled severe problems, such as those associated with alcoholic parents, gross open promiscuity, beating and hunger, fall apart when he is placed in a home where none of this gross pathology occurs. Disruptive behavior is another manifestation of the hostility that erupts when the caseworker or foster parent attempts to build a relationship with the child. One can anticipate such hostile reactions and be psychologically prepared for them, in order to keep to a minimum any counter-hostility as well as to supply adequate controls.

When some reasonable degree of environmental stability, preferably in the child's home, is achieved, the child tends to regress and express direct hostility. This is analogous to the testing-out phase of the parent. Much skill is required in order to remain firm and consistent during this process. Some of the excessive hostility of this stage can be slightly reduced by stressing activity programs (such as trips to buy clothes and going to baseball games) before definitive treatment of the underlying depression is attempted.

Where available and indicated, treatment directed to the underlying character disorder is the next step for the child. In some instances this can be started early in the relationship. Some children will have to be treated in a controlled, therapeutic environment. In other cases combined treatment by the caseworker and the psychiatrist is most effective. This division of responsibility enables the approach to reality control and the approach to fantasy to occur in separate settings.

Summary

A consideration of the inadequacy and pathology presented by the characterologically disordered families who come to the attention of the protective agency has suggested the appropriateness of an analogy to mental topography; to be helpful the caseworker must become, for a time, an effective auxiliary ego for the parent and the child. Viewed in these terms, the caseworker's task with the parent is to help develop modes of functioning which accommodate the impulses of the client, reality demands, and community standards. The optimal focus for such efforts will often be the simple, practical routines of daily life. In work with the child, the task is the difficult one of altering his relationship to his parent without destroying the necessary and constructive elements within it. By introjecting an accepting but realistic view of parental capacity, the child's needs, and community expectations, and by providing protection for the child in spite of his regression and hostility, the worker may initiate in the child a constructive redefinition of self.

12. Testing Dynamic Casework in India*

Helen Pinkus

THE EXPORTABILITY OF social work in the American tradition is now undergoing a practical test. Services that were tailored to our domestic needs have been used as models for programs in a number of the newly emerging nations around the globe. These beginnings deserve careful study since they can help in devising a strategy for our further professional contribution to these nations. What elements in the knowledge, skill, and values that comprise American social work are relevant to the welfare problems in underdeveloped countries?

Many observers have agreed that community organization and group work methods can play a vital role in these areas of the world.[1] There is, however, controversy over the usefulness of the casework method in countries with low standards of living, limited opportunity for self-determination, and cultural patterns markedly different from those characteristic of the United States.

Our knowledge about the potentialities of casework in underdeveloped countries is limited. Relatively few American caseworkers have spent prolonged periods in these countries. The

* Based on a paper presented at the Massachusetts Conference on Social Welfare, Boston, November 2, 1960.
[1] Donald S. Howard, "The Common Core of Social Work in Different Countries," *Social Work Journal*, Vol. XXXII, No. 4 (1951), pp. 163–171.

culture shock encountered on brief visits has probably intensified a tendency to emphasize differences rather than focus on similarities in the programs observed. Examination of actual case records of work with individuals in other countries has been limited because of the language barrier and the relatively few case records available. Because of these factors it has been difficult to determine if individuals and families have been helped through casework services, thus indicating that this method has transfer value.

During a two-year period as a faculty member of a school for social work in India, I had the opportunity to observe programs at the operating level, supervise casework students, and review many case records. Such a firsthand look at the modest beginning of casework services in India affords some enlightenment on the question of transferability of the method.

A Glance at the Background

The common picture of India as a vast country, overpopulated and underfed, is accurate. Widely divergent racial, social, religious, and economic groups comprise the population. Within a radius of thirty miles one can see a group of tribal people, wearing loin cloths and hunting with bow and arrow; a small village of mud huts, its inhabitants bound by the many prescriptions and proscriptions of the traditional Hindu community; and a modern city where little boys in Western clothes clamber aboard the school bus. There are fourteen major languages as well as hundreds of dialects. Wide variations in family patterns include the patriarchal joint family in the north, the matriarchal joint family in the south and the ever-increasing number of unitary families in the cities. The nutrition, housing, clothing, and medical care available to the majority of Indians are, by Western standards, inadequate. The caste system has enforced rigid occupational groupings and the transmission from father to son of special tasks and skills. With industrialization, however, the caste system is becoming somewhat more fluid, affording greater opportunity for economic improvement and upward social mobility.

Problems such as illness, dependency, delinquency, homelessness, and marital discord cut across religious, caste, and other social barriers. Prior to the establishment of the Republic of India these problems were handled by missionary groups, voluntary agencies, or individuals dedicated to a life of service. In India, helping others has been a voluntary responsibility for thousands of years.[2]

Although it cannot be implied that India has a large, well-organized group of agencies for the provision of social services, since independence the central (federal) and state governments have taken strong leadership in increasing health and welfare services through both direct public services and grants-in-aid to voluntary organizations. The first graduate school of social work was established in 1936; there are now at least fifteen graduate schools. The number of hospitals and institutional facilities for special medical problems such as tuberculosis and leprosy is increasing. There are over thirty mental hospitals and a growing number of psychiatric clinics. Programs for the rehabilitation of the handicapped and criminal offenders are underway. Family-planning clinics, family agencies, and institutions for children have been established. There is widespread emphasis on maternal and child health facilities. Although foster care is unlikely to develop rapidly within the caste system of the Hindus, it has been undertaken by other religious groups such as the Parsis who do not have the caste system. In short, there are host agencies similar to those in the United States which can, and in some instances do, provide an opportunity for utilization of the casework method. In 1955 the Government of India published a reference book which sketched the historical background of social welfare and social work in India, summarized current resources, and suggested remedial measures. It clearly differentiated social work from social reform and stressed the need for trained personnel in social work. This report not only recognized the need for casework services but emphasized the need for differential diagnosis and treatment.[3]

The growth in casework programs is not comparable to the nationwide expansion in programs for community development. Community development, although not social work *per se,* has drawn

[2] Evelyn Hersey, "Social and Economic Factors in India's Welfare Program," *Social Casework,* Vol. XXXII, No. 7 (1951), p. 301.
[3] *Social Welfare in India,* Planning Commission, Government of India, Ministry of Information and Broadcasting, New Delhi, India, 1955.

more heavily from the other social work methods than from case-work. Casework, too, may be able to contribute more definitively to this process in the future. For the present, however, it is note-worthy that a number of casework programs have emerged and are undergoing development. Their existence suggests that reservations about the value of casework services have not been uniformly shared.

Doubts about the appropriateness of casework services in India reflect several widely held notions. For example, it is often argued that casework does not apply cross-culturally; that "casework is a frill" which poor countries cannot afford; or that "you cannot do casework with hungry people." Some persons seem to concede that basic principles may apply but must be adapted. Both the logic of these notions and their consistency with the Indian experience can be examined.

Applicability of Casework to Non-Western Cultures

Questions about the applicability of casework in countries with a markedly different culture are defensible to the extent that one regards culture as the basic determinant of behavior. However, only a few of our colleagues in the social sciences take so extreme a position on this issue. Current thinking more frequently follows the premise that dynamic psychology must be utilized in explaining individual behavior as it varies from the characteristic behavior of a certain group: "We cannot throughly understand the dynamics of culture, of society, of history without sooner or later taking into account the actual interrelationships of human beings. We can postpone this psychiatric analysis indefinitely but we cannot theo-retically eliminate it." [4]

In this connection it is worthy of note that psychoanalytic theory does not really ignore the importance of culture. "Freud's own writings contain, essentially, descriptions of how instinctual atti-tudes, objects and aims are changed under the influence of experi-ences. . . . not only frustrations and reactions to frustrations are socially determined; what a man desires is also determined by his

[4] Edward Sapir, "Why Cultural Anthropology Needs the Psychiatrist," *A Study of Interpersonal Relations*, Patrick Mullahy (ed.), Hermitage Press, New York, 1949, p. 247.

cultural environment." [5] Erikson and Hartmann assume the presence of genetically determined drives and theorize that the "society into which the individual is born makes him its member by influencing the *manner in which* he solves the tasks posed by each phase of his epigenetic development." [6]

A more sophisticated understanding of the complex relationship between intra-psychic processes and the environment has come about as knowledge of ego operations has increased. For example, studies of ego autonomy have clarified the extent to which a man may achieve independence from his environment, and the manner in which the environment influences this process. The impetus toward such autonomy derives from man's constitutionally given drives. The conditions that enhance the development of autonomy include safeguards against danger and provisions for the expression of instinctual drives, as well as basic supports for psychological growth.[7] While the Indian culture, like our own, does not represent an optimal milieu, it is a viable culture in which psychological growth obviously occurs. The development of stable processes that mediate between environment and instinctual forces, or ego characteristics, is basic to the human condition. In looking at a case illustration, we find these familiar characteristics.

Hansa came to the clinic dressed in a short white dress, her hair in plaits. She was a slim, pale, neat person who seemed nervous and embarrassed; she was soft-spoken and meek in manner. She told of eating clay and slate pencils, wanting to put water in mud and smell it. She felt sleepy, tired, and fatigued. If she did not eat at least one pencil a day she felt bad. Usually she was able to get a pencil from the school where she taught; if she could not do this she bought a pencil from a shop. When asked about the time she first started to eat the pencils she said her symptoms started about seventeen years ago when she was 6 or 7 years old. She recalled that she and her brother and sister had gone out for a walk; her brother and sister had walked ahead leaving her to follow alone. She ate mud at that time. A little while later,

[5] Otto Fenichel, *The Psychoanalytic Theory of Neurosis,* W. W. Norton and Company, New York, 1945, p. 6.
[6] Erik H. Erikson, *Identity and the Life Cycle,* International Universities Press, New York, 1959, p. 15.
[7] David Rapaport, "The Theory of Ego Autonomy: A Generalization," *Bulletin of the Menninger Clinic,* Vol. 22, No. 1 (1958), pp. 15, 22.

when she had gone to visit her older sister, the sister was sorting grain and eating the stones. Hansa ate some of the stones and liked them; since then she had eaten pencils. She did not like it when people learned of her habit.

At the age of 7 or 8, she had been sent to India from Africa to attend school. She remained in India for twelve years and completed school; during this period she did not see her parents. When asked how she felt about staying away from her parents she said she had been glad to return to Africa after twelve years. However, on her return she found things had changed. Her brother had married and his wife was jealous of Hansa and was not good to her. There were quarrels and the brother sided with his wife.

The patient then had to return to India and had taken a job as a teacher. She felt that her parents could not be firm with her brother because he was the only son and they always listened to him. She also felt that since he was the only son she should not try to come between him and the parents. He was older than she was and used to beat her for eating mud, but while she had been in school he had taken care of her almost like a father; he had paid her fees, had been more interested in her than her father had been. But after marriage he changed.

Hansa thought that if her father had been firmer with her brother right from childhood everything would have been different. She did not want to return to Africa although her family had property there. She had stayed there two years and had worked; sometimes she had organized shows and her brother had liked this, but when he showed his approval his wife made jealous remarks and eventually he turned against his sister. When asked about her parents' open preference for the brother, she replied she did not mind since he was the only son.

She did not want to marry but wanted to be a social worker. In the hostel where she lived some of the older unmarried women said it was better to get married but she was not sure about this. Her school degree was not a recognized one but her father was impressed by this particular institution and had placed her and her sister there. The sister carried tales to her brother about her eating mud and it was then he had beaten her. Last year she had had severe stomach ache and diarrhea. Her doctor had asked her to have her stool examined but she had not done so.

The social worker explained the clinic services. Hansa responded by saying she wanted to know if eating pencils harmed her body; otherwise she did not mind the habit. The worker pointed out that Hansa had spoken earlier about being very compulsive about this habit. The patient pleaded, "You tell me what

211

I should do, please. 'They' tell me it is bad." She could not express what she felt about this compulsion. The worker explained that she did not know the effects on the body of eating pencils but that if the patient was interested in knowing she could come in the following week when the worker would have more information and be able to discuss it with her. Hansa agreed to come. The worker then explained about the need for psychological testing, describing the Bender-Gestalt test. The patient seemed frightened, saying she could not draw.

Impressions: Hansa seemed dependent, childish, anxious, worried. Although she had said she did not like to talk about her complaints she talked easily and the worker had to ask very few questions. She was in touch with reality but seemed confused and anxious, particularly about her future.[8]

A brief analysis of this case suggests familiar psychodynamics and specific cultural influences. Although sleepiness and fatigue are common neurotic symptoms, pica and the wish to put water in mud and smell it may be a more direct expression of the pre-oedipal origins of an obsessive-compulsive neurosis than is commonly found in adults in the United States. In a high caste, wealthy family such as Hansa's, infantile sexuality and aggression would probably be rigidly repressed. A precise dynamic formulation would call for examination of the specific child-rearing practices in both caste and family. One can only speculate on the regressive effects of the child's being sent away to school at age 7, a custom more common in India than in the United States. However, the thinly disguised anal-erotic symbolism seems clear.

It is noteworthy that the onset of the symptoms is clearly linked to the behavior of an older brother and sister, an excellent replica of the oedipal situation, later reinforced by the marriage of the brother and the subsequent withdrawal of his affection and fatherliness. When confronted with the resolution of oedipal feelings, not only toward parents but toward an older brother who has acted *in loco parentis,* one could understand a regression in the face of such overwhelming odds.

Hansa's bland acceptance of the parents' preference for her brother reflects her denial of anger, a necessary defense for many girls. Expression of sibling rivalry toward a brother would be

[8] This case is summarized from *Case Records for Teaching Purposes,* Helen Pinkus (ed.), University of Baroda Press, Baroda, India, 1959.

extremely difficult in India, since the Hindu religion teaches that a son is essential for the execution of certain religious rites at the time of the father's death. She obviously related comfortably to the caseworker and her willingness to return for a second appointment suggests the beginning of the therapeutic alliance necessary for further treatment.[9] Although firm conclusions can be drawn only after a testing of the therapeutic method, the underlying psychodynamics seem to be identifiable and familiar.

Importance of the Relationship

Establishing a relationship has also been seen as a cross-cultural problem in India. Obviously, all casework must take place within the framework of a helping relationship. In India a person is usually viewed as a member of a family and caste rather than as an individual in his own right. The question then arises: How does this traditional emphasis affect his use of the casework relationship? The individual's responsiveness to a therapeutic encounter does not seem to be handicapped by his group affiliation. The uniqueness of being looked upon as an individual may enable the Indian to move—often very quickly—into a relationship and to use it constructively by mobilizing strengths heretofore unused. The following case example illustrates how readily the client forms a relationship.

Suraj, an elderly village woman came to the hospital for complaints of headaches, sleeplessness, fever, and indigestion. At the out-patient department, the social worker noted she seemed confused and disoriented, answering the routine questions with difficulty. When the worker asked why she had not been accompanied by a family member, she seemed upset and said there was no one in her family. The worker commented she seemed very troubled, saying, "Mother, would you tell me what worries cause you pain?" She set erect, opening her eyes wide but not replying. The worker said, "Mother, it seems to me you want to tell me something but find it hard. What bothers you so?" She replied, "Leave me alone. No one cares for me these days. Why are you after me? Why should you take care of me when no one cares for me now?" The worker repeated that it was obvious she was upset, suggesting she tell him about it. Suraj burst into tears

[9] For further elaboration of this point see Erna M. Hoch, "A Pattern of Neurosis in India," *American Journal of Psychoanalysis*, Vol. 20, No. 1 (1960), especially p. 23.

213

and her body trembled as she said, "Why do you call me 'Mother'? My son calls me a witch."

At this point the patient was called to get her medicine and then returned to talk with the worker. He learned she would be taking the train to her village that afternoon and would be at the railroad station; he offered to meet her there later if she wished to talk with him. Suraj looked suspiciously at the social worker and seemed fearful, saying, "No, no, don't be after me, sir. I have not killed her, I have not killed her," and began to cry again. After she calmed down, the worker assured her he was not a policeman and emphasized his role as a social worker and his wish to help. She then asked him to meet her at the station.

This plan was followed. After the worker learned that Suraj had eaten, he asked if she would tell him what worried her so much. The following story poured out: Suraj had been living with her son and pregnant daughter-in-law. Recently there had been a religious holiday which required fasting from both food and water. The daughter-in-law, a religious person, had made her (Suraj) promise under pain of a curse that the daughter-in-law would not be given water even if she asked for it. It happened that during this fast period the delivery occurred and the daughter begged and pleaded for water. But Suraj, fearful of the curse, did not give her any. During the night the girl died by dashing her head against the wall. "Since then I have not slept and my son has called me a witch. Thus, when you called me 'Mother' I was pleased and felt you were a man to trust. It is my fault she died, but this was not my intention. I should not have had such blind religious faith and fear. I am constantly repenting."

The worker and Suraj discussed the matter for some time, with the worker attempting to relieve her guilt, to point out she had not had full responsibility. Suraj seemed calmer. She said she would stop to see the worker next time she visited the hospital and she hoped he could come to her village and talk with her son.*

This is a dramatic case, the specifics of which would probably not be duplicated in this country. Is there not, however, an analogy in situations where family and friends do something detrimental to the health or welfare of others in the family, unwittingly, unintentionally, or through religious conviction? Suraj was helped by pouring out her story to the social worker and through the relation-

* This case is presented by courtesy of the Baroda School of Social Work, Baroda, India.

214

ship was given a sense of being listened to and understood, indeed a precious gift to an old woman who felt herself an outcast and a "witch."

One can easily sense from this brief summary the worker's acceptance of the client, and the quality of the ensuing relationship as manifested in the client's freedom to tell her poignant story. Psychodynamically many questions are unanswered. Was Suraj's behavior culturally determined, that is, motivated primarily by religious superstition, or was there an unconscious wish to be rid of her rival? As an elderly woman did she feel threatened and hence fearful of the daughter-in-law's presence in the home? These questions cannot be answered from the available material; yet it is a truism that people make those choices that are ego-syntonic. As in the case of Hansa, the psychodynamics seem familiar, and one can formulate a beginning diagnosis.

The identifiability of dynamic processes in these cases is certainly consistent with our experience in the United States. We are accustomed to work with widely diversified groups ranging from Kentucky mountaineers to first-generation Japanese. Our attempts to improve services to different ethnic and class groups in the United States have sensitized us to the importance of cultural forces for every individual. In doing so, however, we have continued to rely on the psychodynamic frame of reference for a precise understanding of individual and family functioning.

Although the same basic social institutions exist in both countries, the United States undoubtedly has certain central unifying values and concepts that differ from those of India. Obviously, there are also unique questions posed by Indian culture. For example, how are individual and family dynamics influenced by such factors as the caste system and the joint family? As in the United States, knowledge of the critical cultural parameters is required for the effective practice of casework.

Casework—A Luxury or a Necessity?

"A country with insufficient food or housing can ill afford to concern itself with personality problems until the basic needs of the mass population are met." [10] This statement is based on the

[10] G. Evangeline Sheibley, "Impressions of the International Conference of Social Work," *Social Casework*, Vol. XXXVII, No. 10 (1956), p. 492.

assumption that basic needs can be met without considering personality problems, that personality problems can somehow be separated from "basic needs." Yet we know from our experience in the United States that people do not draw such neat distinctions in their lives. Our experience suggests that programs designed to deal with basic needs are effective to the extent that psychological responses are accommodated. The very use of resources is often related to supporting provisions.

The development of community resources is proceeding at a rapid rate in India; as might be expected, many people are unable to utilize these resources because of ignorance, fear, and superstition. For example, during a famine in India in 1947 people starved to death in the streets of Calcutta. Many starved, not because food was totally unavailable, but because the type of grain available was not the grain eaten in this part of India. People were fearful that this unfamiliar food would cause illness and sterility.

This problem is particularly vivid in the field of medical care. Perhaps a brief example will illustrate the point that casework in India, far from being a frill, must be an integral part of developing health and welfare services if these services are to be used effectively.

Lufta Begam, a 25-year-old Muslim woman, was referred to the social service department of a large general hospital by the physician, so that the social worker might help the patient discuss with her husband the latter's obtaining treatment for venereal disease; the patient had been receiving treatment regularly. The patient talked easily with the worker, explaining she had been married for ten years and had two living children; three others had died in infancy. Her husband was employed as a truck driver. She had encouraged him to come to the hospital, but he had refused. She readily accepted the worker's suggestion that the latter make a home visit.

The worker called at the home at the appointed time but found that Hanif, the husband, had departed early that morning. Lufta talked about general health problems, and the worker recommended blood testing for the children. She also suggested that Lufta consult her husband about another convenient date for a home visit.

The patient contacted the worker when she next visited the hospital and notified her about the date of a second visit. The worker met Hanif, who politely thanked her for the treatment

216

given his wife. He explained that his wife was possessed by a "spirit" from her home village and therefore needed treatment; since the children were "born from her body" they too might need treatment. He was reluctant to be tested or have treatment for himself, commenting that the doctor might be negligent and then he (Hanif) would have wasted his time. He gave many other excuses which the worker accepted, at the same time commenting that though he might feel she was forcing something on him she really was concerned for his welfare and for his family. He finally decided to come to the out-patient department the next day.

He came on time and had a blood test. Later he came to the social service department, where he showed his anxiety about the test results. If the test was positive it would mean injections and he was afraid of the pinpricks. The worker wondered if there was something else he was afraid of, too. Did he think the doctors would punish him for contracting the disease? At this remark Hanif poured out many feelings about doctors—he felt they looked down on patients, blamed them for bad deeds, and so on. He was afraid of being humiliated. The worker assured him that this would not occur.

Prior to his second visit the worker talked with the doctor, explaining Hanif's concern and suggesting he not be questioned about the source of his infection. Hanif and both children were positive for venereal infection and received treatment. Hanif was seen regularly but briefly during his hospital visits. The worker focused on giving him a sense of pride in his fatherhood with some emphasis on how important his health was to the security and well-being of his family. Medical treatment for the entire family was completed.*

This is not a particularly difficult case nor are the techniques especially complicated. A number of areas are left unexplored. The question of how Hanif contracted his veneral disease is deliberately not discussed. Although the details of family and individual dynamics are unclear, one does see a fairly stable family group, on the basis of such evidence as Hanif's steady employment, relatively adequate living arrangements, and the ability of the family to participate regularly in medical treatment once Hanif's fears and rationalizations are handled. Thus the focus is on the medical problem and its solution, a focus often utilized in this country in medical settings. Yet one may predict that had a social caseworker

* This case is presented through courtesy of the Tata Graduate School of Social Work, Bombay, India.

not been available, Hanif would not have received treatment and the cycle of venereal infection would have continued.

The above case illustrates a frequently encountered type of presenting problem. The caseworker is effective in helping the client to utilize a concrete service, which may, for the individuals involved, have far-reaching benefits. Moreover, the long-term benefit of helping individuals to utilize available services has wider implications. An individualized approach becomes more, rather than less necessary, in a country where there is little education, rampant superstition, and a lack of mass methods of communication, such as radio and newspapers. Through the positive experiences of persons like Lufta Begam, many other persons in their immediate families and villages are influenced to utilize these resources. The primary channel of communication in India is still word of mouth, hence as an individual *experiences* a constructive use of a new resource his new attitudes often will be transmitted to others within his social group.

As we have indicated, a companion thought to "Casework is a frill" is "You cannot do casework with hungry people." Perhaps this myth requires a definition of hungry people. Many people in India are hungry; judged by any standards most Indians are underfed and overworked. There is a tremendous need for more food, better housing, better clothing, and more adequate medical care. The question is not whether the Indian people need more of the essentials of life, but whether utilization of casework methods should be postponed until these desiderata have been obtained. Perhaps justifiable concern over the poverty of most Indians—the poorest family in the United States has greater economic advantages than most families in India—has colored our judgment in evaluating the usefulness of casework with hungry people. Certainly the standard of living in India must be improved, but the feelings and expectations regarding basic necessities are somewhat different from those prevailing in the United States. Although this difference in attitude cannot be fully explained, its existence cannot be denied. It can be partially explained by the fact that desires, frustrations, and their expression are related to the society in which they exist—the concept of "relative deprivation" developed by social scientists. The latter theory evolved out of extensive studies of the American

218

soldier which confirmed the truism that being in the army meant different things to different men, but that "the felt sacrifice was greater for some than for others, depending on their standards of comparison." [11]

Another concept that may be pertinent to an understanding of attitudes in a rigid society providing little opportunity for intercaste mingling and upward mobility is found in the statement that "individuals within each stratum will be less likely to take the situation of the other strata as a context for appraisal of their own lot. They will, presumably, tend to confine their comparisons to other members of their own or neighboring social stratum." [12]

In social work terminology these concepts may be paraphrased as the difference between reality and feelings about reality. Thus, while the individual caseworker can do little to alleviate the basic poverty of India or even to provide, by American standards, an adequate diet for those in his caseload, he can, for example, help a boy who had run away from home following his father's remarriage to return to his local village instead of begging in the streets. Or he can aid a villager to take a sick child to a hospital instead of the shrine of the local smallpox goddess. From one standpoint this difference in viewing reality may be a cultural difference that might support the effective use of casework in a society with low standards of living for the *majority* of the population.

It is hoped that the cases presented may reveal the fallacy of some of the myths about casework in India and other underdeveloped countries. Beneath cultural differences we find people with the same needs, emotions, fears, conflicts, tensions, and drives the world over—a world in which casework cannot and must not be considered a "frill" if the goals of new nations are to be reached.[13] It is neither anticipated, nor suggested, that India—or other underdeveloped countries—will in the immediate future develop a vast network of social agencies and clinics to provide intensive casework. It is suggested, however, that casework services, as an integral part

[11] Samuel Stouffer and others, *The American Soldier*, Vol. I, Princeton University Press, Princeton, N. J., 1949–1959, p. 125.

[12] Robert K. Merton, *Social Theory and Social Structure*, Revised edition, Free Press, Glencoe, Illinois, 1957, p. 267.

[13] See Hertha Kraus, "Role of Social Casework in American Social Work," *Principles and Techniques of Social Casework*, Cora Kasius (ed.), Family Service Association of America, New York, 1950, p. 139.

of other expanding social services, have a vital role to play. Most of the clients whose records have been summarized were persons who were, by any objective standards, miserably clothed, meagerly fed, and inadequately sheltered; yet, these problems were not their only concern. Other problems were equally important, and accessible to casework help. And familiar casework principles were effective.

An upward trend in the standard of living is no guarantee of enhanced personal adjustment. Concern for the individual and a psychodynamic understanding of his needs cannot be isolated from social reform and social welfare. Social casework, with its particular knowledge and skill in helping individuals, can contribute to effective social change in two ways: by helping people to utilize technological advances and thereby raise their standard of living, and by providing greater emotional security and freedom from conflict. The disintegration of the joint family, a phenomenon that seems to accompany industrialization, emphasizes the need for individualized enabling and supportive services since "in the old joint family . . . the immaturity and dependency of any individual family member may never become a problem. But the breaking up of joint families into smaller units is likely to expose any lack of independence and wholeness." [14] Re-establishment of individual, familial, and societal equilibrium can all benefit by the utilization of ego psychology and dynamic casework in newly developing social welfare programs throughout the world.

[14] Hoch, *op. cit.*, pp. 14–15.

Part IV

Learning and Teaching
in Casework

13. Ego-Centered Teaching*

Bernard Bandler

THE SUBJECT SELECTED for this paper is central to the main stream of our current clinical and theoretical preoccupations. All respectable therapists work with the ego and all reputable authors make appropriate references to it. It is thoroughly natural that we should attempt to extend our clinical insights and our more systematic conceptual constructs in ego psychology to the field of education and to see what benefits they have to offer. How will they help us in utilizing the maximum capacity of the student, in devising the curriculum with ordered content and sequence, and in improving our methods of teaching? We justifiably anticipate the same gains in our educational programs as are said to accrue therapeutically from contemporary changes in technique.

We all know from experience that the most difficult task in working on any problem is to formulate the right questions. In discussing ego-centered teaching, we might begin by asking: What does this mean? What other teaching is possible? All perception, attention, memory, organization of memories, conceptualization, and judgment are ego functions and activities. Learning is mediated by the ego. To what but the ego can we address our teaching? Is

* Reprinted from *Smith College Studies in Social Work*, Vol. XXX, No. 2 (1960).

there, in short, any teaching that is not ego-centered? The promising topic for this discussion seems to have withered in the first attempt at clarification.

Something obviously seems wrong. But what? Have we made the ego too arbitrary an abstract and, by hypostatizing it into a separate entity, forgotten Freud's reminder that ego, id, and superego are all components of the total personality; that ego is only the organized part of the id, and the superego only a differentiated grade of the ego?

Perhaps an educational example will assist us to a more fruitful formulation of the problem. The second semester of the first year in psychiatry at many medical schools consists of a course on personality development. At one particular medical school, a harmonious relationship had been established in the first semester between the teacher and the class in the introductory course in psychiatry. The content had consisted in the demonstration of the medical relevance of psychology, of the complex structure of the personality, of certain modes of behavior such as denial, projection, and identification, of the strength of the affects and the significance of guilt, of the importance of the unconscious, the meaning of conflict both in its conscious and unconscious determinants, of fixation, and of regression.

These were the limited concepts that the course aimed to develop. The students accepted them and, to an extent, understood them with the minimum of resistance. They entered the second semester receptive and interested. They continued so for the first few lectures of the second semester and participated actively in the small discussion groups into which the class was divided after every three lectures. Then one day the following terse communication was made to the chairman of the department: "The honeymoon is over." A dull, apathetic silence had prevailed at each of the nine sections following that morning's lecture. The students could not be prodded into discussion even to an expression of disagreement. What had happened? The lecturer, a gentle, elderly lady, had discussed for the first time three of the commonplaces of developmental psychology: castration anxiety, penis envy, and the oedipus complex. The students' egos, as a result, suffered an acute decompensation of learning.

224

The Educational Task

Now it is easy to dismiss this example by saying that the lecturer dealt with three major areas of resistances simultaneously; that she discussed phases of development and problems whose existence and solution took place largely in the unconscious and of which, consequently, her audience would have no conscious recollection or experience; that she detonated a quantity of fissionable id and libido content that could not be assimilated at one hearing. Nevertheless, this material was presented to the ego. There is no other way of presenting id content except to the ego, and surely we do not mean, by ego-centered teaching, only the teaching of ego content. What then is the formula to cover this example and to explain the educational collapse of her audience's egos? The formula I would suggest is that the teaching was ego dystonic. It violated the core of personality with which the student works, learns, and develops, those areas of id and superego which are in relative harmony with the ego. We as teachers address ourselves not simply to the student's ego, but to the student's ego-syntonic personality. By ego syntonic I mean all those components of the id—drives, wishes, fantasies, and feelings—that are acceptable to the ego, as well as those elements of the superego and ego ideal that are in harmonious relationship to the ego. The problem to be studied, consequently, is not ego-centered teaching, but ego-syntonic teaching.

Our task as educators is not an easy one; we think of Freud's dictum about the three impossible professions: parents, statesmen, and teachers. We as teachers, insofar as we deal with the psychological core of the human personality, are confronted with a specific difficulty that no other educator shares; we are asking our students to assimilate concepts that deal with powerful forces in their own personalities, with problems and conflicts whose existence and solution took place exclusively in their unconscious, and toward whose revival there are the strongest resistances. By assimilation we mean not mere intellectual understanding, but imaginative, associational, affective comprehension as well, if theory is to be translated into perception, intuition, insight, understanding, and practice. We anticipate such results from a successful psychoanalysis. We are familiar with the opinion of some analysts that such content can

225

only be truly learned through a psychoanalysis. As educators we are challenged to facilitate the students' accomplishing these goals by educational means.

One way of stating the difficult part of our educational task is to say that we are obliged to present ego-dystonic material and to assist the student in its genuine integration. Another way of stating our educational task is to say that we have to enlist fully the student's ego-syntonic personality in overcoming his own resistances. Still another way of stating the problem is that we try to develop the optimal educational tension in each student, that we avoid the Scylla of setting too difficult a task and the Charybdis of asking so little that we fail to tax and to involve his full capacities. We can, in general, anticipate what is ego dystonic and where the resistances lie. Freud, in his introduction to the fourth edition of *Three Essays on the Theory of Sexuality,* observes that:

Now that the flood-waters of war have subsided, it is satisfactory to be able to record the fact that interest in psycho-analytic research remains unimpaired in the world at large. But the different parts of the theory have not all had the same history. The purely psychological theses and findings of psycho-analysis on the unconscious, repression, conflict as a cause of illness, the advantage accruing from illness, the mechanisms of the formation of symptoms, etc., have come to enjoy increasing recognition and have won notice even from those who are in general opposed to our views. That part of the theory, however, which lies on the frontiers of biology and the foundations of which are contained in this little work is still faced with undiminished contradiction. It has even led some who for a time took a very active interest in psycho-analysis to abandon it and to adopt fresh views which were intended to restrict once more the part played by the factor of sexuality in normal and pathological mental life.

Nevertheless I cannot bring myself to accept the idea that this part of psycho-analytic theory can be very much more distant than the rest from the reality which it is its business to discover. My recollections, as well as a constant re-examination of the material, assure me that this part of the theory is based upon equally careful and impartial observation. There is, moreover, no difficulty in finding an explanation of this discrepancy in the general acceptance of my views. In the first place, the beginnings of human sexual life which are here described can only be confirmed by investigators who have enough patience and technical skill to trace back an analysis to the first years of a patient's childhood. And there is often no possibility of doing this, since medical treatment demands that an illness should, at least in appearance, be dealt with more rapidly. None, however, but physicians who practice psycho-analysis can have any access whatever to this sphere of knowledge or any possibility of forming a judgment that is uninfluenced by their own dislikes and prejudices. If mankind had been able

226

to learn from a direct observation of children, these three essays could have remained unwritten.

It must also be remembered, however, that some of what this book contains— its insistence on the importance of sexuality in all human achievements and the attempt that it makes at enlarging the concept of sexualiy—has from the first provided the strongest motives for the resistance against psycho-analysis. People have gone so far in their search for high-sounding catchwords as to talk of the "pan-sexualism" of psycho-analysis and to raise the senseless charge against it of explaining "everything" by sex. We might be astonished at this, if we ourselves could forget the way in which emotional factors make people confused and forgetful. For it is some time since Arthur Schopenhauer, the philosopher, showed mankind the extent to which their activities are determined by sexual impulses—in the ordinary sense of the word. It should surely have been impossible for a whole world of readers to banish such a startling piece of information so completely from their minds. And as for the "stretching" of the concept of sexuality which has been necessitated by the analysis of children and what are called perverts, anyone who looks down with contempt upon psycho-analysis from a superior vantage-point should remember how closely the enlarged sexuality of psycho-analysis coincides with the Eros of the divine Plato.[1]

This observation is still true today. One wonders sometimes whether the ready and almost universal acceptance of ego psychology does not occasionally mask a resistance to the id, a subtle repudiation of motivation which, in the name of the ego, is profoundly anti-psychological. We can fail as teachers just as easily by neglecting to involve our students sufficiently in their struggles with the id as by presenting them, as in my example, with too much id too early, and in too elementary and crude a form, that is, in its primitive, unconscious version.

Areas of Resistance

There are, in general, two areas or levels of ego-dystonic material or of resistances. The first is the ego-dystonic content that refers to developmental phases and problems that have been experienced and solved in the unconscious in the course of growing up. They will have, as a result, no residue in memory to which we can appeal. Since in one way or another they have been individually solved, there is necessarily a struggle against their reactivation. Yet, in some token, derivative, preconscious way they must, I believe, be taken up again by the student, be re-experienced, re-examined, and

[1] Sigmund Freud, *The Complete Psychological Works of Sigmund Freud*, Vol. VII, translated by James Strachey, Hogarth Press, London, 1953, pp. 133–134.

227

once again settled. What I am referring to here is the oedipus complex, including both its libidinal and aggressive components, problems of identification that lead to the desires of each sex to be the opposite sex, ambivalence, masochism, castration anxiety, and penis envy.

This is a large order. If the student does not in some way review his life and relationships in the light of this knowledge, it remains sterile intellectualization. If he does review it, he runs the risk of becoming disturbed. How can we present this content, whether in didactic lectures, case seminars, or field supervision, in an ego-syntonic form? Two principles of psychoanalytic technique, which are also employed in other forms of psychotherapy as well as in case-work, may perhaps be adopted as educational devices. The first is that interpretations start on the surface and deal with derivatives. The word "derivative" may merit some elaboration. We may regard, for example, the problems of adolescence as a second although modified edition of an earlier phase of development culminating in the oedipal struggle. The tasks of adolescence may be considered in their unconscious aspects as derivative from this earlier period. Similarly, current conflicts may be considered derivative from adolescent conflicts, just as disturbances in relationship with individuals in present life may be derivative from the primary figures of the family—parents, siblings, and meaningful relatives. I am not using the word "derivative" in this sense.

Another meaning of derivative is in the topographic sense as it relates to the sequence and ordering of drives, wishes, feelings, and fantasies from the deepest layer of the unconscious through the preconscious to the conscious. Derivative refers to the offshoots and manifestations of the complex interrelationship of motivations, adaptive processes, and defenses as they express themselves in behavior and awareness. It is a commonplace of psychotherapy and casework treatment that we begin with a minute exploration of the current life adjustment, of ego functioning, of reality. This procedure is one of our great strengths, although it may run the risk of becoming superficial if pursued too exclusively. We begin too, with the client, with attempts at clarification of the problem. Such attempts are appropriate and necessary, even though there is danger of one-sidedness if the emphasis is too much on the problem,

228

or the conflict, or the pathology. Interpretations are kept at a minimum. The interpretations that we venture are largely to investigate and to test the client's capacity to respond, to explore what is ego syntonic, and to further our understanding rather than to give insight.

Teaching psychological content proceeds the same way; it begins with derivatives. Since classes as well as individuals differ in their capacities, their responsiveness, and their pace, one necessarily has to test and to experiment to discover what is their optimal ego-syntonic capacity for learning. In indivdual supervision that is not too difficult. It is true that supervision presents a double problem: what is good for the client and what is good for the student. The therapeutic process, as one ideally visualizes it, is not always synchronous with the learning process. But all roads lead to Rome; there are many ways to help patients and it is usually possible to facilitate the student's traveling the road that is traversable by him. We do not have to point out all the roads or to communicate our full understanding, which goes beyond the derivatives into the preconscious and the unconscious. In the teaching that furthers the growth and development of the student the educational task is gradually to introduce ego-dystonic content that does not exceed the ego-syntonic capacities. I know of no formula that would give us the precise timing and dosage as one proceeds from the superficial derivatives to the preconscious and gradually approaches the unconscious. Educational tact, empathy, and judgment are fully as important as their therapeutic counterparts.

Concepts and Percepts

The major areas in which the recognition of derivatives will be helpful are in the teaching of theory and in the application of theory to practice. "Concepts without percepts are empty," observes Kant, "and percepts without concepts are blind." We are all splendidly conceptualized these days—sometimes perhaps a little overconceptualized. It is easy for theory to outstrip experience, to extend beyond percepts, both those past ones preserved in memory, the present ones, and the future ones that we as educators devise and clients offer. How are we to teach the psychoanalytic theory of per-

229

sonality development, structure, and dynamics, as well as the psychoanalytic theories of pathology? Our students vary greatly in their background. Many are familiar with Freud, the social sciences, and psychological theory. Even the most protected students have some verbal familiarity with basic psychoanalytic concepts. They have inquiring minds and good intellects. It is as easy to be seduced into theoretical glibness as to take literally the mother of an asthmatic child, who has a master's degree in the social sciences and is president of the P.T.A., who asks you to explain how she is responsible for her child's illness and avidly awaits your suggestions. It is as easy and just as fatal.

How, for example, should the oedipus complex be taught? The student in all likelihood is familiar with the fairytale-like formula: the son loves the mother and would like a baby by her; he also loves the father, but now sees him as a rival. He is filled with ambivalence and harbors death wishes against the father. Because of fear of castration, he represses his death wishes. In this struggle, repression is aided by identification with the father. This identification plays a preponderant role in the formation of the superego. With appropriate modifications the same struggle and outcome are true of the daughter. The situation becomes slightly complicated by the fact that simultaneously the negative oedipus factor is also at work. The son, through bisexuality and other factors, has a feminine relationship to his father; the mother is now his rival; and so on.

How shall we as educators proceed, whether in the classroom or in supervisory conference? We cannot withhold from the students information that they already have and that they will read in the books assigned to them. First, of course, we can tell them that these are theories derived from psychoanalytic practice, and that the data, the percepts on which the generalizations are based, are available only after long periods of systematic, painstaking analyses of individuals, both adults and children. Since the adventures and processes described take place in the unconscious, they are not available to the student as memories, nor will they be observable in their clients. We may ask the student to think of Coleridge's remark about "that voluntary suspension of disbelief which constitutes poetic faith" and to see whether in the course of time

230

these concepts illuminate experience. Analysands, even after long preparation, do not rejoice at such communications, which, of course, are not presented in the somewhat travestied and archaic form I have given here. There is no reason why students should accept them; to think of themselves and their families in this light is profoundly disturbing.

Ego-syntonic teaching of the oedipus complex through derivatives—and our current concept, of course, has modified the facile formula—would mute the libidinal and aggressive components. It would deal with the daughter's love for her father without undue sexualization, and the struggle and conflict with her mother without murder. It would describe the oedipus complex in the adolescent and child in terms of his overt, describable, subjectively experienced behavior, which the student could confirm through observation and memory.

The second principle of psychoanalytic technique which I suggest as an educational device is "working through." Most simply described, working through means the repetitive and laborious exploration of the many manifestations of a conflict once it has been understood. The analysand has insight, he truly understands, and he begins to achieve freedom from neurotic behavior. But this freedom is not generalized to all areas; there are some areas in which the same neurotic conflict continues to find expression. Further work is necessary to extend the same insight to a different group of experiences and of relationships and to consolidate the therapeutic gains. I believe educational working through is particularly important in respect to ego-dystonic content and casework experiences. It is not merely another example of the familiar educational devices of learning through repetition and of exemplification through varied examples. An additional psychological burden is here put upon the student other than the simple learning of the new and of the unfamiliar. The content is ego dystonic and hence there are resistances to be overcome. The student's failures to apply what has truly been learned in one situation to a dissimilar one that exemplifies the same principle, or even to a similar situation, need not reflect stupidity, psychopathology, or those normal regressions we anticipate in students in certain phases of their training. Failure may simply mean that the student has not been given

231

an adequate opportunity for educational working through. Giving the student such opportunity, with patience and forebearance rather than undue activity on the part of the instructor, may lead to mastery.

Maturational Conflicts

So far we have discussed ego-syntonic teaching largely in respect to id content, the problems solved in the unconscious in the course of growing up, and the resistances generated against their reactivation. There is, however, a second level of resistances that are common to most students and are of a different order. These are resistances in connection with maturational problems and conflicts that are in process of solution or have only recently been solved but are not yet consolidated. They would include such issues as independence, relationship to authority, identification, sexuality, and values. Young adults are once again in the educational mill. Teachers, content, and clients may become involved in current struggles, part of which may be conscious, part unconscious; or they may be experienced as threats to development or a new phase of development which is still precarious. In all phases of development, the most recent advances, the most recent acquisitions in knowledge, skills, insight, and mastery are the most vulnerable and subject to regression. The preservation of genuine gains may be the motive for some of the resistances to teachers, content, and clients.

The danger from the point of view of the teacher is that of educational acting out. I am not here using the phrase "acting out" in the precise, technical, psychoanalytic sense that refers to the analysand's unconscious feelings, fantasies, and wishes that are mobilized by the transference being acted outside the analysis instead of being remembered, verbalized, and expressed in the analysis itself. I am using the phrase in the more general sense commonly employed by psychoanalysts and other psychiatrists when they refer to the neurotic or asocial involvement of other people. Other people are then not perceived or evaluated or responded to realistically. The patient acts out his conflicts in relation to them. Educational acting out would be the involvement of teacher or content or client in the current maturational conflicts of the student, or in their

232

reactivation by the educational process. I should like to stress the word "educational" and the fact that the students' reactions of distorted perceptions and unrealistic responses may be indigenous to the educational process, particularly when that process deals with human psychology. Child psychiatrists, as we know, have been preoccupied for a long time with the problem of the indications and criteria for treatment. The existence of a problem and of a conflict is not an indication; nor is the mere presence of symptoms such an indication. All children have periods of poorer functioning, of temporary regressions, of inhibitions, and of transient symptoms. Some really grow out of them, particularly if they have understanding parents and teachers. As educators we all tend to suffer from a common weakness which is also our strength. We are all clinically or casework oriented; we are all diagnosticians; and we are all therapists or casework practitioners. Our tendency is, then, to see and diagnose the student's difficulties and symptomatology in the same way as we understand the symptoms of our patients and clients. The temptation is to refer the student for treatment.

It would be interesting to know the statistics on how many students are referred to therapy and how they vary from agency to agency, from school to school, and from one region of the country to another. I suspect that students may be referred to therapy more often than is necessary; that on occasion a situation of educational acting out may be misdiagnosed as a neurosis. I realize that no hard and fast line can be drawn, and that it is, in the end, a matter of experience and judgment. But I wonder sometimes whether we have always adequately explored the educational means of helping the student or exhausted the full potentiality of educational resources.

What means and resources do we have that are ego syntonic? Much has been written about the student's fear of change and the threat to identity that change implies. Fear of change is allied to the conservative and regressive forces of the personality; one way of putting it is fear of growth. There is also, however, a desire for change, for growth; this is allied to the progressive forces of the personality. We are all familiar with the human factors that make for growth, that nurture and sustain it. For children—love;

233

for students—benevolent interest and empathic understanding that is experienced as love. For children—gratification of needs; for students—an actively stimulating intellectual pablum. For children —consistency which gives security; for students—an orderly framework. It is hardly necessary to repeat what we all know so well: the delicate proportions of permissiveness and firmness, the permission to make mistakes, the gradual increase of expectations and demands, and the gradual relinquishment of authority to the student's heightened autonomy and mastery.

The primary basis for all these factors is, of course, relationship. Without relationship there is no human growth and development: the body grows; the intellect grows; maturational phases pass through the empty shells of their evolution but without the mortar of emotion which is their reality. For without relationship there is no identity, no ego, no self, no feeling, no love; in philosophy this condition is known as solipsism, in psychiatry, schizophrenia. In "Group Psychology and Analysis of the Ego," [2] the first of Freud's great systematic contributions to ego psychology, he pointed out that the first relationship is that of identification. But he pointed out also in this volume, in which he first introduced the concept of superego, that what binds groups together is libido. The bond that unites groups is love. It is love that leads to identification with the leader, and through that identification, identification with each other.

In teaching the ego-syntonic personality, we are appealing to more than the intellect and to more than the ego. We are also appealing to the ego-syntonic libido and its capacity to love us. That the love is silent, that it is largely unconscious, and that it expresses itself in derivatives such as liking and respect, should not lead us to minimize its strength or its importance. It is the most powerful motive for growth, for facing change, for enduring the ego-dystonic aspects of the educational process in our fields.

Love, however, has its demands, and they are not simply reciprocation and satisfaction. For love above all else is selfless and altruistic. The greatest demand that love makes upon educators is that they

[2] Sigmund Freud, "Group Psychology and the Analysis of the Ego," translated by James Strachey. *International Psycho-Analytical Library, No. 6*, Ernest Jones (ed.), International Psycho-Analytical Press, London, 1922.

be adequate objects for identification. In the example I gave earlier of the benign lady and the medical students, I attributed that particular educational failure to the fact that she introduced too much id content too early in too unmitigated a form and hence mobilized massive resistances. That is only a partial explanation. There is, I believe, a still more significant factor to explain the students' response. By presenting the oedipus complex in its most sexual form, by stressing childhood sexuality, this motherly lady sexualized herself and hence destroyed herself as an object of identification. The shocked silence of the students was that of betrayal analogous to the panic in an army when the general shows cowardice or demoralization of people, or when a trusted political leader betrays his country.

One of our obligations, as well as one of our opportunities as teachers when confronted by educational acting out, is to examine whether we have unwittingly altered the student's image of us as an object of identification. When the negative transference in no way stems from our inadvertences, we know from our work with patients and clients how much we can do, short of interpretation, to shift the transference, by working with the ego-syntonic personality.

14. Psychoanalysis and the Education of Caseworkers*

Selma Fraiberg

EDUCATION FOR SOCIAL WORK, like all professional education, is an education for practice. The theoretical and technical content of this education has always borne a close relationship to the fields of practice. The social agency is the laboratory for the profession. It is through direct work with clients that we feel the pulse of social change and evolve new programs and modify old programs to meet new community needs. It is through direct work with clients that we test new ideas and the applicability of theories and research findings from allied fields to our own profession. When the usefulness of these findings has been demonstrated in practice, the curriculum of the professional school absorbs this new knowledge and makes it part of the professional education.

This means that a good curriculum reflects the best in current practice and thinking and derives its infusions of new knowledge from the work of thousands of practitioners. This means, too, that however restrictive it is to the academic imagination, we cannot be originators of new practices in the classroom and we cannot profess theories in the classroom until they have been tested in practice.

As an applied science, a user of other sciences, social work is obliged to put its borrowings to a pragmatic test. Is this theory useful to our field? we ask. Does it explain things better? Does it

* Reprinted from *Smith College Studies in Social Work*, Vol. XXXI, No. 3 (1961).

suggest new and better remedies for our problems? In asking these questions we are not inquiring about the validity of a theory—which can only be done within its own sphere of operation—we are simply testing its application to our field, which introduces another set of rules. Application implies use; the fact is that whether psychoanalysis or role theory or genetic psychology or cybernetics will find its way into social work practice and social work education will depend upon the usefulness of that particular theory for the performance of the social work job.

For nearly forty years psychoanalysis has been a major influence in the development of social work theory and practice and has supplied the basic psychology taught in schools of social work. It has become so much a part of the fabric of social work theory that we can no longer easily identify many of the elements of our theory that are directly borrowed from psychoanalysis.

In our current appraisals of social work theory and social work education, the contributions of psychoanalysis as well as the contributions from all the behavioral sciences are being examined for their relative value to the professional content of social work. Such stock-taking is an extremely valuable measure to a profession that is coming of age. It gives us the opportunity to separate the components in our social work theory and assign a value to them before we put them together again. It has a stimulating effect upon one's own thinking. As one who believes very strongly that psychoanalysis is the indispensable component in social work theory and practice, I found it an excellent exercise and examination of my own beliefs to ask myself the question, "Why do I think so?"

Then I found myself very much stimulated by a question that is implicit in the Curriculum Study.[1] If the goal of social work is described as "enhancement of social functioning" and "social functioning" is regarded as the unifying concept of social work, as defined in the Curriculm Study (I do not myself favor this definition), what is the place of psychoanalysis within such a formulation? What knowledge does psychoanalytic theory and practice bring to a profession that concerns itself with problems of social functioning?

To answer these questions I found it helpful to review all the

[1] *Social Work Curriculum Study*, Werner W. Boehm (ed.), Council on Social Work Education, New York, 1959.

agency cases that had come to me for consultation during the past year and a few from previous years. In each case I attempted to identify the psychoanalytic knowledge that was employed in diagnosis and treatment, at the same time submitting the data to a test: Will another theory explain these data better or provide better remedies for the problems presented? Although the test was not entirely fair, since I know psychoanalytic theory far better than I know any other theory of human behavior, the process helped to clarify some of my own thinking. I propose to review here a selection from the same cases and see what they may tell us about psychoanalytic content in casework practice. And, finally, I should like to discuss the implications for social work education which can be derived from study of the cases.

A Boy Gang Leader

Some time ago a 9-year-old boy was referred to a school social worker for evaluation. Larry was the leader of a little gang at school that molested other children outside of school and tyrannized younger children through physical attacks and threats. He was a child of good average intelligence and until this year had created no unusual difficulties for the school, although he had always exhibited some minor behavior problems. He was the child of conscientious middle-class parents who were frankly baffled by the complaints from school in recent months. He had always been difficult to manage at home and seemed to be in unceasing battle with his older sister, 11. Often he seemed to be begging for punishment from his parents. But there were strong bonds of affection between the child and his parents and never before had the parents felt that his behavior was something they could not influence.

Both the parents and the school blamed these difficulties in part upon the changing neighborhood in which they lived and in which the school was located. There had been a large influx of Negro families into this neighborhood in a northern city and many of the Negro children who had lived in slums previously had brought with them the code of the street child. A number of small delinquent gangs had sprung up among Negro children of the neighborhood. I should mention that the middle-class Negro children were as threatened by the gangs and their culture as were the white middle-class children.

These are a few of the significant social factors as we knew them at the time of intake. If we now employ a diagnosis based upon the

238

social factors, we may say that Larry and the other middle-class children in this community are reacting to the impact of the street-child culture that has invaded their world. They are threatened by the aggression and tyranny of the newcomers. We can assume that certain middle-class values have been assaulted by the new-comers with their street code and we see this as a conflict between two groups who hold incompatible values and codes of behavior. From the standpoint of the middle-class child, his role as defined by his group is threatened and violated by the alien group.

But now we are confronted with an interesting problem. If we grant that certain factors in the social situation have precipitated a conflict in Larry, we are still left with the question: Why did this externally induced conflict lead to the specific forms of behavior that we observed in Larry? If he is afraid of attack by the tough boys—which is understandable—why doesn't his aggression manifest itself against the enemy in fighting back? And if he forms a little gang, we could understand it if the gang served as a mutual pro-tection association against the danger of enemy attack, but this gang has as its purpose the tyrannizing of younger and helpless children.

Larry is modeling his behavior after the behavior of the delin-quent boys. It might be proposed that Larry has taken the delin-quent as a model because of the power status of the delinquent group within the school community. But, accepting this factor in our tentative diagnosis, we still have no explanation of the fact that Larry and his five gang members have reacted to the new status group by taking on the role of the delinquent; that other children in the school have reacted through an intensification of anxiety and sometimes reluctance to go to school; and still other children have managed to adapt themselves to the presence of the alien group without abandoning their own codes and without suffering paralyz-ing anxiety. Then, too, we are faced with the problem that this diagnosis does not carry with it its own prescription. To say that a child adopts the behavior of delinquent boys because they rep-resent the power group in his community will not tell us what we ought to do about the situation.

Now let us try another diagnostic approach. We begin with the observation that Larry has taken over the behavior of the delinquent boys, that he models himself after them and now tyrannizes younger children in the same way that the delinquent boys have tyrannized him and his friends. We see this behavior as an identification with the delinquent boys and we employ our psychoanalytic knowledge in a tentative formulation that this identification may be a form of defense. The details of this behavior suggest that Larry identifies with the aggressor and actively does to younger children those things that he has passively experienced at the hands of the tough boys. If we are dealing with a defense, we can employ our knowledge of defense in the appropriate treatment, but first we must study this behavior in detail in order to know what needs it serves.

The social worker in this case had a series of interviews with Larry in order to observe his behavior more closely. Larry was a lively, engaging youngster, absolutely on his best behavior during the first three interviews. He understood why he was coming to see the social worker and seemed quite unconcerned about it. He had little guilt about his gang activities and felt that everyone was making much too much fuss about the whole business. The caseworker was attentive to this lack of guilt feelings, knowing that she was dealing either with a defective superego or a defense against guilt feelings, and that the differentiation of these two conditions would be crucial in the formulation of treatment plans.

After a few interviews Larry began to give some surprising glimpses of the delinquent Larry. One day he whispered obscenities under his breath, giggling and casting furtive glances at the caseworker. He grew bolder in the next interview and sang a dirty song under his breath. In the same interview Larry, quite giddy and excited, put on a bad-boy act in which he called himself "Ernie" and raced around the room shouting names at an unseen teacher in Negro accents. The caricature of Ernie was so well performed that the social worker had no difficulty in recognizing the real Ernie, who was a celebrated problem child in the school. Then the caseworker watched with interest as Larry, clowning and excited, began to shadow-box with imaginary opponents, thumping the cushions of the chair and muttering obscenities under his breath. From the mimicry the caseworker understood Larry was now imitating someone else. "Who is this, Larry?" she asked. "Jo-Jo," he said promptly, and now he imitated the random movements and disordered speech of another disturbed child in his classroom.

In watching this strange performance, the caseworker discovered what she needed to know. The play-acting demonstrated very clearly the identification with the "bad" boys; now it remained to test this behavior as defense.

The caseworker said, "All right, Larry, now I think you're getting a little too excited and I'd like to talk with you. Let's sit down." Still in his gremlin mood, Larry dived into a chair and boldly stuck out his tongue at the caseworker. He was preparing himself for a lecture. The caseworker said, "Larry, there are a lot of tough kids at school. I think it must be very scary for you and lots of other kids to be around tough guys and kids who lose control of themselves." Larry was momentarily surprised, then his play-acting came to a stop, and he said with great feeling, "You don't know the half of it!" "I'm sure I don't," said the caseworker, "so please tell me about it."

Larry told his story. He told of the small gangs that attacked kids on their way home from school. He described the extortionist tactics of these gangs and the ways in which many children at school were forced to pay for protection. (Much of this the caseworker knew.) Larry did not mention his own gang at this point. He went on to describe the chaos of his classroom, with Ernie or Jo-Jo running around the room in grinning defiance of the teacher. "We don't even learn anything any more," he said. And there was much more, he hinted, things he wouldn't tell anybody. When the teachers weren't around . . . in the lavatories and the locker-rooms. . . .

Once the caseworker asked Larry if he could not have talked with his teachers about these things. "What good would *that* do?" he asked scornfully. "The teachers are scared of those kids themselves."

At this point the caseworker has learned a great deal. She knows that anxiety is the motive for this pathological identification with the aggressor, and here the diagnosis carries its own prescription. The caseworker knows now how she can help Larry.

In the weeks that followed the caseworker encouraged Larry to talk about the "bad" boys and his fears and carefully protected him from any implication that to be scared was to be a sissy. She helped him to see that his own gang activities were connected with his fears, that he was acting the tough guy because he was afraid of the tough guys and that he was doing to the little kids just what he feared himself from the big, tough boys. And she helped him see that this was no solution to the problem. The caseworker, it was true, could not protect Larry against the danger of attack by the tough boys, but she soon discovered that Larry found much relief in talking

241

about his fears to her and, feeling the psychological protection of this relationship, he began to find better solutions to the problems.

As Larry learned that he could trust the caseworker with any of the things he worried about, he began to tell her about the lavatory and locker-room incidents that he had once thought he could not tell anyone. With great difficulty he described the sexual horseplay in the lavatories, the uninhibited exhibition-ism of the tough guys, playful threats against the genitals, dirty jokes, incestuous name-calling.

The caseworker began to understand that the street-child code was a sexual as well as an aggressive threat to the middle-class child and to Larry particularly. Then, through tactful questions, she learned that Larry had sometimes participated in these games and, with this admission, the one-time tough-guy Larry displayed the most agonizing guilt.

Now we understand that there was another motive for identifica-tion with the "bad" boys. Larry believed that he, himself, was a bad boy and by behaving like the "bad" boys he was making a con-fession. Now, too, we understand one of the motives in his provoca-tive behavior and simultaneously we know why he did not show guilt feelings about his "bad" behavior. He regularly made his confession of guilt and invited punishment. When he received punishment from his teachers or his parents his guilt feelings were satisfied and he was free to renew the cycle of crime and punishment.

With casework help Larry gave up his gang activities and settled down to work in his classroom. Larry's parents were helped to gain a better understanding of his problems and to find more satisfactory ways of handling his behavior at home. With the caseworker's knowledge of the guilt-punishment mechanisms in Larry's person-ality she was able to give specific help to the parents in the area of discipline. Larry's behavior at home improved significantly.

We may say, then, that casework achieved its goal of more effec-tive social functioning in the case of Larry. But, in order to do this, the caseworker needed a precise and finely differentiated diag-nosis. The factor of identification with bad boys could be estab-lished either by employing role theory or psychoanalytic theory during the first descriptive phase of diagnosis. But only psycho-analytic theory could establish the motive for the identification, and only through discerning the motive could casework treatment be effective. The motive, we found, was highly complex. This is not because Larry's case was more complex than others; it is because all human motives are complex. If we only know that Larry identifies with bad boys we have a description of the behavior, one that is perfectly valid as description but cannot tell us how we shall bring about change in the behavior. In order to modify behavior we must know its meaning exactly.

In Larry's case we saw that identification served as a defense against both an external and an internal danger. The external danger was represented in the threat of the delinquent boys; the internal danger was represented in the child's own aggressive and sexual impulses. We derived this from the data in the case, but it is also useful to remember that identification is one of the defense mechanisms that operate simultaneously against inner and outer dangers.

How useful are these case findings outside the case itself? Are these analytically derived data generally applicable? From my own experience with delinquent boys I would say that the factor of "identification with the aggressor" is one of the most important keys to an understanding of the "contagion" of delinquency. It is not, of course, a middle-class phenomenon. The delinquent street children who initiated the gang activities at school were also doing unto others what had been done unto them. Before they became the persecutors they had been the persecuted, the victims of older child gangsters. And the tyranny of the child culture is itself modeled after the tyranny passively experienced by many of these children in their own homes.

From the case of Larry we must also observe the external conditions that call forth the defense. The failure of adults—the teachers and parents—to protect Larry and others from the danger of attack and seduction created anxiety in each child that summoned his characteristic mechanisms of defense. This suggests another application of the psychoanalytic case findings to prevention and treatment on a larger scale. When adults lose their protective role and function, the child is forced to fall back upon primitive defenses. If Larry's teachers had been equipped to handle the new problems that the delinquents brought to the school and had retained their role of adult protectors, the disorganizing effects of the street child on the middle-class child might have been minimized and the spread of delinquency checked. Even such a simple measure as adult supervision of lavatories and locker-rooms may be highly effective in curbing anxiety if we understand how aggressive sex-games and incestuous name-calling can create both excitement and guilt in children who have not yet successfully repressed their oedipal strivings.

Casework Treatment of a Mother on Behalf of the Child

Let us look at another case, one from a family agency, in which a mother sought advice in handling the problems of her 8-year-old daughter.

The presenting problem was Margaret's reluctance to go to school, a problem that had existed since her kindergarten days and now had reached serious proportions. Margaret complained of headaches and nausea each morning and begged her mother to allow her to stay home. Each morning a weeping, nearly hysterical little girl was dragged off to school. Once there she managed somehow, her mother said, and sat mute and docile in her seat, not taking in half of what was said in class. Her school grades were considerably below the expectations for a child of better than average intelligence.

When the parents were able to get Margaret to talk about her fears in connection with school, she could only say that she was afraid that the teacher might get angry at her. Since her teacher was not unduly severe with children, this explanation was not very helpful.

At home Margaret was described as a cheerful, well-behaved child who presented no unusual problems to her parents. If it were not for the difficulty in getting her off to school the parents would have no complaints. She occasionally wet the bed, her mother recalled. Margaret's strongest ties were to her mother, but her father had much affection for his children and was indisputably head of the family. There was an older brother, 10, whose school performance was very good, and Margaret often compared herself unfavorably with him.

Margaret's problem is one that the social worker sees very often in school and family agencies and in child guidance clinics. If the social worker's job is to bring about more effective functioning in the area of school and learning, the first question is: How shall this be done? If Margaret's problem were clearly a reaction to a severe and punitive teacher, we might help the teacher acquire more

244

understanding of Margaret and be more lenient in her expectations of the child. But here there is no evidence that the teacher enters into the conflict on a real basis, and we are left with a child's unreal fears. We may, if we like, tell Margaret that her fears are unreal. She will not believe us.

Some theories may be mentioned here. Suppose we say that Margaret has failed to adapt herself to the role expectations of a school child, that she sees herself as the baby of the family and prefers to remain dependent upon her mother. This may be true. If we now employ this diagnosis in treatment we should try to help Margaret become independent and to find that being a big girl has greater satisfactions. If this is only a dependency problem, the method may work. But we shall find that if we attempt to make Margaret independent of her mother her anxiety will increase and we shall move further away from our goal of restoring social functioning. The dependency, we must reason, is only one facet of the problem.

What we need is a diagnosis that takes into account the factor of *dread* in Margaret's avoidance of school, dread of an imagined danger. The diagnosis needs to account for the fact that an 8-year-old child is a model of good behavior in her home and that she fantasies dangers when she is at school. The diagnosis must account for the outbreak of anxiety when Margaret is obliged to go to school and for the conversion symptoms that appear at these times.

The diagnosis "school phobia" is correct here and immediately comes to our aid in treatment. If we understand the structure of a childhood phobia, we shall know that a conflict that originated in a child's relationships to his own parents is displaced onto objects outside the home. The original ambivalence to parents vanishes, the dangerous aspect of the parent is split off and attributed to teachers and to the school itself. The child's own repudiated hostile impulses are projected outward and experienced as coming from the outside, and the child himself becomes free of conflict within the home as long as he can avoid the danger outside—the school. Again the diagnosis carries its own prescription. We must locate the sources of conflict in the child's relationships to his parents and help parents and child find new solutions to the conflict.

In Margaret's case the family agency chose to work with the

parents, particularly the mother who seemed to be in the center of this invisible conflict.

The caseworker began to help the mother to see Margaret's docility and obedience in another light. Gradually the mother was able to see that the child had acquired her obedience through completely surrendering naughty or aggressive impulses and that this had been achieved at great cost to the child. Margaret was afraid of anger, of her own anger and the anger of others; this was one of the elements in the school phobia. When the mother understood this she began, with the caseworker's guidance, to become a more lenient mother. She could allow Margaret to express feelings of anger when this was appropriate and ease the child's fear that anger would bring loss of love or monstrous retaliation.

As we might expect, when Margaret was given permission to feel anger toward the mother whom she loved, the conflict that had been displaced from home to school returned to home ground where now, with the help of the caseworker, better solutions could be found. Margaret's fear of school diminished rapidly. Within a few months the conflict was successfully withdrawn from the area of school, and school functioning improved markedly.

In the case of Margaret the casework treatment was aimed at "improvement of social functioning." The underlying phobia was not dissolved through this treatment. Margaret, for example, still had night fears. But this treatment was effective in bringing about the restoration of ego functions that had been restricted by the phobia. So we see that even such a simple objective as getting a child back into school and improving her scholastic performance depends upon a diagnosis that discriminates and organizes details. The psychoanalytic diagnosis not only describes but it explains, and when the caseworker understands the meaning of the behavior he can formulate the appropriate treatment.

A Family Conflict

Mrs. B came to the family agency for counsel. Her problems were almost too many to enumerate. Her 5-year-old son, Jon, was a bully and was generally regarded as a neighborhood menace. Neither she nor her husband seemed to have any influence over him. Jon was passionately jealous of Lydia, the 2½-year-old daughter of the family. Lydia herself was a feeding problem and refused to go to bed at night. There was considerable conflict between Mrs. B and her husband, most of which centered around

246

discipline of the children and the interference of Mrs. B's parents in their marriage.

Mrs. B's parents had battled as long as their daughter could remember. Her father would take refuge from the abuse of his wife by spending several days a week at his daughter's house. He would take over the cooking of evening meals at her home in shy apology for his too frequent visits and in an attempt to make himself useful. Mrs. B's mother was erratic and opinionated, and ruled her husband and her daughter by means of paralyzing guilt-producing tactics. Mrs. B's husband had grimly endured the involved relationships with in-laws for twelve years and now this long-suffering husband had made his own blunt protests. Something needed to be done.

Mrs. B, after several interviews with the caseworker in which she described the chaos of her home, finally began to see clearly that her problems as a wife and a mother were inextricably bound up in her problems with her parents. As long as she could remember she had been in the center of their own marital conflict and had been used by one or another of the parents as refuge and confidante and, as the only child, the sole reason for continuing the marriage. She was the peacemaker, or the trucemaker, and carried the intolerable burden through childhood of keeping her parents together.

Now, as a grown woman, she was still bound to them. She was weary of their quarrels. She was tired of her father's constant presence in her household and sympathized with her husband. But she could not discuss this with her father. Her mother's incessant demands and her interference in Mrs. B's family life exhausted Mrs. B, and impotent rage against mother and father made her a distracted and petulant wife and an erratic mother.

She could not even understand this tie to her parents, she confessed to the caseworker. Her mother and she had very little to say to each other. Her mother would call her frequently on the telephone and Mrs. B, who often longed to end these conversations, could not terminate the calls because of her guilty feelings. Sometimes, she said, her mother would call and say nothing, and each would hold on to the phone, in complete silence, unable to say good-bye.

We have no difficulty in understanding why Mrs. B is unable to function as wife and mother. As long as her infantile ties to her parents are not dissolved she cannot be a wife or parent in her own right. She repeats the infantile conflict with parents in her adult life, and with the best will in the world she cannot prevent herself

247

from doing it. She is tied to her parents through guilt. The telephone calls from her mother become a pregnant symbol; neither one can break the connection.

This constitutes our preliminary casework diagnosis. We might need a second thought to realize that everything that we have said derives from a psychoanalytic diagnosis. As we have indicated, psychoanalytic thinking is so closely woven into casework theory that we often cannot even identify it without a close look. We recognize in Mrs. B's relationships with her parents an unresolved oedipal conflict. The unconscious repetition of infantile patterns we have learned to identify through psychoanalysis; the neurotic guilt feelings that bind this woman to her parents and form an indispensable part of casework diagnosis were first identified and described by Freud.

Let us examine the casework treatment method employed in the case of Mrs. B. The caseworker began to show Mrs. B the repetition of certain patterns in her behavior toward her parents. She did not interpret these patterns but she brought them to her client's attention. (This is an application of a psychoanalytic technique to casework.) Mrs. B responded by examining for the first time in her life certain patterns of conduct which seemed so much a part of her personality that she had never even questioned their existence. (This, too, is a borrowing from psychoanalytic therapy. We create the conditions for self-observation and make the irrational behavior the object of inquiry.) Now the question "Why?" was raised in the casework interviews. "Because I feel so guilty if I don't do these things!" said the client.

The caseworker now needs to make a judgment. To what degree can this pathological tie to parents be modified through casework treatment? There are compulsive patterns in Mrs. B's behavior. She seems too concerned with orderliness and cleanliness. Are we dealing with a compulsion neurosis? If we are, any attempts to alleviate Mrs. B's guilt feelings will only plunge her deeper into illness. In an unobtrusive way the caseworker collects data over a number of interviews and is finally satisfied that there are no systematized compulsions and that orderliness and cleanliness can be abandoned under a number of circumstances without creating anxiety in the client. (Here the caseworker makes use of the psychoanalytic theory of neurosis in order to safeguard her work with the client and to justify the use of casework treatment.)

From this point on the caseworker employs a method of treatment that in no way resembles psychoanalytic therapy and yet makes use of psychoanalytic knowledge in certain identifiable ways. The caseworker supports Mrs. B in her wish to be free of this paralyzing tie to her parents. She gives her permission, as it were, to be free.

> Mrs. B, through the support of the caseworker, begins to take active steps in freeing herself. She becomes firm against her parents' intrusions and their provocation of guilt in her. But with each step her own guilt feelings come to the surface and are brought to the casework interviews for clarification. As a consequence the relationship between Mrs. B and her husband is strengthened and their conflicts diminished. There is considerable improvement in the behavior of the children and Mrs. B demonstrates greater confidence and understanding in her handling of them. (There are, however, indications that Jon may later require treatment for himself.)

In casework terms, the treatment method employed here might be called supportive, although in certain areas treatment was directed toward modification of adaptive patterns. But our description of the method does not in itself describe the dynamics of this treatment. In a scientific casework we want to be able to know exactly why a method works in a particular case or group of cases in order that we can duplicate the results under similar conditions. Here, again, psychoanalysis helps us to understand the dynamics of this treatment. The positive transference to the caseworker is employed for a kind of re-education of conscience. Through the relationship with the caseworker new standards of conduct and new attitudes are introduced to the ego, and the caseworker as a benevolent mother figure and authority has the effect of softening the harsh strictures of the tyrannical mother who was, of course, the original model for conscience. The unconscious sources of guilt feelings remain untouched by this treatment method, but this educational approach, which utilizes conscious attitudes and feelings, may be successful in freeing certain areas of functioning from their paralyzing effects.

Psychoanalytic Perspectives on Adaptation

In each of the cases we have reviewed we began with a disturbance of social functioning, but the restoration of function could only be achieved after careful diagnosis of internal as well as external motives. Psychoanalytic insight provided a precise diagnosis, made the behavior meaningful, and prescribed the corrective measures. The psychoanalytic diagnosis made full use of the data pertaining to the social stituations and the interaction of personalities.

Both psychoanalysis and social work are concerned with problems of adaptation. The study of adaptation has been at the center of psychoanalytic study during the past thirty years. Adaptation, in the psychoanalytic view, is a complex process that involves both external and internal regulation by the ego. Although adaptation is largely the function of the ego, each of the mental institutions— ego, id, and superego—serves adaptation in special ways.

Psychoanalysis shares with other psychologies an interest in the ego's regulation of relationships to the environment and the effects of environment upon the ego's adaptive capacities. But psychoanalysis sees the ego as the regulator of internal as well as external processes, and adaptation in this view is given dimension and complexity. This means that adaptation is achieved not only by the ego's regulation of its relationship to the environment but by its regulation of the internal relationships between the mental institutions.

We can easily see the advantages of such a formulation. A disturbance between the ego and id, for example, can affect the relationship between the ego and the environment. (The classic example of such a disturbance and its effects upon adaptation may be seen in adolescence.) Similarly, a disturbance between the ego and the environment may affect the equilibrium of the mental institutions. (We saw this in the example of Larry, when the conflict with the delinquent boys reactivated an inner conflict between ego and id.) And in the psychoanalytic view the ego's own functions that subserve adaptation may be disturbed if they are drawn into conflict. (An example would be Margaret's impaired learning.)

Such a view of adaptation is extraordinarily complex, but we find that because it is more complex than other theories it is more useful. It obliges us to consider adaptation as a process that engages every part of the personality. A failure or a disturbance in adaptation cannot be attributed to "a weak ego" or "environmental stress," but must be discerned through the most careful study of the internal and external processes that work for adaptation. In order, then, for the social worker to support the adaptive tendencies in personality or to modify adaptive patterns, he must know which parts of the personality are involved. The social worker does not need to be a psychoanalyst to make his assessment. Internal conflicts can be deduced through a study of the ego, as we saw in the case reports we have reviewed, and their relative significance in a disturbance of functioning can be ascertained.

Such a comprehensive view of adaptation gives us a more stable diagnosis than one that measures behavior alone. I know a rebellious and hot-headed little boy who was placed in an institution at the age of 9. Within a year he was perfectly adapted to the requirements of the institution. He was well behaved and polite and no longer gave anyone any trouble. He gained thirty pounds during that first year and began to wet his bed nightly. When I saw him at the age of 11 he was passive, obese, and still a bedwetter. If we judge this adaptation by external signs this child was much improved in his behavior and was well adapted to the requirements of the environment. But the psychoanalytic view of adaptation requires that a successful adaptation be assessed impartially by internal as well as external criteria. An adaptation that results in improved relationships with the environment at the cost of internalized conflict, symptoms, and a shift in the personality from active to passive aims is not a successful adaptation in the psychoanalytic view.

We social workers are always in the position of making crucial decisions in human lives. We make these decisions not through advice-giving but through a diagnosis and the treatment plan that grows out of it. A diagnosis that is based upon social functioning alone can be a perilous undertaking for a mental health worker. And a theory of social functioning and adaptation that does not take into account the inner mental processes that work for adaptation can lead us into the position of manipulators of social roles which calls for a divine wisdom that will not be achieved in two years of graduate study in a school of social work.

251

Teaching and Learning Psychoanalytic Theory

What does a social worker need to know about psychoanalytic theory in order to make effective use of this knowledge in practice? If we use only the case examples I have cited, let us see what knowledge was necessary for diagnosis and treatment. A knowledge of ego and libidinal phases of development, of the structure of the ego and the mechanisms of defense; an understanding of transference phenomena and the repetition compulsion; knowledge of symptom formation and the structure of neuroses—all this is explicit. But we also find that implicit in this knowledge is the theory of drives, the concept of mental energy, primary and secondary mental processes—and before we have completed the list we shall have covered nearly the entire structure of psychoanalystic theory!

I am not advocating, of course, a full curriculum in psychoanalytic theory in the two years of social work graduate training. We are satisfied if we can provide our students with the fundamentals of psychoanalytic theory, even as we are satisfied if we can provide them with the fundamentals of other aspects of social work theory. What, then, constitutes the fundamentals of psychoanalysis for students of social work?

In the present curricula of schools of social work the major concepts and theories of psychoanalysis are presented as part of a course called "Human Growth and Behavior," or "Growth and Development," which is designed to cover physical, mental, and emotional growth throughout the life span. The scope of this course is so vast that it is usually taught by a team of specialists in medicine, psychiatry, anthropology, and psychology with a social work faculty member serving as co-ordinator. The number of lectures specifically dealing with psychoanalytic theory may be a very small fraction of the total. In this respect psychoanalysis fares no worse than other disciplines represented at this smorgasbord. Out of this melange of ink-blots, chicken pox, chromosomes, cortisone, ego, libido, and the Trobriand Islanders, the exhausted student may very well emerge with a disease that I once discovered in an examination paper in this course. It was called "prostrate trouble" and I was so touched that my student found this way of telling me what was wrong with my course that I could not even bring myself to correct his spelling.

There is general dissatisfaction with this course among both faculty and students in schools of social work, and at a time when nearly all schools are considering new ways of teaching this material I should like us to consider that part of the course content that deals with psychoanalytic theory. Because of the vast scope of this course the psychoanalytic content as well as the material from other disciplines is often so general as to be useless. In the short time available to discuss every aspect of human functioning the psychoanalytic content becomes "psychoanalytic information" instead of psychoanalytic theory.

What concerns us most is that students emerge from their introduction to psychoanalysis with a terminology that seems to have very little meaning for them. The student knows the terms "ego," "id," "superego," "oedipus complex" and "libido." He has learned the names of defense mechanisms with the same dutiful feeling that he once learned the Latin names for plants and with as little expectation that the knowledge will do him any good. He often misuses this terminology in ways that reveal his uncertain grasp of concepts.

If we analyze the typical errors of terminological usage of our students, we sometimes get valuable clues to the learning difficulty. We find that many of our students treat the concepts of ego, id, and superego as if they were geographically defined regions in the psyche or even as if they were anatomical structures. The dynamic relationships between the mental institutions are then lost in the student's theory. "Psychic determinism," in the student's view, means that personality is "determined" in early childhood. "Anxiety" is a bad thing to have; a mature person shouldn't have it. Mature people don't have "repressions" either. Defense mechanisms are known to our students in the descriptive sense and are frequently understood in the layman's sense, not the scientific one. "Denial" for example is often understood as "to deny," following ordinary usage. "Reaction formation" is used as a synonym for "reaction." "Undoing" is used to cover a wide variety of acts which have nothing to do with defense, in which an action "undid" or negated an earlier action.

253

On more than one occasion students have shown me how my elementary exposition was responsible for their own untidy thinking. A few years ago when I was teaching a course in "Normal Development" I had introduced students to the mechanisms of defense by identifying and illustrating the types of defense and showed them how anxiety created the motive for defense. I noticed that nearly all the students seemed quite unilluminated by this discussion, and as we were discussing reaction formations, our discussion was particularly fuzzy. Finally one student asked, "What made the defense so strong in the example you gave? Why did it need to be so strong?" This was an excellent question. The problem of quantity could not be explained through the descriptive presentation I had given. And the mechanisms of defense could not be explained without quantity. I had not intended to go into energic concepts during this introductory phase of the course, but I now saw how my elementary exposition was creating its own confusion.

At this point I began to discuss the concept of mental energy and illustrated how a defense "borrows" energy from the warded-off instinctual wish. The students were then able to see how the strength of a defense was a crude measure of the strength of the repudiated wish. From the questions that followed I knew that the students were beginning to grasp the principles of defense. We were also able to make a practical application of these principles to casework treatment. In order to support or to modify defenses in casework treatment, we need to be able to judge the relative strength of a defense and to make inferences regarding the impulse warded off in defense.

On another occasion in a casework class, we were discussing a case of learning disability in a child and got off into a theoretical discussion of sublimation. We saw that sublimation was a special form of displacement. I remarked parenthetically that in defining sublimation we no longer used the phrase "from a lower to a higher goal" because value judgments have no place in a scientific definition. At this point one of my students said, "I don't get it. Then what makes sublimation different from any other form of displacement? If I'm mad at my boss and I come home and kick the door or yell at my wife is *that* sublimation?" This was an excellent question. When I told my student that his question put him in excellent company among psychoanalytic theorists he looked terrified. But now consider the dilemma of the teacher. The elementary presentation got me into trouble again. Yet, to answer the question I needed to lead the students into rough theoretical territory. Hartmann's concept of "neutralization" which could lead us out of this tangle could just as easily bring our class into chaos.* Hartmann, understandably, is not on all casework reading lists.

I enlisted the help of the students. "All right," I said, "what do we need to explain the difference between sublimation and displacement?" Some students thought we would have to return to evaluation of the act, after all. This was argued down by the purists in class. Then someone hit on the notion that the difference could not lie in the displaced goal, but, using the first student's example, in what happened to aggression. Aggression, she thought, would be changed, too, in the sublimated act. In what way? Well, she wasn't exactly sure, but she thought that it would lose some of its aggressiveness; it certainly wouldn't express itself in kicking a door! And there we had it—a homely but practical way of stating the concept of neutralization of energy. With a few more examples we were able to demonstrate that in sublimation there was a displacement of goal with a corresponding change in the mode of energy, that is a "desexualization" or a "deaggressivization" of the energy. When we now returned to our case the child's failure to acquire sublimations took on fresh meaning. With this much understanding of sublimation we could understand the child's failure, and the casework remedy suggested itself.

These are only two of many classroom examples that illustrate the perils of oversimplification of theory. The fragments of theory had no meaning when they were plucked out of the context of the larger theory. My students' defense-mechanism jargon was not a measure of their intelligence or studiousness but a reflection of my own teaching. There is no possibility of understanding defense mechanisms or sublimation or any aspect of ego psychology without introducing the student to the theory of drives, the concept of

* For further discussion of neutralization see Louise Bandler, "Some Casework Aspects of Ego Growth through Sublimation," Chapter 5 of this volume.

mental energy, unconscious mental processes—in short to give unity to these ideas and to show the interrelatedness of mental processes.

My third semester students in casework once had a lively discussion that centered around the use of psychoanalytic knowledge in casework practice. There was general agreement among the students that psychoanalytic ego psychology had demonstrable value to the caseworker, but what about dream theory? What about unconscious processes? Since social workers never deal with unconscious material, they said, was there any need to learn about these things?

I chided them for being so thrifty in their attitude toward knowledge, but I took up the challenge. I reminded them that one cannot divide the mind into geographical territories. The very conception of an ego in psychoanalytic psychology implies the existence of drives and unconscious forces. Where there are no drives there are no mental processes. When the caseworker deals with the ego he must take into account unconscious mental processes even if he does not make them the object of his investigation as does the analyst. A social worker does not need to become expert in dream theory. But knowledge of unconscious mental processes is essential not only because it gives coherence to the study of psychoanalytic theory but because in practice we are obliged to take unconscious motives into account. When we observe a client's behavior, or his defenses, or repetitious patterns in his life, we make inferences regarding unconscious motives. These inferences serve our diagnosis and treatment even though the unconscious motive is not the object of our study.

Although a student may never interpret a dream in his professional life, he may find it profitable and rewarding to become acquainted with the psychoanalytic writings on dreams because there is no better way of understanding unconscious mental processes. The dream, of course, is the model of unconscious mental functioning. If he understands the principles that govern unconscious mental functioning, he will be able to understand defense, symptom formation, transference, and delusional states, and he will also understand the relationship of the ego to the id, which is a significant part of ego psychology.

I have described some of the hazards in learning and teaching that may be attributed to our educational approach in the graduate school. A "psychoanalytic information" course can easily lead to fragmentary and inexact comprehension of psychoanalytic principles, which adds to the confusion of the learner and limits the possibility of applying these principles to social work practice. And, I should add, the best gifts of the teacher may be exhausted in the attempt to present coherent theory within the framework of a course that covers nothing less than the whole of human functioning.

If psychoanalytic knowledge is to be made useful to our students we shall need to find ways in which the fundamentals of psychoanalytic theory can be taught as a coherent body of knowledge, and ways in which we can promote transfer of learning from theory to practice.

I do not envision such a theoretical course or series of courses as a formal series of lectures. It would seem to me most satisfactory to teach this material on the basis of lecture-discussion in classes that should not exceed twenty-five or thirty students. The lecture, if used at all, should not deprive the student of the necessity to acquaint himself with basic writings in psychoanalysis. In our present teaching the psychoanalytic lecturer has served as a kind of readers' digest for the student, and it is not at all unusual for students to admit that they have never read a single work of Freud's. (When we persuade our students to read the neglected works of Freud on their course bibliographies, they are always surprised to find that Freud is more lucid than his elucidators.) Perhaps much of the time that is now spent on lecture-digest of psychoanalytic concepts and theories might be more profitably spent in the libraries. The classroom time might be used for discussion of reading, and clarification of problems. Lectures or exposition by the teacher might be employed to bridge gaps in the students' reading or pull together materials that are not otherwise available to students or are too difficult to place on a student's bibliography.

In a course for social workers it would seem very natural that the teaching should encompass not only the theory but the applications of psychoanalytic theory to social work practice. Illustrative case and group material from social agencies are excellently suited to demonstrate applications to diagnosis and treatment. Although we also expect that the students are studying applications of theory in their methods courses, we should not wish to create rigid divisions in theory and practice. The students' learning will be enhanced throughout if, in each of the teaching areas, we demonstrate the interrelatedness of theory and practice. It is just as advantageous for the methods teacher and the field teacher to discuss problems of theory when this is appropriate.

If we value the contributions of psychoanalysis to social work, we shall need to make it the object of proper study in our professional schools. I do not think that anything less than serious study will yield returns to the student. And as our profession moves toward its objective of a scientific social work we are under a clear obligation to teach the component sciences of social work as science.

The student who understands psychoanalysis as science will know that it is not a speculative system but a body of knoweldge that is derived from observation. He will learn to observe behavior with close attention to detail and be able to draw inferences from it. Having studied the complex processes that enter into ego functioning and social functioning, he will not seek simple remedies and will understand that effective social treatment must take into account the complexities and dimensions of human personality. He will understand the general principles of mental functioning, but he will also know that each personality is uniquely constituted and reacts to its environment in ways that are its own. He should be able to discriminate through a scientific diagnosis between those conflicts that may be relieved through modification of the environment, those that can be helped through understanding and support of adaptive tendencies in personality, and those that require modification of the adaptive patterns themselves. The student who understands all this will also know that professional intervention in a human life carries deep responsibilities and makes severe demands upon his scientific knowledge.

All in all, these benefits of a sound education in psychoanalytic psychology strike us as very familiar. They are, of course, identical with the objectives of a sound professional training in social work.

15. New Frontiers in the Teaching
of Social Casework*

Virginia S. Bellsmith

CASEWORK PRATICE TODAY is undergoing multiple and pervasive changes. While the knowledge base from which practice draws is constantly broadening, the field of forces in which practice is carried on is altering markedly. Professional education must be oriented to these realities of today and to their implications for tomorrow. The impact on education of the behavioral sciences and of the newer extensions of ego psychology has been frequently noted and discussed. Somewhat less attention has been given to the educational implications of the changing context for casework practices. What has happened to the patient and the worker in the mental hospital will furnish one illustration of my thesis.

Mental-Hospital Care Today

It seems only yesterday that a patient with a mental illness of some severity had a predictable fate. As long as his behavior made him a possible danger, to himself or others, he remained institutionalized. The hospital in which he lived for a relatively long period of time was geographically distant from a population center, often housed over five thousand patients, and rarely had sufficient staff

* Presented at the Massachusetts Conference on Social Welfare, Boston, November 1, 1961.

to give more than custodial care. Admissions were largely involuntary and the hospital was a closed social system. The pitifully few professional staff members—including social caseworkers—were part of a vast, humane, holding operation. Some casework was done with individual patients in the hospital, but generally patients were not assigned to a caseworker until immediately prior to, or after, discharge. Casework service utilized familiar techniques of psychological support, designed to strengthen the patient's tie to reality and to extend his ego boundaries; the focus was on helping him move out of, or back into, the hospital, and on working with his family to permit his re-entry into the home. During this time the community was not increasing the size of staff, but was expending ever larger sums of money on physical plants merely to contain mentally ill patients.

Now, all over the United States, there is a veritable revolution in the care and treatment of the mentally ill, without any significant extension of knowledge into the causes of mental illness or even about modes of therapy. The schizophrenic, the manic depressive, or the senile arteriosclerotic is still sick and we still know little about why he is sick. What, then, has happened?

Two things have struck the mental hospital in the recent past. . . . The first [is] that acute clinicians in a few centers have been able to show that practically all of the physical restraints and restrictions used in mental hospitals in the past have been unnecessary—locks, bars, camisoles, packs, involuntary certification—and, the deteriorated, soiling, aggressive, panicky, distraught patients are rapidly disappearing from our mental hospitals.[1]

The second factor is the introduction of tranquilizing drugs into mental-hospital practice with very similar effects on both hospital and patient. The change in the mental hospital has been aptly characterized as a shift not to an open door, but, rather, to a "revolving door." [2] The ramifications of the open hospital, the therapeutic milieu, and the use of chemotherapy have led to a variety of innovations in mental health care.

The caseworker in the mental hospital, like the rest of the staff, is very conscious of what the new order demands of him. The

[1] Ernest M. Gruenberg, *New Developments in Community Mental Health,* Proceedings of a Conference, Massachusetts Department of Mental Health, Division of Mental Hygiene, November, 1959, pp. 13–14.
[2] *Ibid.,* p. 14.

open-ward mental hospital now differs less markedly from other kinds of hospitals. The emphasis is on using all professional staff members for assignments that will strengthen the therapeutic milieu. The caseworker may have responsibility for participation in a patient self-government group, or as a consultant for the halfway-house staff which meets in the community, as well as for casework contact with patients. His direct work with patients and their families reflects the sharp change in philosophy from one of containment to a continuous and multidimensional treatment process to make hospitalization as short and as therapeutically effective as possible, to keep the home fires burning, and to support the mentally ill patient in the community. The mental patient is now in and of the community; the tenacious vestiges of Coventry and Bedlam are at last disappearing.

Caseworkers are working in all the new programs for the mentally ill. Experience indicates that traditional work patterns are not always adequate or even appropriate to this new set of circumstances. Classical casework treatment with the individual is not necessarily the treatment of choice in some of these programs. Our perception of the mental patient has altered as we have seen how we can adapt to his treatment needs, and as we have observed him in an open hospital building or on the grounds unattended by staff. Through our work as consultants to community groups we have been further compelled to evaluate health and illness in new and different terms.

Other Currents in Practice

A comparable movement to that already transforming the agencies and institutions working with the mentally ill is under way in the field of corrections. The expansion of theories about social deviation as well as experimentation in the community, in reformatories, and in prisons give evidence of important changes. If these developments continue, the community will be involved to a much greater degree in preventive care and rehabilitation of the social deviant. The correctional institution will no longer be viewed solely in terms of containment of offenders or as a security operation. Social work—casework, group work, and community organization—will thus be challenged to re-evaluate its theory and treatment strategies and to adopt or create methods specially suited to these developments.[3]

Similarly, in child welfare, if we are going to work with dependent and neglected children in their own homes, as Meier [4] and others suggest, we must do more than prevent family break-up and the child's removal from the home. We must augment our main treatment centers, foster homes, and institutions by introducing a variety of community services designed to support family strengths and to meet children's basic needs. To achieve this end, we shall have to do more than teach the child welfare worker to think "family," and the public welfare worker to think "family and child"; we shall have to extend theory and develop practice skills that will permit us to reach, hold, and help families and children more effectively.

At present, activity group therapy and interview group therapy are practiced by caseworkers in so many settings that they are accepted without question as alternate treatment modes for clients. Family-centered therapy, in which the whole family is seen at the same time is appearing in more settings every year; so too is family life education. A number of agencies have provided special advanced training for staff using the new methods of intervention. Transactional treatment,[5] multiple-impact therapy,[6] crisis intervention,[7] and the life-space interview [8] are all examples of treatment methods that have been recently adopted in traditional social work settings. Experimental demonstrations are still being devised to test or retest these techniques in practice and to proceed with the task of theory development.

[3] J. Douglas Grant, *The Case for Studying Interactions Between Kinds of Treatments*, Unpublished document, California Department of Corrections.

[4] Elizabeth C. Meier, *Focused Treatment in Behalf of Children in Their Own Homes*, Paper delivered at National Conference on Social Welfare, Minneapolis, Minnesota, May, 1961.

[5] Roy R. Grinker, and others, *Psychiatric Social Work: A Transactional Case Book*, Basic Books, New York, 1961.

[6] Agnes Ritchie, "Multiple Impact Therapy: An Experiment," *Social Work*, Volume 5, No. 3 (1960), pp. 16–21.

[7] Howard J. Parad and Gerald Caplan, "A Framework for Studying Families in Crisis," *Social Work*, Volume 5, No. 3 (1960), pp. 3–15.

[8] Nicholas Long, and others, "Life-Space Management of Behavioral Crises," *Social Work*, Volume 6, No. 1 (1961), pp. 38–45.

Educational Implications and Trends

It would seem evident that both schools of social work and training agencies will have to do at least two things with some immediacy: (1) consider thoughtfully whether classroom and agency teaching are actually preparing the student for practice today and five years hence; and (2) study the implications of a range of therapeutic innovations for present theories of practice.

The expansion of courses, in some schools, to include third-year and doctoral programs, with emphasis on advanced practice, research, and the social sciences has profoundly affected social work education. These schools have graduated a crop of new teachers who are introducing studies of theory and method which will influence the master's curriculum in schools of social work throughout the country. This development, combined with other professional activities, has promoted changes in courses in social work methods, personality theory, and the social services. All the courses taught are increasingly weighted with theoretical formulations; current offerings are less descriptive, deal less with "how to do it."

There have been additions to the curriculum, too. Social science courses, for example, were not part of most curricula in schools of social work in the 1940's. Now they appear in a number of school catalogs. Change is in the air; in several schools of social work there is now a standing curriculum committee to assess courses continuously rather than at five- or ten-year intervals. The curriculum committee reviews the content of a course or a sequence in relation to the total content of a graduate student's experience and then makes recommendation for the rentention, expansion, or in some cases, excision of a course. At best, such committee action can establish educational priorities for a given period of time only, for in the professional school the problem of "what to teach when" can never be permanently solved as long as the theoretical framework and method of practice in the profession are subject to scientific scrutiny and experimentation.

Casework Teaching

The casework teacher has his own particular responsibility in relation to the curriculum. He cannot address only the challenge posed by the new. He is bound by the reality that the student practitioner has to master enough of the available knowledge during his two years of training in class and field to be able to meet the needs of his clients. As knowledge increases, the instructor finds it increasingly difficult to cover even the core content in the time allotted. He has to decide whether the inclusion of new material may crowd out established substantive content necessary for practice competence. But he also recognizes that if the practitioner is to achieve a professional status in the social work community, social work education must obviously do more than turn out a social work artisan. One of the ways in which we can ensure the graduation of a *professional* social worker at the end of the two-year period is to expose him continuously to the impact of the fact that social work philosophy, theory, and method are part of an open system of knowledge subject to continuous artistic and scientific exploration, and that only by exploration of the system are knowledge and skill increased. It is not enough to convey this to the student implicitly. Part of our all too brief teaching hours in the methods courses must be devoted to a critical consideration of some of the new frontiers.

The temptation in exploring new material with a class is to start with formulations that seem translatable into the professional social work vocabulary. Both teacher and student are lulled into believing that the writer from another discipline is merely putting into his article or book what every well trained social worker knows and practices. For example, when Otto Pollak did his first study at the Jewish Board of Guardians in New York City some years ago, he made a strong, well-documented case for the inclusion of fathers in the over-all treatment plan in child guidance clinics.[9] The most universal reaction in the professional group outside the Jewish Board of Guardians was that the sociologist was belaboring the obvious. Every social worker knew that fathers were important in families. With few exceptions, however, the field has not yet come to terms with the strategic and methodological consequences that follow if fathers indeed are made an integral part of the treatment unit in child guidance clinics or other social agencies. Our acknowledgment of the importance of fathers in the lives of clients

[9] Otto Pollak, *Integrating Sociological and Psychoanalytic Concepts,* Russell Sage Foundation, New York, 1956.

does not simply mean that we work with them as we do with mothers.

The casework teacher who is trying to introduce content with which he has, at best, only a secondhand, often purely intellectual, acquaintance (in contrast to his intimate knowledge of casework) has to acknowledge this to himself and to the class and to emphasize the necessity for analysis of new material as a first step. He must also acknowledge that even if the new material is clinically tested and found to be of value, fusion with current formulations may not always be possible. Scientific history is replete with illustrations of new theories supplanting older ones and then in turn being extruded by still different formulations. Social work cannot be spared the consequences of evolution, but we can increase the likelihood that when change occurs it will move us toward better service for clients by inculcating in students a genuine spirit of scientific inquiry. They will then be able to discharge their responsibilities as practitioners by subjecting all theories and methods to rational inquiry.

Skepticism and Learning

Unfortunately there are still some reservations about whether one ought to promote a spirit of scientific inquiry in caseworkers. Sometimes the view is offered that practice competence involves only a single-minded commitment to certain well-defined courses of action in behalf of the client; that an approach which is based on skepticism, inquiry, and logic would, at the very least, inhibit the caseworker and, at the worst, make him so anxious that he would be unable to give appropriate service to clients. Towle [10] and others have commented on the inevitability of anxiety in professional learning. There is no question that student anxiety may be intensified as social work education becomes more rigorous and makes more and different demands upon students. However, the more clarity we are able to achieve about the orthodox and heterodox content for which the student is to be held responsible, the greater are the chances that his anxiety will be mastered within the ordinary learning and practice situation. In social work, as in

[10] Charlotte Towle, *The Learner in Education for the Professions*, University of Chicago Press, Chicago, 1954, pp. 27–31.

265

all helping professions, some anxiety will be endemic just as long as practitioners search for answers to the how and why of their activity. Possible student anxiety cannot be used as an excuse for putting blinders on the profession. In fact, our training is designed to help practitioners deal with uncertainties. The student who is equipped with the best methods we can teach him *now* to help clients can assume his share of responsibility for recognizing the gaps in knowledge, and the experimentation necessary to move the profession ahead.

Theoretical Mastery

With all the upheaval in social work and the behavioral sciences, the student has to have an anchor to windward, if he is to retain his balance. In my opinion, stability is derived from the fact that, as a student, he is held accountable for achieving mastery of only one "theory-practice" formulation. In most schools this means that a student is expected to *learn* diagnostic casework as deeply and thoroughly as he can learn it, and as we can teach him. There is an assumption that concentrated study in depth will permit the student subsequently to learn theories and methods other than the one to which he has had primary exposure in a disciplined, scientific fashion. On the master's level, not only are diagnostic casework courses and a Freudian psychiatric sequence prescribed for all casework students, but their field teaching also synchronizes with such an approach. In contrast they learn *about* other theories and methods through classroom exposure only.*

How can students in a time-limited training experience, in which major emphasis is placed on one line of theory, learn about the many relevant alternative formulations? In my own casework teaching I have found it convenient to make use of a bibliography developed especially for this purpose. A review of my experience may illustrate the problems and possibilities of such an approach.

---

* On the third-year and doctoral level, students are held accountable for learning a much wider range of *theories*. For example, they are faced with the fact that neo-Freudian psychiatry, and the other behavioral and social sciences have not been exploited as fully as the Freudian and diagnostic formulations in practice, so that their applicability is perforce in the experimental state, if it has been demonstrated at all.

266

Use of Bibliography

A supplemental bibliography is assigned, with selected references relevant to both theory and practice. The class is asked to read an article, monograph, or book and analyze the material for: (1) relevance to casework process; (2) application to a case being used in class discussion or one of their own cases; (3) relationship to "classical" casework literature—similarities, overlaps, differences; and (4) suggestions for bridges where there are significant gaps. I require oral reports from specific students and take considerable responsibility for organizing and summarizing the content of these.

As might be anticipated, some students have acted as if any departure from the basic bibliography is an attack on the true faith or is at least vaguely subversive. They want to "prove" that the secondary references are not important. Others in the group have welcomed the opportunity of following any will-o'-the-wisp of theory or practice to get away from learning required content. Most of the class, however, have completed the assignment carefully. Discussion has tended to be increasingly well documented as the semester proceeds. The pay-off—if there is any—has come in term papers that reflect an expanded but also a better focused discussion of theory and practice than would otherwise be possible.

First Semester

In the first semester, when students begin to try to winnow out the grain from the chaff as they learn the social study process, the content for which they are held accountable is derived from *Theory and Practice of Social Work* by Hamilton.[11] Two outlines, along with the theoretical formulations on which they are based, are introduced to facilitate the study process; these two are "extras" and are so designated. One developed by psychiatrists is an outline of the data necessary to help in determining whether an individual can be described as normal, neurotic, or psychotic.[12] The

[11] Gordon Hamilton, *Theory and Practice of Social Case Work*, (2nd Edition), Columbia University Press, New York, 1951.
[12] Edward Weiss and O. Spurgeon English, *Psychosomatic Medicine*, Saunders, Philadelphia, 1957.

student's attention is directed to such considerations as the individual's ability to make decisions, his work capacity, his ability to love someone other than himself, and the absence of somatic symptoms of neurotic origin. The differentiations between health and illness and the connection of symptomatology with object world relations and adaptive patterns are meaningful to students as they try to organize a mass of seemingly inchoate study data.

The second outline, derived from sociological study, is focused on family functioning and individual participation in the family.[13] Here the student's attention is directed to those aspects of family life, functional and dysfunctional, with which caseworkers are normally concerned. The material contains a description in detail of the processes that give shape and coherence to the bewildering array of events, perceptions, emotions, actions, learning, and changes which the members experience. For example, the idea is advanced that in every family it is possible to identify how the unit deals with significant biosocial issues in each family's evolution of definitions of male and female and "older" and "younger." It is suggested that each family establishes the boundaries of its world of experience; that to know the individual, one must know his family. All the categories are described in enough detail to allow a student to begin to observe and to ask questions in an interview, or, as he reads a record in class to gain further understanding of the outline's usability in the social study process.

These two outlines of individual and family behavior patterns are used to supplement Hamilton's social study material. They serve to suggest some new dimensions and combinations. The first suggests the interrelationship of the individual's psychodynamics and his adaptation or maladaptation, without designating stress points. The second develops a number of sociocultural variables in the family, suggesting how they can accommodate to, or produce strain in relation to, the psychodynamics of the individual. Recognition of some of these factors is all the beginner can encompass. As he reads more widely and is exposed to other courses and has even limited experience as a practitioner, he may be able

[13] Robert D. Hess and Gerald Handel, *Family Worlds: A Psychosocial Approach to Family Life*, University of Chicago Press, Chicago, 1959.

to test some of these formulations. However, even in the first semester, questions are raised as to whether the outlines are too facile. Students recognize that the answers can come only from careful study of these two instruments in practice. They also realize that such study would be justified only if these outlines showed, from preliminary use, that they were worth further attention. Use of this material has forced them to look at the client-family-problem through a much wider lens; the concept of interaction, as well as the social study data needed to document it, seems more vivid and infinitely more complicated than they had previously considered it to be.

Second Semester

By the second semester, students have finished a variety of courses which may include the history and philosophy of social work, social welfare, the introductory course in the sociocultural sequence, and the beginning psychiatric course in growth and development. Their field experience inevitably places a demand upon them for service that often surpasses their ability to respond appropriately. This is often a period of accelerated learning throughout the curriculum. The casework-course plan is designed to take advantage of this momentum. Class discussion, written assignments, and all the teaching materials used during this semester exploit this increase of professional involvement.

A bibliography of diagnostic casework concepts is assigned. The extensive literature from the functional school of casework is assigned, at the same time, as additional bibliography. Special emphasis is placed upon the theories of Freud and Rank as they have been presented by Mullahy, Hendrick, and Munroe.[14]

I have sometimes used a panel discussion or a written assignment in which the students analyze both approaches and point out the major theoretical differences in both personality theories and casework concepts, and attempt to develop the major methodological and service implications stemming from each philosophy. Such an

[14] Patrick Mullahy, *Oedipus: Myth and Complex*, Hermitage Press, New York, New York, 1948. Ives Hendrick, *Facts and Theories of Psychoanalysis*, (2nd Edition), Knopf, New York, 1939. Ruth L. Munroe, *Schools of Psychoanalytic Thought*, Dryden Press, New York, 1955.

assignment has the advantage of highlighting one of the few illustrations of two explicitly presented theory and practice formulations. The students can start with classical references in casework, from both schools of thought, and then move on to recent publications of both schools so that it is possible to get a dynamic picture of the present status of both philosophies and methods.

Because this reading assignment is so heavy, students do not have much library time to invest beyond that needed to cover the required reading about the diagnostic process on which they are focusing during this semester. However, they are also asked to read one brief report on a service demonstration program in which the diagnostic activity of the caseworker plays an important part. The report deals with an emergency treatment team, consisting of a psychiatrist, a psychiatric nurse, and a psychiatric social worker, which makes a home visit to a patient who would usually be referred directly to a psychiatric hospital.[15] Discussion centers on the diagnostic responsibility of the team which includes assessing the interaction of the patient's psychopathology, physical status, family relationships, and sociocultural factors as they are reflected in his illness and as they bear directly on the decision about hospitalization *versus* home care.

Second Year

Characteristically, the second-year student approaches course and field work with increased sophistication and trepidation. His main concern is that he will not know what to do with what he has previously learned. He wants to learn more about the theory and practice of casework treatment, so that he can help clients more effectively. His classical diagnostic references are heavily weighted with treatment implications; the cases used in class are selected to demonstrate methods and levels of treatment. In the fourth-semester casework course the student typically asks for a recapitulation and deepening of basic content which will make synthesis

[15] Virginia S. Bellsmith, "A Psychiatric Team Home Visit," unpublished teaching material, New York School of Social Work.

possible on a more complete basis than previously. Here, too, the theme he wants to elaborate is invariably that of treatment method.

Through additional reading assignments (in the third or fourth semester) he learns about such developments as milieu therapy,[16] family-centered therapy,[17] and treatment of the multiproblem family,[18] since these seem to be the newer forms of treatment which have already involved caseworkers to a significant degree. In the fourth semester, the class chooses transactional therapy or crisis intervention for discussion purposes. *Social Casework—A Problem-solving Process*, by Perlman,[19] has been used in either the third or fourth semester, to foster the student's analytical ability through use of functional as well as diagnostic literature. The difference between problem-solving and crisis-theory formulations is considered. Problem solving proposes resolution of a range of difficulties through limited intervention with the individual client. The crisis approach involves the development of a model strategy applicable to a specified phenomenon which may occur in a range of clients. The difference between both these approaches and diagnostically oriented casework can be developed.

These selections and their placement in the sequence are not to be regarded as blueprints. They need to be shuffled about and replaced as more useful material becomes available. This experience has suggested the educational advantages of using social work and non-social-work sources interchangeably. Furthermore, this plan strengthens the student's image of the profession as being involved with new themes and the growing edges of practice as they are reflected in the literature. The fostering of a critical approach to our literature (often conspicuously absent in our field) is a valuable by-product.

[16] Morris S. Schwartz, "What Is a Therepeutic Milieu?" *The Patient and the Mental Hospital*, Milton Greenblatt and others (eds.), The Free Press, Glencoe, Illinois, 1957, pp. 130–144.

[17] Nathan W. Ackerman, *The Psychodynamics of Family Life*, Basic Books, New York, 1958; and John E. Bell, "Family Group Therapy," *Public Health Monograph*, Number 64, United States Department of Health, Education, and Welfare, 1961.

[18] Ludwig L. Geismar, "Three Levels of Treatment for the Multiproblem Family," *Social Casework*, Volume XLII, No. 3 (1961), pp. 124–127.

[19] Helen Harris Perlman, *Social Casework: A Problem-solving Process*, University of Chicago Press, Chicago, 1957.

Obviously, a guided tour to new landmarks in social work, *via* bibliography, cannot solve all the pedagogical problems engendered by the growth and development of a profession. The reading and subsequent discussion serve mainly as vehicles for teaching that social work theory building and practice demonstration are a never-ending process. Hopefully, we shall move from what are often symbolic exercises to the actual infiltration of emerging content into schools of social work. As was suggested in the New York School curriculum study,[20] this end can be achieved through seminars (open to qualified students) where faculty members and students can, over a period of years, collaborate on problems of theory and practice. If substantial content ultimately emerges from such a joint venture, it will then be considered for inclusion in formal academic courses and in field teaching.

Another way of breaking the still-tight, student chrysalis might be to re-establish participant observation as a respectable mode of social work learning. We know that two-way screens, tape recording, films, and staff seminars can teach the student in ways different from those of the supervisor and the classroom teacher about the complicated world of theory and practice. Why not try making them *the* teaching tools in some settings and assess their effect on student learning and performance?

Regardless of our methods, we must transmit our body of knowledge fully and freely. If in the process we do not inhibit the spontaneity and creativity of the student entering the profession but, instead, provide him multiple opportunities for growth and the incorporation of professional values about self-discipline and the commitment to the pursuit of excellence in service for clients, we shall virtually guarantee that new frontiers will continue to be acknowledged, explored, and settled by succeeding generations of social workers.

[20] Herman D. Stein, *Curriculum Study*, New York School of Social Work, Columbia University, 1960.

16. The Changing Role of the Supervisor*

Lucille N. Austin

THE QUESTIONS CURRENTLY under debate about supervision in the social work profession are related in part to the status that can be achieved by the practitioner, and in part to the design of the administrative structure best suited to a profession that is practiced under agency auspices. For many years the system accepted by agencies and workers alike had as its core the "close" supervision of the practitioner at all levels of experience. Administrators approved of such a system because it reinforced, rather than disturbed, the hierarchical structure of the agency, which was based on the current principles of administration. They believed that organizations should operate under a formal, logical, rational design, and that organizational efficiency is increased when agency activities constitute a hierarchy in which the activities of persons in the lower section are directed and controlled by those at the top.[1] Workers approved the system because the tutorial supervisory situation was accepted as the means for achieving technical competence. Supervisors concurred because their superior position in the hierarchy was recognized.

* Presented as the Fifth Annual Lecture of the Smith College School for Social Work Alumnae Association, Philadelphia, April 22, 1960.
[1] Chris Argyris, "Some Propositions about Human Behavior in Organizations," *Symposium on Preventive and Social Psychiatry,* Walter Reed Army Institute of Research, Washington, D.C., 1957, p. 218.

In recent years, however, particularly since 1953, dissatisfactions have been expressed with the system, by the practitioners generally and at times by supervisors. [2] Practitioners are asking for more autonomy in their work—for the rights and responsibilities of decision-making and self-direction. They are asserting that their place in the agency hierarchy should not be at the bottom of the pyramid. They want the practice job recognized as one that merits substantial status and salary, and is not merely a channel for promotion to positions in supervision and administration.

The Status of the Practitioner

The first topic, dealing with the status of the practitioner, should be discussed before we move on to the second subject of innovations in organizational structure and administrative practice. It is generally assumed that the practitioner in any profession is its most important member because he administers the service to the client. The status jobs in social work, however, have been those of supervision, administration, and teaching. This situation came about because social work, as a new profession, required its skilled practitioners to move into teaching and administration in order to induct new members, and to work in the agencies on method development.

As long as the most promising workers are drawn off into supervisory work and practice is left in the hands of beginning workers or those of average ability, it will follow that practice can reach only a certain level of competence; that practitioners cannot undertake validation of prescribed methods or innovation on an experimental basis. Until the practice job is given full status, professionalization is not completed. It seems that the time is at hand for agencies to implement the aims of the professional group and enhance the career of the practitioner. The crucial questions center around the status of the new graduates at the master's level, the beginning workers.

At what point in his career is the practitioner capable of assuming a truly professional role, with the autonomy usually implied by this

[2] See Charlotte G. Babcock, "Social Work as Work," *Social Casework*, Vol. XXXIV, No. 10 (1953), pp. 415–422; Esther Schour, "Helping Social Workers Handle Work Stresses," *Social Casework*, Vol. XXXIV, No. 10 (1953), pp. 423–428; Lucille N. Austin, "An Evaluation of Supervision," *Social Casework*, Vol. XXXVII, No. 8 (1956), pp. 375–382.

term? Does the achievement of the master's degree in social work prepare the student to begin actual practice in his profession? There is a growing body of evidence that the answer is "Yes." Agencies are now attempting to define the job of the beginning worker and to set up appropriate criteria for judging performance. Credit is being given to what the worker knows and can do, rather than judging him on what he does not know and still has to learn. The concept of an internship period following graduation has been pretty well discredited in favor of realistic definition of a beginning job. [3] Social work education in the master's program has been steadily enriched by the growing conceptualization of social work methodology, and the formulation of a body of transmissible knowledge which facilitates the teaching and learning of a process. Today's graduates, therefore, are better prepared than those of ten years ago.

Despite these positive achievements, some doubts about the capacity of the beginning worker still exist. We hear that "They know a lot but there is so much to learn." "Young people of today are not as dedicated as we were." "They want privileges but not responsibility." "The professional responsibility to serve clients is so great it cannot be entrusted to beginners." "The accountability of the agency to its sponsors can only be guaranteed by close inspection and is too serious a matter to be delegated to the initiate." The question under discussion here concerns the means by which the desired end of professional excellence can be achieved.

Independence and self-confidence cannot be nurtured in an overanxious and perfectionistic climate. In many agencies the climate is not dissimilar to that in a home where the overprotective mother, well known to us all, cannot free her child. The reciprocal role of a timid or negativistic child in that situation is paralleled in a worker who is similarly restricted and similarly acculturated. A 6-year-old child who was asked, "What is the nicest thing about being six years old?" replied, "To go on your own once in a while." Surely at 22 or 32 the pleasure and the right to go on one's own and take the consequences are not too much for the professional to ask.

[3] See Frances H. Scherz, "A Concept of Supervision Based on Definitions of Job Responsibility," *Casework Papers, 1958,* Family Service Association of America, New York, 1958, pp. 18–32.

A review of the assumptions that constituted the rationale for the traditional supervisory system reveals the attitude that the practitioner has not been regarded as fully a professionalized person, although many reason can be given for its defense. [4] The established system has rested on the belief that:

1. The beginning worker needs a long period of tutorial instruction following his master's degree.

2. Close supervision is the best medium for teaching workers at any stage of development. The supervisor can know the worker and his caseload intimately, and can teach him in accordance with his individual needs. Workers therefore learn and improve their practice in direct relation to the quantity and quality of supervision.

3. Social work learning and practice arouse personal conflict and anxiety. The worker needs self-awareness in order to help others, and the supervisor is in the best position to help him gain it and to give him needed support.

4. Administrative responsibility is delegated to the supervisor in the chain of command and he is, therefore, accountable for the work of staff members assigned to his care. The supervisor is logically the primary, and often the sole, evaluator of the worker, because he knows the work of his supervisee intimately.

5. The supervisor as administrator is responsible for implementing and interpreting policy to the staff, and for seeing that it is carried out. He, in turn, represents the staff in channeling their ideas about policy and program to the central administrative group.

It is well to remind ourselves of the professional self-image which we hold by right of being professional men and women, and which we seek to inculcate in our students. A professional person has a philosophy, a code of ethics, and a body of specialized knowledge to use in the service of clients. Only he can weld these three components into a scientifically based art of practice. A professional person must be in a work situation where his expertise is held in respect and where he is given room for self-direction.

[4] Lucille N. Austin, "Basic Principles of Supervision," *Social Casework*, Vol. XXXIII, No. 10 (1952), pp. 411–419; Sidney S. Eisenberg, "Supervision as an Agency Need," *Social Casework*, Vol. XXXVII, No. 5 (1956), pp. 233–237.

A new set of concepts that reflect these ideas is now emerging. [5] These may be summarized as follows:

1. The master's degree in social work is the recognized degree of the professional in social work. It entitles its holder to the usual "rights, privileges, and immunities" pertaining to this rank.

2. The tutorial situation is useful at times in any stage of learning, but group learning, contacts with many individuals, and the learning that can only come from experience are equally important. The worker therefore must assess his needs and determine what use he will make of available resources and stimuli to further his skill.

3. Learning and improvement in skill are not necessarily directly related to the quantity and quality of supervision. They may be more closely related to self-motivation and the aptitude of the worker.

4. Self-awareness is important in understanding others. If the worker has a problem in the work situation this must be called to his attention. If he needs therapy he must seek it outside the agency. Prolonged supervisory support too often obscures the need for specific therapy or the individual's basic inadequacy.

5. The work situation is inherently anxiety-producing. Support from a structure that provides incentives that ease strain, such as adequate salaries, reasonable leeway in time arrangements, and professional recognition by colleagues will go far in reducing work tensions.

6. The professional social worker is capable of understanding and abiding by policy and procedure, and is in a key position to contribute directly to policy making because of his firsthand contact with the clients.

7. The professional worker can be held accountable for his own work. He should be able to recognize the need for an objective evaluation and to relate to evaluation procedures that respect his internalized ethic of accountability, define criteria, and designate suitable evaluators.

[5] Lucille N. Austin, "An Evaluation of Supervision," *op. cit.;* Frances H. Scherz, *op. cit.*

If the practitioner's job is defined in these terms, there are implications for change in the supervisor's role. Obviously, if one position in the structure is redefined, other positions and the system as a whole will be affected. As new sets of relationships between the jobs are studied, the function of the supervisory job will be determined.

Organizational Theory and Its Implications for Administration

Before we discuss the proposals for change that have already been made, it would seem useful to develop a relevant, theoretical frame of reference about organizational structure and administrative practice. Social work is still an agency-centered profession, although private practice has been increasing and some group practice associations have been formed, partly as a result of dissatisfaction with existing organizational restraints. It seems likely that agency-centered practice will continue to be the major form of social work, because of the very nature of its relationship to the community and the larger society, and the professional commitment to meet needs that involve the provision of social services. Hence, the social work profession is vitally concerned with organizational form, as it affects both the professional maturation of its members and adequate services to clients.

The need for a purposive formal organizational structure in a well-run agency is clear. Social work is not immune to, or unaffected by, the trend toward bureaucracy in other institutions in our society. Stein points out that "bureaucratic theory is now being looked to as the major source of understanding organizational problems in social work administration." He goes on to say, "This theory makes it possible to speculate about the functional and dysfunctional consequences of the formal organizational system and to design research that will yield facts for use in further planning." [6] Vinter has also written about the social structure of services. [7]

[6] Herman D. Stein, "Organization Theory—Implications for Administration Research," *Social Science Theory and Social Work Research*, National Association of Social Workers, New York, 1960, pp. 80–90.

[7] Robert D. Vinter, "The Social Structure of Service," *Issues in American Social Work*, Alfred J. Kahn (ed.), Columbia University Press, New York, 1959, pp. 242–269.

Bureaucratic theory is significant for small agencies as well as large, since the model in larger agencies is accepted as a pattern even when it is not fully put into operation. The informal structure of the smaller agency has its problems, as Polansky has pointed out; the small happy family is not always so happy.[8]

It may come as a new idea to social workers to hear their agencies called bureaucracies. To many workers loyalty to "our agency" is as much a personal matter as a professional matter. Perhaps necessary organizational loyalty will be strengthened and made appropriate if the agency can be viewed in objective terms. A first suggestion is that the criteria used in student evaluations need examination. The criteria may read: (1) ability to work within the framework of the agency; (2) ability to accept policy, procedures, and agency "limits." Should the criteria also include the student's ability to be critical of agency policy and procedures as they affect his work and service to clients? This idea, so often said to be implicit, needs to be explicated. Too often we have protected the agency from criticism and shut the student off from an important area of learning about administration and policy making.

What is a bureaucracy? In its popular definition it is a rigid organizational form with emphasis on red tape and depersonalized ways of dealing with employees. Theoretically, it is a formal organizational system which strives to clarify roles, distinguish between superiors and subordinates, and locate power in proper centers. Also, in this sense the organizational system is seen as a social system and can be studied as such. Like other social systems it has value orientations, defined role relationships, rewards and punishments, prescribed forms of behavior in set situations, and channels of communication, which shape the behavior of its members and give it character. Seen in these terms, social work administration can no longer work within a narrow set of concepts and principles. It must envisage the intricate network of social interaction in the work situation. It must study the consequences of administrative structure and actions for both the staff and the clients of the agency.

[8] Norman A. Polansky, "The Professional Identity in Social Work," *Issues in American Social Work, op. cit.,* pp. 293–318.

279

This perspective impels one to consider other modes of organization or the restructuring of patterns in the existing mode.[9]

Some sociological research, particularly in the mental hospitals and correctional institutions, is pointing up the significance of bureaucratic theory as a source of new insights for adminstrative changes and program planning. [10] Social work literature includes new considerations about the effects of agency policy on clients selected for treatment, about the role expectations for the "good" client, and about the ways in which the worker's perception of the clients is affected by the institutionalized versions of hopefulness or despair concerning the outcome for clients with varying diagnoses. It is hoped that some of these new concepts may be more widely used to study the formal and informal organizational structure of the social agency and its influence on the performance of staff members and on service to clients. It is sometimes hard for supervisors and administrators to raise questions about the existing system because it has been good *to* them, though perhaps not as good *for* them as they may think.

Sociological research on bureaucratic structures outside social work, particularly in industry and some government agencies, has pointed up some of the dilemmas plaguing social agency administration. Argyris, in a paper on "Some Propositions about Human Behavior in Organizations," analyzes the basic properties of formal organizations and properties of the human personality. [11] He concludes that there is a basic incongruence between the needs of a mature personality and the requirements of formal organization. The incongruence increases as: (1) employees are of increasing maturity; (2) the formal structure based on principles that form a rational design is made more clear-cut and logically tight for maximum effectiveness of the formal organization; (3) one goes down the line of command; and (4) jobs become more and more mechanized,

[9] See Herman D. Stein and Richard A. Cloward (eds.), *Social Perspectives on Behavior,* The Free Press, Glencoe, Illinois, 1958, pp. 560–609.

[10] Alfred H. Stanton and Morris S. Schwartz, *The Mental Hospital,* Basic Books, New York, 1954; Lloyd E. Ohlin, Herman Piven, and Donnell M. Pappenfort, "Major Dilemmas of the Social Worker in Probation and Parole," *National Probation and Parole Association Journal,* Vol. II, No. 3 (1956), pp. 211–225; Harold L. Wilensky and Charles N. LeBeaux, *Industrial Society and Social Welfare,* Russell Sage Foundation, New York, 1958, pp. 233–282.

[11] Argyris, *op. cit.,* pp. 222–225.

that is, take on assembly-line characteristics. Argyris says the dilemma between meeting the needs of the individuals and the demands of the organization is a basic continual dilemma posing an eternal challenge to the leader. His analysis of what happens to workers in a tight system that molds their behavior toward the organization's objectives, and thereby makes them passive, and dependent on and subordinate to the leader, is paralleled by the reports in social work literature on the effects of prolonged supervision. His analysis of worker responses to conflict, frustration, failure, and short-time perspective—culminating in the choices of leaving the organization, climbing the organizational ladder, manifesting such defense reactions as daydreaming, ambivalence, regression and projection or becoming apathetic and disinterested toward the organization, its make-up, and goals—can also be applied in social agencies. These studies confirm the fact that the system influences employee behavior. They discredit an exclusive diagnosis of personal hostility attributed to workers who express criticism or dissatisfactions.

Gouldner, in his analysis of bureaucratic structures, factored out two types of bureaucracy: the representative bureaucracy and the punishment-centered bureaucracy. "The representative bureaucracy is, in part, characterized by authority based on knowledge and expertise. It also entails collaborative or bilateral initiation of organizational rules by the parties involved; the rules are justified by the participants on the ground that they are means to desired ends, and persuasion and education are used to obtain compliance with them." This is in contrast to the punishment-centered bureaucracy characterized by authority based on incumbency in office which requires subordinates to do things that are divergent from their own aims. [12]

It is apparent, in terms of social work philosophy and in terms of the attributes of a profession, that the representative bureaucracy is the type of organization congruent with social work needs. It is important to know whether social agencies are indeed of this type, to what extent, and the consequence where it is not so.

[12] Alvin W. Gouldner, "Organizational Analysis," *Sociology Today*, Robert K. Merton, Leonard Broom, Leonard S. Cottrell (eds.), Basic Books, New York, 1959, p. 403.

Insights from sociological studies are available on other kinds of strain inherent in integrating professional roles into an organizational structure. Wardwell, writing on the subject of bureaucratization and the professions points out that professional roles in general resist bureaucratization. He says, "A professional man, such as a doctor or lawyer, does not need delegated authority and the weight and sanction of an authoritarian organization to support his professional decisions. . . . The appropriate basis of social organization for a profession is therefore the group of equals pattern of the professional association, rather than the bureaucratic type of organization. [13] The social work profession is now struggling more consciously than before with the question of how the "group of equals pattern" can be harmonized with formal organization patterns. The questions were not raised as sharply before because social work practice was not yet fully professionalized. Now that it is, it is inevitable that the practitioner should be more aware of the effects of an administrative structure on his work than was the practitioner of an earlier day. Wardwell points out that it is probable that the professions, with their philosophy and humanistic patterns, can provide the integrative forms and skills needed to build harmonious interrelationships between professional and bureaucratic ideologies.

Proposals for Change in the Organizational Chart

With this background it becomes apparent that the influence of the formal structure in the agency is far reaching. The immediate task is to see if job definitions and organizational arrangements can be restructured in a satisfying formal organizational pattern that will be consistent with professional goals and values. Consideration must be given to some of the questions about job autonomy, suitable specializations and their interrelationships, and accountability by all members of the agency. Because the pyramid has been used in many organizations and perhaps meets their needs, we have tended to think of it as the only possible structure. But change is always possible. The administrative pyramid may be changed to another

[13] Walter I. Wardwell, "Social Integration, Bureaucratization and the Professions," *Social Perspectives on Behavior,* Herman D. Stein and Richard A. Cloward (eds.), The Free Press, Glencoe, Illinois, 1958, pp. 572–576.

form if the practitioner and the executive use new channels of communication with each other, if the practitioner is presumed to have a voluntary relationship with the persons concerned with staff development, and if authority is delegated to him for making decisions in matters of professional practice. Delegation of authority downward is quite a reversal from the earlier model. Obviously, the supervisor's job as it is now defined will be vitally affected if many of his functions are removed and transferred to the practitioner, that is, if he is not held responsible for the worker's performance, or for sharing responsibility for decision making in the individual case.

An analysis of the supervisory job and one possible new pattern for experimentation was projected in my 1956 paper, referred to above. I pointed up some of the negative factors in the existing system by stating that: (1) the assimilation of knowledge and the internalization of standards by the worker are weakened by an emphasis on extreme controls; (2) the caseworker's professional contacts within the agency are too limited; (3) the assignment of two major functions, teaching and administration, tends to a concentration of power in one person; and (4) this dual function leads to an overly complex assignment for the supervisor. I projected in a purely theoretical way some of the possible means by which the supervisor might be freed to carry out his basic responsibility for staff development, and for enabling workers to perform as adult responsible professional persons. A separation of the administrative and teaching functions was proposed. The suggestion was made that the title of supervisor should be retained for designated administrative personnel, skilled in administrative leadership and knowledgeable about the professional process to be administered. The teaching function would be assigned to staff development personnel without line authority. This definition of a new set of administrative persons called for respect and knowledge about the administrative process. It implied that performance as an administrator involves the mastery of particular knowledge and a set of skills, and is of such importance that it cannot be obscured by a mixed assignment which makes it secondary to the teaching assignment. The plan located the evaluative responsibility in administrative hands in order to remove it from confusion with

283

an educational appraisal and teaching device. The need for a change in the system of communication between practitioners and the administration on matters of policy and program development was emphasized.

It was further assumed in this proposal that the teaching personnel would be related to the administrative structure of the agency in proper ways, but their primary responsibility would lie in improving the skills of staff members, with a focus on the development of professional method in the interest of the clients of the agency. They would use all the skills developed in social work teaching particularly related to practice learning. They would teach in a tutorial relationship and in group situations as requested by the staff members, with attention to immediate case problems and ongoing conceptualization of professional methodology.

The problems to be dealt with in such an organizational departure are those of co-ordinating the work of the staff development personnel (who are outside the line of authority) with the administrative personnel, since each group relates to staff in different ways. New ways will need to be worked out for achieving effective communication about those matters requiring decision which occur at different levels of operations and which have significance for the agency as a whole.

The proposed plan involves a radical change. All the factors now operative indicate that there will be a gradual shift in this direction even if the change is unplanned. The experiments of some agencies now trying the plan should be made known to the field. Organizational theory holds that specialization of an activity inevitably leads to a separation of functions. This seems to be the trend in social work practice, administration, and teaching. Research has entered the field as a specialization and is seeking a definition of its place in the structure.

Recently, Frances Scherz described an experiment in supervision in the Jewish Family and Community Service in Chicago.[14] She defines supervision as an administrative job with the teaching function "integrated with management, rather than as one of *two* functions assigned to the supervisor." The administrative aspects of the supervisory job are clearly analyzed and a new dignity is given to the

14 Scherz, *op. cit.*

284

supervisor's administrative role. She also emphasizes the importance of high-level conceptual teaching but assumes that the skills of administration and teaching can be mastered and the tasks best performed by one person, the supervisor. She makes it quite clear that the practitioner, including the first-year worker, is esteemed for his competence and is held responsible for his own work. He is free to use the agency's staff development resources voluntarily in the interests of improving his practice, but he must be accountable to the administration.

If this agency succeeds in elevating the administrative role in the supervisor's assignment, the teaching assignment may fall into a secondary place. However, if the administrative role is not elevated in fact, the teaching role may again be in the ascendancy, and there will be a return to the status quo. Role confusion has been minimized in this blueprint. The issues of role conflict and centralization of power in the supervisor's job have not been factored out, nor has the complexity of the assignment been assessed. Further publication of this agency's experiences will be of interest.

Reports of other experiments with new organizational arrangements are making their way into the literature. [15] These include so-called group supervision, peer supervision, and consultation, rather than supervision for experienced workers. Such experiments are important because they are attempts to introduce into the formal structure various new ways to relieve strain. They have limitations in that they are, for the most part, undertaken without relation to the question of their consequences for the organizational system as a whole, and they bypass important administrative issues. For example, having members evaluate each other in group sessions is obviously not a substitute for an administrative evaluation. Similarly, there would seem to be role discontinuity in a system that holds workers under "close" supervision for a long period and then releases them to the freedom of consultation at a late age.

At any rate, the ice has been broken, and a flow of ideas will continue until some new forms are evolved.

[15] See John Wax, "The Pros and Cons of Group Supervision," *Social Casework,* Vol. XL, No. 6 (1959), pp. 307–313; Arthur L. Leader, "New Directions in Supervision," *Social Casework*, Vol. XXXVIII, No. 9 (1957), pp. 462–468; Carl M. Shafer, "The Family Agency and the Private Casework Practitioner," *Social Casework*, Vol. XL, No. 10 (1959), pp. 531–538; Ruth Fizdale, "Peer-Group Supervision," *Social Casework*, Vol. XXXIX, No. 8 (1958), pp. 443–450.

Administration as a Specialization

The need for some further analysis of the specialized nature of administration and teaching emerges as we try to set up criteria for various positions. It is true that we have been slow in developing a body of knowledge about administration and its related skills. A practical and theoretical discussion of the subject leads us to the realization that administration is a specialization in social work. The recent study by the Council on Social Work Education points out that few courses in this subject have been offered in the schools, and that field work in training for administration has been almost non-existent.[16] Questions must be answered as to whether such education can be conducted at the master's level or whether it can only be offered at the doctoral level. Meanwhile administrators have grown into their jobs through apprenticeship or, more often, through learning on the job. Social work administrators have a body of knowledge and work competence which they have not always defended, because they were intimidated by the expertise of the practitioners and supervisors. Supervisors with line authority have constituted the largest number of administrators in the profession. Yet because they conceived of themselves as teachers, and were held responsible as administrators only in limited ways, they did not advance administrative methods as they did educational methods. In their alignment with the staff, supervisors often undercut the administrator, or kept issues from full discussion by trying to placate both groups.

In large agencies as well as in small ones the existing pattern, in which the executive works with the community and the board and the casework supervisor concentrates his attention on the staff, has served to put distance between the administrator and the staff. The casework supervisor, as assistant to the director in many agencies, has held a power position. She (more often than he) achieved the position and derived her status from her knowledge of method, and was delegated administrative authority which allowed her to develop an empire of which the executive knew very little.

[16] Werner W. Boehm, "Objectives for the Social Work Curriculum of the Future," *Social Work Curriculum Study*, Werner W. Boehm (ed.), National Council on Social Work Education, New York, 1959, p. 138.

The administrator must think anew about his role. What does he want to delegate, and why? What does he know about what is going on in his agency? How is the informal structure militating for and against the aims of the formal structure? What does staff turnover signify about morale? Can he accept as valid the supervisor's statement that a resigning worker is not suitable for the agency, or is it possible that the worker is a professionally able person who cannot function within the limits of this agency? How can the administrator get to know what the students and clerical staff know about the internal stresses? When are agency need and agency loyalty antithetical to the professional career of an individual worker? How can objective criteria be established for rating performance in a variety of jobs? What is the effect of size of the agency on participation and worker satisfaction? What is the effect of centralization or decentralization of service units on clients in different parts of a city?

If able administrators begin to open channels of communication with the practitioners, rather than speaking only with supervisors who represent the staff, will vitality flow into the tasks of program planning and policy making? Will practitioners place their technical preoccupation in new perspective if they are directly involved in program planning? Will new knowledge and experience with clearly designated administrative personnel open up career choices in administration for those who have interest and aptitude? Do students need this opportunity as well as staff? These and many other questions should be engaging the administrator. The time is ripe for the administrator to claim respect and status in the profession.

Relevant organizational theory, as I have suggested, must be studied by administrators for its import. It is a dynamic theory and can do for administration what a dynamic personality theory has done for practice. The integration of a theory of agency structure and function with a theory about the needs of professionals in agency work situations would be a major contribution to the profession from administrators. If supervisory personnel begin to realize the import of their function as administrators they will be inspired to do the same creative job for administration that they

287

have done in developing educational method in social work. Only when they become knowledgeable about the theory of administration will they perceive the source and the reality of some of the strains they are experiencing.

Teaching as a Specialization

Lest the teaching function fall into a secondary place because of enthusiasm about administration, I must speak about this specialization. Agency teachers have developed a high degree of specialized pedagogical methodology and have contributed to educational theory. Agency supervisors as well as social work educators in the schools have related psychoanalytic personality theory to learning theory, and devised individualized teaching techniques that facilitate learning. Agency supervisors and experienced practitioners have also conceptualized casework methodology on a clinical practice level and on a general theory level.

There is a vitality in the agency teaching assignments in terms of the immediacy of the application of concepts. The demands on attention, imagination, and ingenuity are high because there is no ready-made syllabus. Order is achieved through the teachers' strong hold on a conceptual framework. There are few other supports. Combinations of assignments which distract rather than feed into the central task of teaching are not conducive to good results. The selection of teachers is another matter of vital importance. Only he who loves to teach and has particular aptitude for communication of ideas should be entrusted with this mission.

Exactly what is involved in "conceptual teaching" in an agency? This means not only teaching the case in all its immediate significance for the clients involved, but it also means teaching the case in terms of its implications for method development. An organized body of knowledge that makes it possible to carry over learning to other similar cases depends on the construction of working hypotheses that can be tested out in practice.

Work on identifying and systematizing knowledge derived from practice is the specific task of the practice and teaching groups in the agency. The formulation of a specialized method for the treatment of character disorders is an example of the way in which generaliza-

288

tions growing out of practice in several agency settings were systematized and made available for further testing.

The agency practitioners and teachers are also concerned with using and developing a general theory of method focused on social study, diagnosis, and treatment. A look at the theory of social study, with its emphasis on scientific methodology directed to the ascertaining of facts and deriving inferences, shows the close interrelationship between clinical theory and general theory. A theory of social study becomes a guide to the formulation of principles about case management during the initial stages of the case. It poses many questions. What kind of data is relevant to the understanding of the problem? What sources of data will be utilized? How can the study be conducted at the same time that immediate needs are met and crises handled? What short-cuts to full study are productive? What data are so significant that other data can be ignored? Within the theoretical assumption that there is need for understanding the total personality and total social situation of the client, what partialization can be made that will define a proper unit of attention within the broad field? New ideas about psychosocial diagnosis are emerging as work is focused on better ways of correlating personality diagnosis and social situational factors. Questions are arising about family diagnosis and treatment.

The need for new formulations about treatment methodology is pressing, since attention to new variables introduces new dimensions and suggests new techniques. Suffice it to say that the teaching personnel in the agency need more time than is now available for concentrated attention on educational method and practice content. They need time for association with the educational groups in other agencies and the schools, if they are to give leadership in their advantaged position in the profession. They also need to be related to research endeavors in their own agencies, as well as to other research in the field. A narrow agency focus can be dysfunctional for the agency as well as for the profession. Agency teaching, therefore, must be provided a properly structured role.

Implications for Social Work Education

Many implications for social work education emerge from this discussion. How can the student be better prepared for the position

289

he will hold? How can the transition from student to professional be facilitated so that it represents a continuous orderly progression? An analysis of the present situation does reveal that the professional schools and the social agencies must strengthen their partnership in social work education. Collaborative work on curriculum content is needed for better teaching by the classroom faculty, and for improved field instruction in the agencies. The current effort to establish within agencies a specialized position of field instructor whose major responsibility is the training of students is an important step in the right direction. This should reduce the turnover of field instructors and should build a group of experienced field teachers. The educational principle of learning through involvement points the way to more contact between administrative personnel and students in regard to policy making, program planning, and community activity. How can this be implemented?

The professional schools recently have been putting a greater premium on the student's capacity for self-direction. We have been moving steadily toward encouraging students to question and be critical of practice, and of agency programs and policy. Today's students are fortunate in having access to new social science formulations at the beginning of their careers. They are benefiting from the rethinking of methodology in conceptual terms which is a natural concomitant of effective field instruction and classroom teaching. They will be bringing to the agencies a new stimulation which should be welcomed, however upsetting it may be.

It is always more comfortable to be one step ahead of young people, but we must never underestimate their capacity to bring about change if the climate encourages this. If students and young workers had not spoken up in the last decade, the questions about their status might have been a long time in taking form.

Conclusion

In summary, the definition of the supervisory role in social work is undergoing change. If professional recognition and salary scales are re-evaluated so that the practitioner is given status equal to, if not superior to, that of the administrator and teacher, a different climate and administrative structure will be apparent in the agency.

290

Administrative practice in social work is facing new demands for creative leadership within the agency as well as in the community. New insights from organizational theory, role theory, and communication theory, combined with a dynamic psychology of human relations, should place administration in a position to become a fully professionalized specialization in social work. A proper structuring of the agency teaching role will facilitate the transmission of knowledge built up in practice, and increase the agency's contribution to practice innovation. Practitioners, teachers, and administrators must be willing to experiment with new organizational patterns that will further their common professional goals.

17. Understanding Ego Involvement in Casework Training*

Yonata Feldman

THE PRACTICE OF CASEWORK had its beginning when philanthropy discovered that man cannot live by bread alone. It developed and broadened as the behavioral sciences, especially psychoanalysis, made valuable contributions to the knowledge of man's psychological needs. These contributions aided practitioners not only in understanding how man may grow and find increasingly better ways of meeting his needs, but also in recognizing that man may find ways to destroy himself through inappropriate behavior or mental or emotional illness.

Increasing sophistication about the nature of man made it clear to caseworkers that goodness of heart alone is not sufficient equipment for helping others. To supplement an attitude of helpful interest, the worker must have an understanding of the emotional and physical needs of people. Toward this end, schools of social work today offer an impressive body of knowledge about man as well as supervised field work experience to develop skill in implementing this knowledge.

* Presented at a meeting sponsored by the Chicago Chapter of the Smith College School for Social Work Alumnae Association, October 23, 1961.

The Need for Supervision

The social work profession in the United States has never assumed that training ends with the student years, but has accepted, *de facto,* that it must be extended into the job situation for an indefinite period of time, depending on the individual worker's capacity to apply himself. This continuing training task, assigned to the most experienced workers, is known as supervision. Although supervision has been undergoing critical re-examination, I find ample justification for continuing and strengthening the present arrangement to foster professional development through extended supervision. My conviction results from a consideration of the forces at play in the therapeutic transaction and from observation of the usual course of professional development.

Let us consider some of the demands the caseworker encounters. He is expected to be able to understand, tolerate, and relate therapeutically to the client's expression of primitive feelings, and to utilize for the benefit of the client both aggressive and libidinal impulses as they are projected upon the caseworker through the casework relationship. These are indeed imposing demands and they confront caseworkers in every setting. Neither the level at which treatment may be offered nor the auspices under which the worker functions can insulate him against them.

All types of human needs that come to the attention of the social worker require of him a fundamental understanding of psychological forces. Although the stress that caused the need for help may be located in the environment, the reactions to stress inevitably include psychological implications. These reactions must always be considered, even in situations in which the major casework effort is directed toward environmental change. Indeed, the ability to recognize or to rule out the need for psychological help in itself requires considerable diagnostic skill.

A large proportion of the clients who come to social agencies, however, have problems that are primarily psychological in nature. Often these problems are deeply rooted and the clients are unconscious of their source. Even though their requests for service may look simple and uncomplicated, such clients cannot be helped unless the social worker extends himself therapeutically. Therefore

293

the caseworker's training must focus on understanding the nature of the casework relationship and how to utilize it for the benefit of a specific client.

Performance of the Beginning Worker

In training caseworkers, supervisors have often observed a curious phenomenon. The initial impression of the new worker's performance is that he has a good understanding of what the client is trying to communicate, and responds in a therapeutically correct manner. Thus, after the prescribed probationary period, the worker receives a favorable recommendation for extension of his appointment. As time goes on, however, the supervisor finds that the worker's performance has become very uneven. Instead of improving, the worker begins to display serious blocking in his ability to understand his clients; this blocking is sometimes extreme enough to cause the supervisor to question whether the worker should have chosen casework as his profession.

Several years ago a group of supervisors at the Madeleine Borg Child Guidance Institute of the Jewish Board of Guardians in New York City conducted an exploratory study of the performance of a group of beginning workers. The workers selected were well recommended when they were employed, were considered gifted and promising after their probationary period, and were thought to have lived up to these expectations at the time the study was made. The study showed that, in the very beginning of their careers, all these workers seemed to have been doing well. Then for a period they became increasingly restrained and rigid, showing less understanding of their clients' communications. Even the best workers, with the best supervision, seemed to have gone through such a transitory stage.

An explanation of this paradox may be found in the increasing emotional demands upon the caseworker as the casework relationship develops. Many social workers believe that the establishment of a casework relationship depends on them, on the decisions they have to make and implement. Actually, when a person applies to a social agency for help, his action is usually a last resort; all his own efforts have failed and he finds himself helpless. The caseworker's offer to extend help psychologically recreates for the client a situation of early childhood when he was helpless and his parents seemed all-powerful and able to help. The client's readiness to enter into a casework relationship gives the worker the opportunity to study the client's past (although he himself may have forgotten much of the detail), to understand what interfered with his emotional development, and thus to be able to provide him with a corrective emotional experience.

Once promised help, the client often expects that all his difficulties will be solved as if by magic, and he responds to the worker positively. The worker also responds positively to the idea of being needed and wanted by the client. Because of this mutually positive response, there is often an intuitive understanding which is conveyed to the client. Furthermore, because the initial phase of treatment calls forth early childhood memories, the emotional needs of the client are also those of an earlier stage of development. The worker's interest in the client, his permissive, non-critical attitude, his giving of time, his concern, all constitute psychological feeding and thereby symbolically meet the psychological needs of the client. Thus, the worker may, with only a beginning intellectual understanding, have a beneficial effect on the client. Frequently, after one or two interviews, the client's symptoms lessen or disappear and he at once feels much better. However, this state of affairs cannot last very long. Under the impact of the worker's permissive, non-critical attitude, the client becomes free to express forbidden feelings, originally directed toward important persons in his life, and now projected on the worker in a way that may be disturbing and troublesome to him.

A crucial task faces the beginning worker. He must, through learning, move from a superficial, intellectual understanding of the client to a therapeutically meaningful, deepened, dynamic grasp— from partial awareness to emotional acceptance. If the worker's ego is to incorporate learning effectively, growth in emotional responsiveness and theoretical knowledge must be simultaneously fostered by the supervisor.

Understanding Communication

To help the client effectively, the worker has to learn to understand his indirect as well as his direct communications. Analysis of the interaction of the initial interview makes clear the need for such understanding.[1] In the initial interview, when the client makes a request for a concrete and specific service, he is expressing an emotional need or a primitive wish which he expects the worker to fulfil. It is these underlying needs and wishes that the worker must explore and understand. The request itself, if met, may be a destructive one for the client. But even when meeting the request appears constructive to the worker, he may fail to fulfil the client's childish expectations. Unless the meaning of the need is understood by the worker and worked through with the client, the experience may leave the client with a feeling of deprivation rather than the satisfaction that would contribute to his maturity.

What is the meaning of this indirect communication? Since the content refers to feelings not permitted direct expression by the client's ego, it must therefore be transmitted indirectly and symbolically. The reason the new worker fails to understand the hidden meaning of the communication is twofold. First, the indirect communication refers to developmental phases in the client's life which, because of conflict or traumatic experiences, could not be fully integrated. Dr. Bandler, pointing out the resistance that students typically show to classroom teaching of the phases of emotional development, emphasizes the importance of "the ego-dystonic content that refers to developmental phases and problems that have been experienced and solved in the unconscious in the course of growing up. . . ."[2] Even though the groundwork has been laid in classroom teaching and the social work student has accepted the concepts involved, often it is primarily an intellectual acceptance. The forceful attack on the worker's ego comes later, in practice, when he is exposed to the onslaught of the client's continuous emotional discharge in the interview.

Second, the failure to understand may be a defensive maneuver on the part of the worker. There are, of course many ways by which a worker can defend himself against such understanding. He may

[1] For further discussion see Yonata Feldman, "Learning Through Recorded Material," *Ego Psychology and Dynamic Casework,* Howard J. Parad (ed.), Family Service Association of America, New York, 1958, pp. 203–215, and Yonata Feldman, "Integration of Psychoanalytic Concepts into Casework Practice," *Smith College Studies in Social Work,* Vol. XXX, No. 2 (1960), pp. 144–156.
[2] Bernard Bandler, "Ego-Centered Teaching," this volume, p. 227.

protect himself by understanding only the client's direct communication. That is, he may tend to think only in terms of the reality factors that confront the client. By becoming deaf to the expression of forbidden feelings that lie hidden in the story, the worker wards off a distressing experience. This response is shown in the following fragment of an interview.

Mrs. A had brought her 5-year-old daughter to the clinic because she refused to speak in kindergarten. Mrs. A soon disclosed that she, too, was shy, could not speak, only whispered. Her history pointed to severe repressions of aggressive and libidinal drives. She started the interview by asking the worker for advice. Her 2-year-old daughter was smarter than the 5-year-old. When the 5-year-old began to read, the 2-year-old corrected her. Should she permit the younger to boss the older?

Superficially this might seem, to an untrained worker, to be a perfectly legitimate child guidance question, but it would take skill in deduction from former material, plus this interview, to understand that the mother was referring to her conflict about whether her 2-year-old childish wishes should control her or the superego commands appropriate to the age of five.

The worker may, by what seems to him a logical question and a rational need for information, interrupt the client's communication and thus prevent a revelation that may cause distress to the worker. Such defensive maneuvers often express themselves in the unevenness of the worker's performance. Amazingly, the worker may record both the client's and his own important communication correctly, but understand the meaning of the client's and his own words and behavior only superficially. Or the worker may give a correct interpretation of the dynamics in the case, but in his behavior toward the client during the interview act as if he were totally unaware of the meaning of his own interpretation.

As an example of this phenomenon let us examine the case of Stevie, age 5, carried by a beginning female worker.

The worker recorded that the child was referred for aggressive behavior, hitting his brother and misbehaving. She stated, "He bites his mother and she bites him back hard." The child had fears and nightmares. In describing Stevie's mother, the worker stated, "She is in a sadomasochistic relationship with Stevie." In reading the interviews the worker had with the child, one is at once impressed with the positive feelings the worker had toward the boy. A very verbal child, he stated that he would "rather talk than play." He knew he was coming to the agency because he was "bad." Although the child said, "Now is the time to talk," the worker encouraged him to play, apparently not ready to have the child tell her in what way he was bad. In his play with paint, water, but mostly with guns, he symbolically expressed castration fears and a great deal of sexual preoccupation. In fact, an experienced person would have suspected from Stevie's play that the child must have witnessed the primal scene. The worker saw only the aggression and she encouraged it, even though Stevie said he did not "wish to kill." Stevie was very affectionate with the worker, would box around with her, jump up and down in rhythmic fashion, and then run to the washroom "to wash his hands." The worker recorded that often when he left her office, he ran quickly to his mother, jumped into her lap and started hugging and kissing her.

Because the worker did not understand the sexual implication of the indirect communication of the child, she created a situation that was too anxiety-provoking to him. In one interview he began to scream at her. The worker's record reads:

Stevie looked down at the drawings, mumbled "cuckoo" and and then with a very angry expression, he pulled down his paintings and said he was not coming back. He glared at me and screamed that he'd like to screw me. I said I liked him and would like to have him stay. He said no, he was taking his things and was never coming back.
I could hear him screaming in the waiting-room. A few minutes later he walked to my door and grinned in a coy way. I told him I would like him to come in. After showing some reluctance, he came in. I told him I knew he was quite angry and this was a place where he could get angry. He said no, he was not angry, he just got a little too excited.

Although the worker recorded the sexual material and her observation of the mother-son relationship, she treated the child as if he were too severely disciplined by his own mother and needed an experience with a more permissive and loving parent. Although she recorded the words "He screamed that he'd like to screw me," she became aware of their meaning only when the supervisor called her attention to them.

Such a reaction to material is not unique to this particular worker and did not represent a personality difficulty. I have since used this case for teaching, and experienced social workers have often read aloud the child's words "screw you" and have reacted to them as if they did not exist in the text, thus indicating how difficult it is for us to accept infantile or childhood sexuality. It is not easy to accept that a charming child of five could have used a phrase like this, even more impossible to believe that a small child could be sexually aroused, and horrible to think that this was in reaction to the worker's expression of positive feelings toward him. Yet the worker, in her statement that the son's biting the mother and the mother's biting the son hard indicated a sadomasochistic relationship, must have had an inkling of the sexual nature of this relationship.

Enhancing the Worker's Awareness

The worker may at times be emotionally aware of the client's feelings when anxiety does not permit him to become fully enough aware to deal with them. The worker's ego boundary at the time is such that he is not ready to recapture an earlier ego state of his own—a state his client is at present experiencing. Not being able to recapture the early feeling, he cannot develop empathy with the client. If the supervisor considers the probability that the worker will at first react with anxiety to her explanation of the meaning of the material, she will not expect that, in the next interview or even the next few interviews, his approach will change for the better. On the contrary, one may even expect more rigidity. To counteract this tendency it may be advisable for the supervisor to tone down the shock by saying that her idea may not be right and need not be accepted as definite, but that the worker should keep on testing, observing, and experimenting with his own ideas. This approach gives the worker time to absorb the idea and gradually perceive for himself what the client is saying. If the supervisor tries to be too convincing and puts too much effort into making the worker understand the client's real emotions, it may constitute an attack on the worker's defensive mechanisms. He may then interpret her desire to train him quickly as an unloving criticism, and his ability to learn will decrease.

As the worker becomes more rigid and more guarded during the interviews, the client often senses the worker's anxiety and becomes less frank in his statements. When this happens during the period of training, the recording often begins to be a problem to the worker; he suddenly finds no time to record or his recording gets brief or confused.

The breakthrough of the worker's anxiety because of his inability to accept the meaning of the client's communication may lead to the closing of a case. One beginning male social worker, when discussing his work with the mother of a difficult child, was told by the supervisor that his client was trying to tell him she was in love with him and craved his response. It was obvious, even during the conference, that this statement made him very uncomfortable. Very soon he reported that the case had taken such a turn that it had to be closed. Even though the case had started successfully, the worker had created a situation where treatment had to be broken off because of the anxiety aroused in him. This supervisory effort was poorly timed since the worker was not yet at a stage where he was able to understand transference phenomena effectively; as a result he became fearful about his own responses.

Assessment of the worker's readiness to absorb and integrate a new idea will depend on the supervisor's skill. One social worker, when participating in the discussion of the case of Stevie, could not accept his colleagues' idea of the sexual meaning of the material. He maintained that Stevie had picked up the significant word from the street and did not know its meaning. This worker obviously was not ready to integrate a new idea at this point.

How can a supervisor help a worker accept and integrate the emotional expressions of his clients when he is not ready for this step? In the beginning stages of casework treatment the worker may react to the client's communication in a correct way as if fully aware of its meaning. But when asked to explain, he often indicates only a limited understanding of the underlying meaning. He often responds to the supervisor's query by saying, "It just felt right to react this way." The fact that he reacted correctly would show that in the area of feeling the worker's ego is ready to admit stimuli to conscious perception, although the ego is not fully conscious of its own operation. If the supervisor first explains what the worker has already reacted to correctly, the worker will have a fuller understanding with an accompanying feeling of discovery and mastery.

300

The positive remark of the supervisor is a pleasurable experience to the worker, opening his mind to absorption of less familiar ideas from the supervisor. This is in keeping with Federn's concept that a new idea cannot transcend the ego boundaries unless the ego boundaries are libidinally cathected.*

I have observed that explaining to a worker why he has reacted to a client correctly enables him to react appropriately to more threatening material—material that points to more remote developmental stages. Again, although he has reacted correctly, he continues to need explanation. It would seem as if approval and patient explanations by the supervisor—but most of all his ability to demonstrate by his own attitude that he can face feelings, talk about them, and still have full control—will strengthen the worker's ego and enable him to master anxiety. He can then, without fear of harmful countertransference, permit his client to express feeling directly. Through the experience of supervision the worker gains confidence that he will be able to manage his own feelings and thus be in a position to help his client to achieve control.

Development of Tolerance and Empathy

A fundamental task in casework training is to help the worker develop real empathy with the client. This phase of training must proceed slowly and cautiously. In the beginning the worker must be protected from the onslaught of the client's primitive, poorly repressed feelings—from becoming too quickly aware of the full depth of the meaning of the clinical presentation or of transference phenomena. The supervisor's aim is to help the worker gradually develop a tolerance toward emotional discharge, a tolerance that goes hand in hand with intellectual understanding. Without this training a worker will be unable to develop the capacity to provide a proper emotional climate for his client.

Such training must be based on a thorough understanding of a worker's total performance. In other words, the supervisor must study the worker's personality as it reflects itself in his work. The supervisor's explanation of the case, based on thorough understanding, frequently evokes a surprise reaction from the worker. The

* I am indebted for a fuller understanding of this phenomenon to a seminar given by the late Dr. Paul Federn in the years 1948–1950.

worker is convinced of the truth of a concept not by the supervisor's explanation, but by the next interview with his client in which the worker hears the "truth" from the client himself. He reacts as if to a revelation—his revelation, not his supervisor's. It is never the supervisor who can transmit to the worker how people really feel; it must be the client. The supervisor, however, through knowledge of the case and understanding of the worker, can suggest situations to the worker that will enable him to help his client discharge feelings, but only feelings that the worker, at a particular stage, can tolerate and understand.

It is usually inadvisable, therefore, for the supervisor to give the worker a long intellectual explanation of the dynamics of the case. When, in the supervisor's opinion, the worker is ready to tolerate a discharge of feeling, the supervisor may offer a concrete suggestion about what to say to facilitate the client's release of feelings so that the worker may experience emotionally what he previously has known only in theory.

For example, a beginning caseworker could not tolerate aggression on the part of her clients but was often blind to its expression. One of her clients, mother of a child in treatment, often broke appointments. The worker would usually wait until two successive appointments were broken before writing to inquire what had happened. The client would then come in and give a lame excuse —and the whole story would repeat itself. The worker knew the client was showing resistance, but did not know the cause or what to do about it. When the client, in one interview, remarked that she did not see much purpose in coming, the worker became alarmed and consulted the supervisor. Without giving any explanation, the supervisor suggested that the worker try a new method: take the blame upon herself; tell the woman that she had neglected her by not telephoning her to find out why she had failed appointments. The worker, intrigued, tried this approach, and the client broke down in violent crying. She said she felt the worker did not care for her, only for her children; nobody cared whether she lived or died. For the first time she told of her barren childhood, void of love and attention, and her great need to be important to somebody. To the worker this outpouring was all a revelation.

In a subsequent supervisory conference, the worker admitted she had had an uneasy feeling toward this woman. She did not like her and when the client broke appointments, the worker was relieved to have a little extra time for her dictation. Now, after the woman had felt free to express all her hate and aggression toward the worker, along with her need for acceptance and concern, the barrier was broken. This client taught the worker how emotions and feelings stored up by a person and originally directed toward parental figures could be transferred to her, a lesson she previously had learned only intellectually. From then on the worker was able to see this woman, not as a cruel mother who neglected her children and offended the worker by breaking appointments, but as a "child" who needed care. And she saw herself as the person able to meet this need. There were no further broken appointments and there was definite progress in the case.

The following example also shows how the tolerance of feelings must be developed simultaneously with intellectual understanding.

Lila S, a 5-year-old girl, would speak at home, but not in school or outside the home. Her mother, Mrs. S, also had difficulties in communication. The mother, the oldest of six children, had immigrated to the United States alone at the age of 16 and served as a domestic until the age of 25. She told her first worker that she was shy and had always been hesitant about speaking. "My mother," said Mrs. S, "used to make me sit in a corner and be quiet." Mrs. S had thought that she would never marry; she had been afraid of getting into trouble if she went out with men.

The first worker remarked that when Mrs. S spoke about angry feelings or sex, "she always whispered." Mrs. S and Lila had had several workers before the worker whose training we wish to demonstrate took over the case. The following two interviews are excerpted from the worker's own record.

First Interview: Mrs. S said she had a lot to talk with me about when we were alone. She expressed a great deal of negative feeling and concern about Lila's school and teacher. She also questioned how long I would be here, hoping it would be for a while. I reassured her and commented that it had been hard for her to have so many changes in workers. She said it was not hard for her, but it was hard for Lila. Lila had had four different workers. Mrs. S said she certainly enjoyed Miss D (her former worker). She "just loved" Miss D.

Second Interview: Mrs. S started by saying Lila had talked about me this week. She wondered why her mother's worker was changed so often. Mrs. S said she explained to Lila that Miss D had to leave, and that she only saw Miss T temporarily. She told Lila that she would be seeing me for a while now. I agreed with this.

When the supervisor asked the worker's reactions to the two interviews, she replied that Mrs. S expressed her own concern about losing her worker, but she seemed to take it sensibly even though she loved Miss D.

The supervisor said if Mrs. S loved Miss D, why had she stated that it was *not* hard for her when Miss D left? Was this not an insult? A loved person left her and it was not hard? Did she have no feeling?

The worker agreed that there was hidden anger in this phrase and added that perhaps Mrs. S's expression of negative feelings toward school and teacher really extended to the clinic and to the worker. The worker then added that in the second interview Mrs. S was apparently still talking about her own feeling about the worker's leaving, not Lila's.

The supervisor then said to the worker, "If this is so, if she is using Lila to describe how she herself felt as a child, then what do you think of explaining away such an injury? The worker starts treatment, makes promises of help, and then leaves because of her own needs. Isn't the worker supposed to represent a good mother to this client? How can such conduct ever be explained to a child?" As the supervisor said this she raised her voice in anger.

The worker looked very frightened. She asked, "You do not mean to suggest that you would express yourself to the client with so much feeling?" When the supervisor asked, "Why not?" the worker replied that anger as expressed by the supervisor would frighten the client. The supervisor then responded by saying that if anger was, in the worker's opinion, frightening, then it was perhaps better for Mrs. S to keep on whispering.

In a subsequent conference the worker stated that the supervisor's strange behavior and remark while discussing the S case had made her think a great deal. She admitted that the supervisor's loud voice and emotionality frightened her, and she had wondered, if Mrs. S had screamed and angrily accused her in the interview, how would she have taken it? It would have upset her. She would have

304

thought something she did was wrong, that the client did not like her; she did not know whether she then could like the client. The supervisor said that perhaps the client's mother did not like it either when Mrs. S, as a small child, could not accept the attention her mother gave to the newborn babies. Perhaps Mrs. S had screamed and stamped her feet and had a tantrum. Perhaps it was then that her mother made her sit in a corner and told her to shut her mouth. Being afraid of losing her mother's love, Mrs. S had shut her mouth so hard she could only whisper ever after.

The worker understood then that it would be therapeutic if Mrs. S could feel free enough with her to shout, scream, and accuse her; and if the worker could tolerate this aggression, not be annoyed, not stop her and punish her, but accept her anger as a natural reaction of a child who resents a new baby in the family. The worker was now concerned about how she could encourage such behavior in the client. The supervisor told her that she need not do anything at all, as long as she was no longer afraid to listen to screaming and childish tantrums in an adult.

We see here that the worker's ineffective response to what her client wished to express in the interview was based on her own fear of aggression. The supervisor dramatized the client's aggression and realized that in doing so she frightened the worker. The supervisor's statement—that if the worker would be frightened by the expression of aggression, it might be best for the client to whisper—stimulated the worker to work on her own attitude toward aggression. In the second supervisory conference the worker was able to face her own problem about aggression, thus making additional use of her growing theoretical knowledge.

Conclusion

This paper has dealt with selected phases of learning and teaching in the supervisory process. Effective training for casework practice is not determined by how much knowledge must be taught and how fast we wish to impart it, but by the quality and rate of the worker's absorptive capacity which is in turn determined by the dynamic structure of his personality. With our current understanding of ego psychology it would be erroneous to say that a caseworker should be expected to be able to work independently after graduating from a school of social work or that we can arbitrarily determine the number of years after which a worker should be permitted to work independently.

Properly carried out, supervision is an aid to independent, free, and creative performance because the freedom of expressing oneself individually and uniquely in the therapeutic situation is a fundamental prerequisite even for the beginning worker.

In general, when a worker has mastered the skills needed to investigate the conscious and unconscious forces operating within a client, and is maturely aware of the meaning of his own activity, he is able to work independently.* It is at this point in the worker's development that supervision might well be superseded by consultation. Since the threat involved in any form of psychotherapy to the worker's ego is ever-present, consultation should be easily and regularly available. Although the following quotation, clearly outlining the need for such a protective device, refers to the role of the analyst, it is equally applicable to the caseworker:

Since the analyst is the instrument of method, his own mental hygiene must also be considered. It is a problem whether enough individuals have a personality that tolerates the demands of daily psychoanalytic work. There are some professions which are dangerous, not in respect to life or physical health, but in regard to character health. Whenever a professional worker constantly deals with people who look up to him, or are dependent on his help and judgment . . . or who are inferior in strength, education or are younger than he, he may become seduced into narcissistic inflation.[8]

The learning process in dynamic casework is a never-ending one; and self-training is a fundamental part of the process. Because of the very nature of casework as a form of psychotherapy and because of the constant degree of ego involvement of the caseworker in the therapeutic transaction, the availability of guidance by a skilled third person—whether he is called supervisor or consultant—continues to have proven value.

* See paper by Florence Hollis, Chapter 1 of this volume.
[8] Paul Federn and Heinrich Meng, "Psychoanalytic Prevention versus Therapeutic Psychoanalysis," *Searchlights on Delinquency*, K. R. Eissler (ed.), International Universities Press, New York, 1948, p. 29.

Index